Media Ethics at Work

True Stories from Young Professionals

Second Edition

Lee Anne Peck
University of Northern Colorado

Guy S. Reel
Winthrop University

Editors

FOR INFORMATION:

CQ Press

An imprint of SAGE Publications, Inc.

2455 Teller Road

Thousand Oaks, California 91320

E-mail: order@sagepub.com

SAGE Publications Ltd.

1 Oliver's Yard

55 City Road

London, EC1Y 1SP

United Kingdom

SAGE Publications India Pvt. Ltd.

B 1/I 1 Mohan Cooperative Industrial Area

Mathura Road, New Delhi 110 044

India

SAGE Publications Asia-Pacific Pte. Ltd.

3 Church Street

#10-04 Samsung Hub

Singapore 049483

Printed in the United States of America.

Library of Congress Cataloging-in-Publication Data

Names: Peck, Lee A., editor. | Reel, Guy S., editor.

Title: Media ethics at work : true stories from young professionals / Lee Anne Peck, University of Northern Colorado, Guy S. Reel, Winthrop University, editors.

Description: Second edition. | Thousand Oaks, California : CQ Press, [2016] | Includes bibliographical references and index.

Identifiers: LCCN 2016010217 | ISBN 9781506315294 (pbk. : alk. paper)

Subjects: LCSH: Journalistic ethics. | Mass media—Moral and ethical aspects. | Journalistic ethics—Case studies. | Reporters and reporting—Case studies.

Classification: LCC PN4756 .M355 2016 | DDC 174/.907—dc23 LC record available at https://lccn.loc.gov/2016010217

This book is printed on acid-free paper.

Acquisitions Editor: Terri Accomazzo

Editorial Assistant: Erik Helton

Production Editor: Olivia Weber-Stenis

Copy Editor: Tina Hardy

Typesetter: C&M Digitals (P) Ltd.

Proofreader: Theresa Kay

Indexer: Hyde Park Publishing Services

Cover Designer: Karine Hovesepian

Marketing Manager: Ashlee Blunk

MIX
Paper from responsible sources
FSC® C014174
www.fsc.org

16 17 18 19 20 10 9 8 7 6 5 4 3 2 1

Media Ethics
at Work

Second Edition

The editors would like to dedicate this edition of Media Ethics at Work *to the memory of media professor Daniel Reimold who died August 20, 2015. He and his contributions to student journalism will be missed.*

Contents

About the Editors

Lee Anne Peck, Ph.D., is a professor of journalism and media studies in the School of Communication at the University of Northern Colorado, Greeley. Peck has taught English, journalism and communications courses. Before teaching at UNC, she was an assistant professor of international communications at Franklin University Switzerland, Lugano. Peck's research focuses on the best way to teach students ethical decision making.

Peck's professional experience began as a correspondent for the Moline (Illinois) Daily Dispatch. After graduating with her bachelor's degree in technical journalism from Colorado State University, she edited, and then managed the Northern Colorado Choice Magazine of the Front Range. In the mid-1980s, she edited and wrote for publications in Indiana and Delaware; she has worked for the Fort Collins Coloradoan as an editor and a columnist and for the now-defunct Rocky Mountain News as a copy editor. Peck has also worked as an intern at the now-defunct Tampa Tribune's online product, Tampa Bay Online, and at Microsoft's now-defunct online publication, Denver Sidewalk. Peck continues to do freelance editing, writing and public relations work via her company Little White Dog Communications.

She holds a doctorate in mass communication from Ohio University, a master's degree in philosophy from OU, a master's degree in mass communication from the University of South Florida and a master's degree in English from CSU. She has been active both regionally and nationally with the Society of Professional Journalists for more than 20 years.

Guy S. Reel, Ph.D., is a professor of mass communication at Winthrop University in Rock Hill, South Carolina. A former newspaper reporter and editor for The Commercial Appeal of Memphis, Tennessee, Reel teaches journalism and mass communication and has written extensively about issues in journalism and communication history. He is author of "The National Police Gazette and the Making of the Modern American Man, 1879–1906" (2006), a study of portrayed masculinities in 19th century tabloids. He received his doctorate from Ohio University, his master's from the University of Memphis and his undergraduate degree from the University of Tennessee.

About the Contributors

Giselle A. Auger is an award-winning professor of public relations at Rhode Island College. She received her Ph.D. in Mass Communication from the University of Florida and holds an M.A. in International Relations and Strategic Studies from the University of Lancaster in England. Her research focuses on advocacy and nonprofit organizations, transparency, the strategic use of social media, and academic dishonesty. She has more than 20 years' experience in communication industries and her teaching reflects the intersection of practice and academia, making theory and research relevant for her students.

Lucinda Austin is an assistant professor of strategic communications at Elon University where she teaches courses in health communication, strategic communication campaigns, strategic writing and communications research. Austin's research focuses on social media's influence on strategic communication initiatives, namely health and crisis communication, and explores publics' perspectives in organization–public relationship building. Her professional experience includes work for the Center of Risk Communication Research at the University of Maryland and for ICF International, a firm offering communication support to Federal government and nonprofit organizations, including the CDC, HHS, FEMA, and the American Red Cross. Austin has published work in several journals.

Lois A. Boynton is associate professor in the School of Media and Journalism at the University of North Carolina at Chapel Hill, where she teaches media ethics and public relations courses and is a fellow in the university's Parr Center for Ethics. She worked for 14 years as a reporter, editor and public relations practitioner before pursuing a teaching career. She has published in Journal of Mass Media Ethics, Communication Yearbook, Public Relations Review and PRism. She has a doctorate and master's degree from UNC-Chapel Hill.

Cailin Brown worked as a reporter at The Troy Record, the Albany Business Review and the Times Union in Albany. She is an associate professor at The College of Saint Rose in Albany, where she teaches media ethics and journalism, and advises the student newspaper, The Chronicle. Brown has a Ph.D. from the State University of New York at Albany.

Beth E. Concepción is the dean of the School of Liberal Arts and chair of the writing program at the Savannah College of Art and Design. She has more than 25 years of experience in journalism and public/media relations, and her areas of expertise are news and promotional writing, social media marketing and writing for new media. Concepción earned a B.A. from Oglethorpe University, a B.S. from Mississippi State University, an M.A. and M.F.A. from SCAD, and a doctorate from the University of South Carolina.

George L. Daniels is associate professor of journalism in the College of Communication and Information Sciences at the University of Alabama. Before attending graduate school, Daniels worked as a local television news producer in Cincinnati, Atlanta and Richmond, Virginia. His research interests include diversity in the media workplace and diversity in journalism and mass communication education. He received both his master's and doctorate degrees in mass communication from the University of Georgia.

David R. Davies is director of the School of Mass Communication & Journalism at the University of Southern Mississippi. He holds a doctorate from the University of Alabama and master's degrees from Southern Miss and Ohio State University. He teaches courses in mass communication history, and he is working on his third book, an analysis of press coverage of race, for Northwestern University Press. Before joining academia he was a newspaper reporter for 10 years in Arkansas, most recently at the Arkansas Gazette.

Deni Elliott holds the Eleanor Poynter Jamison Chair in Media Ethics and Press Policy at the University of South Florida, St. Petersburg, and is the chairwoman of the Department of Journalism and Media Studies. Dr. Elliott has written, produced or edited 10 books and documentary films in practical ethics and has written or co-written more than 190 articles for the scholarly and trade press. Her current books in process include "New Ethics for New Media" and "What You Think You Know Can Kill You: Busting the Myths of Breast Cancer." She received a master's degree in philosophy from Wayne State University and an interdisciplinary doctoral degree from Harvard University with a focus in teaching ethics.

Nathaniel Frederick II is an assistant professor of mass communication at Winthrop University. His research and teaching interests are in media law, media history and cultural studies. He has presented and published works focusing on the intersection between media, cultural production and social protest during the American Civil Rights Movement. He received his master's in media studies and his Ph.D. in communication from Pennsylvania State University.

Nancy Furlow is the chairwoman of the Department of Accounting, Economics, Finance and Marketing and professor of marketing at Marymount University, Arlington, Virginia. Furlow's research interests include product placement, environmental labeling, cause-related and social marketing, and "green" advertising. She received her doctorate in mass communication from the University of Southern Mississippi and her master's in journalism from Louisiana State University.

Scott R. Hamula, associate professor and chairman of the Department of Strategic Communication at Ithaca College, New York, has worked in advertising sales and radio station management in Michigan and New York. Hamula spearheaded the development of the integrated marketing communications major at Ithaca and has served as adviser for the American Advertising Federation student chapter and for Ithaca's award-winning Ad Lab. His research interests include audience and client promotions, advertising sales management, and radio and TV station branding strategies. Hamula has a master's degree in marketing from the University of Chicago.

John H. Kennedy has been a print journalist for four decades as a wire service reporter and editor, an award-winning reporter and an editor for a major metropolitan newspaper, a freelance magazine and newspaper writer and a nonfiction book author. Since 1994, he also has been a college instructor at several institutions. In 1999, he launched a communication major at an American college in Switzerland and in 2003 at Rosemont College in suburban Philadelphia. He has traveled to East Africa to help teach journalists investigative reporting techniques, computer-assisted journalism and ethics. He currently is a lecturer in Boston University's journalism department.

Jan Leach is an associate professor in the School of Journalism and Mass Communication at Kent State University. She is director of Kent's Media Law Center for Ethics and Access, which annually hosts the Poynter KSU Media Ethics Workshop. Leach is an Ethics Fellow at the Poynter Institute for Journalism Studies in St. Petersburg, Florida. In 2014, she did media ethics training for the U.S. State Department for students and professionals in four different cities in India. Before joining the faculty at Kent State, Leach was editor and vice president of the Akron Beacon Journal. She recently was named to the Cincinnati SPJ Journalism Hall of Fame.

Aimee Pavia Meader is an assistant professor at Winthrop University with a doctorate in journalism. She teaches courses in multimedia and storytelling production and advanced broadcast journalism. Meader's research examines the psychology of media, ethics in multimedia and selective exposure. As a journalist, she worked for six years at KUSI news in San Diego where she produced a two-hour newscast. Meader has a master's in mass communication from San Diego State University and a Ph.D. in mass communication from the University of Texas at Austin.

Donica Mensing is associate professor at the Reynolds School of Journalism, University of Nevada, Reno. She teaches media ethics, interactive publishing and critical analysis of media. Mensing has published on the topics of journalism education and networked journalism. She has a master's in science, technology and public policy from George Washington University, and a master's in journalism and a doctorate in political science, both from the University of Nevada.

Joe Mirando is professor of communication at Southeastern Louisiana University in Hammond, Louisiana. He is a former newspaper reporter and copy editor and a former high school teacher. His doctoral dissertation analyzed the lessons on ethics published in college news reporting textbooks, and his research has appeared in the Journal of Mass Media Ethics among other publications. Mirando earned a doctorate in communication from the University of Southern Mississippi and has accreditation at the Master Journalism Educator level from the Journalism Education Association.

Ray Niekamp is associate professor in the School of Journalism and Mass Communication at Texas State University–San Marcos. Prior to university teaching, Niekamp worked in television news and developed an interest in the effect new technology has on the news-gathering and news presentation processes. His current research focuses on the use of new media in broadcast journalism. His doctorate in mass communication is from Penn State University.

Michael O'Donnell is associate professor of communication and journalism at the University of St. Thomas, St. Paul, Minnesota. He teaches website design, publication design, photojournalism and visual communication. He has advised student media at St. Thomas for more than 10 years and helped lead the transition from a printed newspaper to an online-only student news site, TommieMedia.com. O'Donnell has nearly 30 years' experience as a sports reporter, editor and page designer at papers such as the St. Paul Pioneer Press and the Chicago Tribune. His master's degree is from Iowa State University.

Frances Parrish worked on the student newspaper at Winthrop University as a staff writer and then editor-in-chief. She interned at The Greenville News and Urban Home Magazine in Charlotte. After graduating from Winthrop in 2015, Parrish began working as the education reporter for Independent Mail in Anderson, South Carolina.

Kathy K. Previs is an associate professor of Communication at Eastern Kentucky University where she teaches public relations. She is also an online instructor at West Virginia University in the integrated marketing communications program and the Reed College of Media. Her research interests focus on public relations campaigns and ethics, social media and science and health communication and the role of PR in those discourses.

Kelly Scott Raisley is a lecturer in the School of Communication at the University of Northern Colorado. She teaches strategic communication courses, including media planning and research, political communication, intercultural communication, persuasion and advertising principles. She earned her master's in communication studies from UNC and is pursuing a doctorate in Higher Education and Student Affairs Leadership, also from UNC.

Daniel Reimold died Aug. 20, 2015. At the time of his death, he was employed as an assistant professor at St. Joseph's University. Reimold was an adviser to The Hawk, the student news organization of Saint Joseph's, and founder of the influential blog College Media Matters, an Associated Collegiate Press resource on student journalism. Reimold's first book, "Sex and the University: Celebrity, Controversy, and a Student Journalism Revolution," was published in 2010 by Rutgers University Press. His doctorate is from Ohio University, and his master's is from Temple University.

Adam Rhew is a communications professional with experience in journalism and public relations. His career has included stops at television and radio stations in Charlotte; Richmond, Virginia; Charlottesville, Virginia; and Chapel Hill, North Carolina. His public relations experience focuses on strategic communications, message development and crisis communications. Rhew is a graduate of the University of North Carolina's School of Media and Journalism.

Gary Ritzenthaler, a visiting assistant professor of journalism and new media at the State University of New York at Oswego, teaches courses in online/mobile journalism and the effects of new media. He has spent almost two decades working in the field of online journalism with large media chains, smaller design firms and startup web companies. He has done graduate work at the University of Florida, and his research interests include the history of journalism on the World Wide Web, social and mobile media, and the evolving integration of virtuality into everyday life.

Cassie Rodenberg writes at the intersection of poverty, mental illness and trauma. While conducting her four-year project in South Bronx, she completed a master's in education and taught public school in the neighborhood. Her writing on addiction has been included multiple times in "The Best Science Writing Online" anthology series. She is currently pursuing a doctorate in sociology at State University of New York at Albany and teaching at nearby colleges.

Vinny Vella is a staff writer for the Hartford Courant, specializing in coverage of crime, poverty and urban affairs. He graduated from Philadelphia's La Salle University in 2012. After graduation, he worked at The Denver Post and was a member of the staff that won the Pulitzer Prize in 2013 for Breaking News Reporting. Most recently, he served two years on the night cops-and-crime beat for the Philadelphia Daily News.

Richard D. Waters is an associate professor in the School of Management at the University of San Francisco, where he teaches marketing and public relations, fundraising and nonprofit organization management. His research interests include relationship management between organizations and stakeholders, the development of fundraising theory as it pertains to charitable nonprofits and the use of Web 2.0 technologies by nonprofit organizations. He is a former fundraising practitioner and current consultant to Fortune 500 and Philanthropy 400 organizations throughout the United States. He has published more than 45 research articles and book chapters. He has a doctorate in mass communication from the University of Florida.

K. Tim Wulfemeyer is a professor and coordinator of the journalism degree program in the School of Journalism and Media Studies at San Diego State University. He has worked as a radio and television journalist in California, Iowa, Texas, New Mexico and Hawaii. His research interests include ethics in journalism, the content of radio and television newscasts, the content of news websites, audience interests and content preferences, mass media literacy, advertising aimed at children and sports journalism. He is the author or co-author of six books, four book chapters and 30 journal articles. He has a master's from Iowa State University and a Doctor of Education degree from UCLA.

Preface

For instructors: During the first week of my media ethics courses, I show my students the class blog, www.iwantu2boutraged.blog spot.com,[1] and point out posts about recent ethical lapses by people working in the media professions.[2] As the semester progresses and I add new posts, a pattern emerges: Students show much more interest in the cases involving student media or young professionals than they do in the well-publicized cases involving experienced professionals at major organizations. As they're working to develop their own standards, students want to discuss the actions of their peers. The question "What would *you* have done?" leads to lively debate.

When Whitehouse and McPherson noted in a Journal of Mass Media Ethics article that media ethics casebooks "ask media ethics students to take the dramatic mental leap from being undergraduates preparing for their first jobs to becoming leaders of companies,"[3] co-editor Guy Reel and I thought they had a good point. We believe too many books present

---

1. You can create a free blog for your class via www.blogger.com. You act as the guest host and aggregate information on your site.

2. I receive daily Google Alerts for the terms "media ethics," "journalism ethics," "public relations ethics" and "advertising ethics" for finding current ethical dilemmas, both national and international, for my class blog. I also subscribe to daily e-newsletters from various media organizations such as Poynter's Morning Mediawire and MediaBistro's Morning Newsfeed.

3. V. Whitehouse and J. B. McPherson, "Media Ethics Textbook Case Studies Need New Actors and New Issues," *Journal of Mass Media Ethics,* 17, No. 3 (2002).

students with the kinds of ethics cases faced by experienced media managers rather than the kind young people are likely to encounter in school or in an internship or first job. "Students need cases reflecting issues faced by entry-level media professionals," Whitehouse and McPherson said in their conclusion. "They must know how to take responsibility for their own ethical decisions, and they must be able to express their views from low positions of power."[4]

This book provides those entry-level cases along with the tools to help students reason through them. In these pages, authors tell the true stories of young media professionals who struggled with an ethical dilemma early in their careers in public relations, advertising, and print, broadcast and online journalism. These young people face a wide range of difficult choices. Some are perennials, such as what to do when a source tries to "take back" what he's told you for a story or when you discover that your supervisor is manipulating publicity material. Others are permutations for the digital age: for instance, is it OK to go online pretending to be someone else? Should you remove a story from a web archive at a source's request?

Much has been written about the ethical lapses of young professionals in the fast-paced, increasingly competitive media world. Classic high-profile cases involved Jayson Blair, formerly of The New York Times; Stephen Glass, formerly of The New Republic; and Janet Cooke, formerly of The Washington Post. These young writers lied, fabricated stories, embarrassed their news organizations and damaged the credibility of everyone working in the media. They knew what they were doing was wrong, but they did it anyway.

In contrast to those cases, most of the young people featured in this book—like many young professionals—had good instincts. When confronted with an ethical issue, they wanted nothing more than to do the right thing. They just weren't sure what the right thing might be or when to trust their instincts.

The underlying issues in the dilemmas encountered by young professionals—dishonesty, bias, sensationalism, conflict of interest— are the same issues that continue to pose challenges throughout any media career. The difference is that younger professionals with their

---

4. Ibid.

limited experiences in the working world may not recognize the ethical dimensions of a situation before they act in whatever way seems appropriate at the moment.

Even when they do recognize an ethical dilemma, young professionals have fewer resources on which to draw. The issue may seem far too big to tackle—never mind resolve—from their entry-level position in the organization. They're not sure what questions they should ask, whom they should ask or when they should ask them. They may feel ill-equipped to brainstorm about options for action beyond the first ones that come to mind. Not wanting to look ignorant, they might not have the courage to speak at all.

That's where this book's true stories play a role. Written in a narrative style, the chapters take readers through ethical dilemmas as they actually unfolded—from the perspective of the young person involved and with only the information available to him or her at each point. Readers can stop at each stage and reflect on the questions "What would I do if this happened to me?" or "What alternative might have worked?" As they follow the case and discover how the young professional resolved the situation, readers will develop strategies and patterns of thought that will better prepare them for their own inevitable ethical dilemmas.

Because the issues these young professionals encountered cross over all media professions, the chapters are arranged not by profession but by theme: honesty, sensitivity and balance. The cases can be assigned in any order; create your own path through the material by following the connections you want your students to make. For instance, you can look for cases that resemble something currently in the news or choose a case to discuss via the philosophical theory recently discussed in class.

I recommend during the first week of classes pointing out recent ethical dilemmas being reported in the news before tackling theory. (Creating a blog as I did provides an easy place to continually post news of dilemmas as you learn about them.) Most students don't realize how widespread these issues are and how damaging they can be to their chosen profession. In my experience, they become more willing—even eager—to tackle the decision-making tools that will help them with their own dilemmas in the future.

Depending on how you teach the media ethics course, this book can work as a primary text or a supplement. As a stand-alone text, it offers enough content for a semester-long course with its explanations of the Western ethical theories typically taught in media ethics courses, discussion of what ethics codes can and can't do and examination of moral development. It also offers more than 25 cases involving young people, something no other media ethics textbook does, many of them addressing the ethical complications resulting from new technology. Because you can choose the cases you want to discuss as a class, the book can be a good supplemental text for a media ethics course, backing up whatever primary text you might use. If this is the first time you have taught the course, all the parts that make up each chapter will help you create class discussions, quizzes and essay tests or reflection pieces.

In introductory courses, such as media writing or public relations, the book can work as a supplement. Although in these lower-level courses you might not cover all the decision-making tools discussed in the first chapter, exploring some of the cases will help alert students to the principles of their professions and to the situations they might encounter in the working world, providing fodder for discussion. Teaching the beginning skills of writing a press release or a news report is important, but it's also important to simultaneously begin students' understanding of ethics in their fields.

If you do use this as your main text, you'll find easy-to-understand explanations of Aristotle's Doctrine of the Mean (virtue), Kant's Categorical Imperative (duty), Mill's principle of utility, John Rawls' theory of justice and more. Each theory includes examples of how it might apply today to the work of a media professional. You may want to spend more time on some sections of the decision-making chapter, asking students to read the original texts by the philosophers mentioned. Many websites provide these readings at no cost, and putting copies of original readings on reserve at the library is always an option.

Codes of ethics are discussed in this chapter as a good starting point for young professionals. You can also opt to work through any case with your students by choosing an ethical theory and showing how it can provide a deeper answer than the principles stated in a code. "Tool for Thought" boxes highlight a certain code or theory, showing one way to deliberate the case.

However you approach ethical theory, we do not recommend covering all the theories in one class session or sitting—or even in one week of classes. Discuss a theory, then choose a case in the book, and the chapter does not necessarily have to cite that specific theory. Work through the case using the theory recently discussed and those previously discussed; keep building from there. Chapter 2 takes you through the stages from early ethical decision making to moral sophistication, as illustrated by the story of a young reporter who found herself in a clash between her own ethics and those of the profession, ultimately creating an opportunity for self-reflection and moral growth. The example helps students see themselves in her dilemma.

Within the case chapters, additional features offer more perspectives. "Thinking It Through" questions help students review the case and the actions of the young person involved. In some chapters, a "Tool for Action" box provides practical tips such as how to use blog posts in information gathering. Chapters also include related web links for more information, and an appendix lists the web addresses of all the ethics codes referred to in the case chapters. Finally, "What If?" scenarios offer a related situation designed to push readers' thinking about the issues further. Unlike the true stories that are the center of each chapter, these "What If?" cases have no resolution, leaving the decision making to the reader.

All the stories told in the case chapters are true; the chapter authors obtained the information, including a summary of the thinking process, directly from the young professional involved. When we began soliciting contributions for the book, we planned to use only real names of people and companies. Doing so, however, did not prove possible in every chapter. In some cases, the young professional still works with some of the people who made questionable decisions and, thus, must be cautious about reflecting on these decisions publicly. In others, the entry-level employee was not in a position to know the full reasoning behind a company's or individual's chosen course of action, and the people involved have left; thus, background could not be checked to the degree required to eliminate libel concerns. In each chapter in which names have been changed, a note at the end of the introductory summary clearly says so and explains the reason. If you see no such note, the names are all real.[5]

---

5. If instructors would like a sample syllabus or sample essay test created by Peck, contact her at leeanne.peck@unco.edu or call her at (970) 351-2635.

We hope this unique book helps your students find the guidance and courage they need to make ethical decisions and thus do their part to maintain high standards in the news and persuasion media. With the basics in hand and with the practice the book offers, students and young professionals can connect what's learned from reading and class discussion with the changing realities they'll face.

Today's fast-paced, ever-changing media scene makes finding the ethical course of action more difficult—not just for new professionals but sometimes for their bosses as well. If young people can enter the workforce with an ethical framework built on sound theory and moral reasoning, they won't instantly know what to do in every situation, but they'll be confident enough to reason through it.

ACKNOWLEDGMENTS

Peck would like to thank her mentors for being influential in the way she teaches media ethics today. They include Garrett Ray, former media ethics professor, Colorado State University; Bob Steele, Poynter Institute's values scholar; Jay Black, former Poynter-Jamison Chair in Media Ethics, University of South Florida; and Clifford Christians, media ethics scholar, University of Illinois. She would also like to thank her professors in Ohio University's graduate philosophy program for helping her understand ethical theory more thoroughly.

Reel would like to thank his colleagues at Winthrop University, including Drs. Lawrence Timbs and William Click, and former student Frances Parrish.

SAGE Publishing gratefully acknowledges the contributions of reviewers Paula Hearsum, University of Brighton; Barbara J. Irwin, Canisius College; and Joey Senat, Oklahoma State University.

Introduction

A ndie Peterson, a 2015 journalism school graduate, really wanted to do an internship during the summer between her junior and senior years of college. Her work interest? Anything to do with advertising. Peterson, a Colorado native, had already worked as an account representative for the university's student newspaper during her junior year, but now she hoped to intern at a Denver ad agency. During spring semester of her junior year, she applied for many openings she found listed through the Denver Egotist website. Finally, at the end of the semester, a small agency offered her a position for the summer. She was ecstatic—especially because alumni from the business school of her university operated the business.

Peterson worked three days a week for the Christian-centered company with two other interns. After a couple weeks, though, she realized that the internship for which she had paid summer tuition was not only a waste of money but also a waste of time. Peterson got lunch for her supervisors and wrote social media posts for clients that her supervisor OK'd. To make matters worse, she and the other interns realized that the members of the so-called God-based agency seemed to be hypocrites. For instance, the agency represented an alcohol company, promoting one of its new products, a spiced rum; Peterson was also asked to "create" positive reviews for clients on the rating sites of Yelp and Google. The ultimate goal: More stars! Her bosses had boasted the agency could improve ratings on these sites. Under little direction, Peterson created seven different Gmail identities.

Toward the end of her internship, she noticed her fake reviews were not anywhere to be found on Yelp or Google.

"When I first noticed, I didn't say anything because I was thinking I could probably fix this or maybe I wasn't seeing them published because there was a system error or something," Peterson says. "I told my supervisor after a little while, saying I couldn't see my comments anywhere. He didn't say or do anything at first, but then one client realized nothing was being posted and that's when he approached me." Peterson emailed Yelp first. This is the response she received:

"Hi there,

I'm writing to let you know about our Support Team's decision to close your user account. Your account has been closed because of Terms of Service (http://www.yelp.com/violations), including creating multiple accounts."

She had been "caught."

"If you fake anything," Peterson says, "they will kick you off the site—forever."

In the meantime, another intern who was fed up with the shenanigans had already quit. The graphic design intern quit mid-July. The three were getting no constructive experience or feedback, and the promised networking was nonexistent. Peterson, however, persevered.

All in all, Peterson says, she learned nothing of any value—except the consequences of pretending you are someone whom you are not. "The final slap in the face was when I had to advertise for my own replacement."

Did Peterson do the right thing by staying—even if she felt uncomfortable with what she was asked to do? If you think she did do the right thing, how would you justify her actions to others? If you think Peterson made a bad decision by staying, what might she have done instead?

These are the kind of questions you'll be asking yourself, and learning to answer, as you read this book. They're also the kind you might encounter—if you haven't already—while working in student media, doing an internship or at your first job as a young media professional. As your career begins, you might face issues similar to these:

- What do I tell an editor who wants to sensationalize my copy?

- What if a PR client wants me to omit facts or lie in a press release?

- What if I'm asked to stretch the truth in ad copy?

Of course, people who have worked in the media for years face similar dilemmas. The difference is that when you're new to a job, it's harder to recognize an ethical challenge when you see it and harder to know what to do. You're just learning about your profession in general and your employer in particular. If you want to voice your concerns, whom do you talk to and when? Being new to a profession means you're learning new skills—and moral reasoning needs to be one of those skills.

This book presents stories of young people who had to wrestle with an ethical dilemma at the beginning of their careers in the news or persuasion media. By following along as these young media professionals make their choices, you'll begin to understand how to ask yourself questions, envision alternatives and justify the decisions you make.

All the stories in the book are true. The authors of the chapters know the individuals involved and have interviewed them to get details on what they thought and did as they tried to resolve their ethical dilemma. We had hoped to use real names throughout the book, and about half the chapters do use them. However, ethical issues involve debate and controversy, and sometimes it's not possible to tell a complex story from one person's point of view without making others look bad in ways that may not be fair. Therefore, in some cases, including the story of Andie Peterson in this introduction, the young media professional has asked us to change the names of people and companies.

As you read each chapter, ask yourself how you would have responded in that situation. Right now, you have the luxury of deliberating cases in the classroom with your peers. Practicing ethical thinking now will better prepare you for making decisions later in the craziness of deadlines at a news organization, ad agency or PR firm.

Before you get to the book's cases, you'll find a chapter that covers philosophical theories and codes of ethics. These decision-making tools will help you not only with your discussions of how the young professionals in the cases acted but also with your future deliberations in the workplace. We encourage you to explore original readings of philosophers mentioned and to read the entire codes. Chapter 2 then offers insight into how one builds character via moral development; it includes the story of a young woman who had to make tough choices about the way she approached her job.

Because the problems encountered by the young professionals in the book—including dishonesty, bias, sensationalism and conflict of interest—could happen in any media workplace, you'll find the chapters organized not by profession but by types of issues. Even if you don't plan to be a public relations practitioner, you can learn from the situations a PR professional encounters and how he or she handles them. Plus, it always helps to get acquainted with the tasks done in other professions as you enter the working world.

Within the case chapters, you'll find "Tool for Thought" boxes that show how certain theories or codes could be applied to the situation in the chapter. Sometimes the boxes use a combination of tools because when you deliberate a dilemma, more than one way of thinking may help. You'll also find a variety of other features among the chapters, including discussion questions, web links and quick tips on practical matters such as whether it's OK to use information you found on Facebook.

This book will help you build professional character, and part of building character is realizing that you're going to make mistakes. For example, Peterson, who now works as a personal banker, wondered if she should have left with the other interns. The fall semester after her internship she took her required media ethics course. Because she hadn't taken the course yet, she believed she "didn't know how to talk" to her supervisors about doing tasks that made her uncomfortable.

"I should have stuck up for myself. I wanted more experience in advertising, but what I got was something different," Peterson says. "I also learned that bosses aren't always right." And that last comment is key.

Young people who encounter a work-related ethical dilemma usually recognize that what they're doing isn't right but often do it anyway for a variety of reasons: not wanting to look stupid, not having the courage to confront or confide in supervisors or just not knowing how to think through the dilemma or explain their reasoning. Helping you learn to deal with these roadblocks is why we compiled this book—and why Andie is a more confident employee today.

From your first day on the job, you're as responsible as anyone for the work your organization produces. Professionalism includes taking that responsibility. When you're the intern or the "new kid," obviously you don't want to lecture people who have twice your experience about how to do their jobs. But if you have questions, it's your responsibility to ask them. It's never safe to assume the questions will be asked and answered somewhere higher up the line.

The pace of change in today's media means that when ethical issues arise, even your boss may not be sure what to do. Each professional is the architect of his or her own credibility, and each individual's credibility is key to establishing the credibility of the media as a whole. If you can build your ethical framework on sound theory and moral reasoning, you won't instantly know what to do about every situation that develops, but you'll be agile enough and confident enough to reason through it.

CHAPTER 1

Tools for Ethical Decision Making

Lee Anne Peck

"This doesn't seem right," you think. You're the youngest and newest person in the office, but all your instincts tell you that something about the story or the project you've been assigned is not quite, well, ethical. Whom should you talk to? What should you do?

Not to worry. You're not alone. You have colleagues, professional associations and their codes, plus centuries of ethical theory on which to draw. Exploring tools and ethical theory now will help you reason through the dilemmas you'll face in the future. Otherwise, you might jump into decision making with only a gut feeling. Learning to think through a dilemma will not only make you more confident and comfortable with your decision; it will also help you justify to others why you acted the way you did.

The Western philosophical theories shared in this chapter include many that students tend to embrace. That doesn't mean you and your instructor or colleagues should not explore others, such as the Judeo-Christian perspective and the Golden Rule, but these will get you started. Along with each philosopher's theories in this chapter, you'll find examples of how their ideas might apply to situations that today's media professionals face.

The chapter begins with some basic definitions, followed by a discussion of ethics codes. It continues with the beginnings of Western ethical thought and then moves into concrete theories you might use while reasoning through a dilemma. You'll see that many of the theories embrace similar key concepts, such as justice, fairness, empathy and equality. You may just find yourself using them in your personal life, too. Who knew you were an Aristotelian?

TERMS TO KNOW

Some of you have taken a philosophy course or two, so this will be a review, but for those who haven't, let's start with the basics. The study of philosophy can be broken into three areas:

1. What is being? (ontology)
2. What is knowing? (epistemology)
3. How should one act? (ethics)

This book, of course, focuses on how one should act—and in particular, how one should act while working in one's chosen profession. Based on the Greek word ethos, ethics explores the philosophical foundations of decision making. When you reason through dilemmas, you think about morality, which comes from the Latin word mores. Morality refers to the way in which people actually behave or act. Therefore, ethics is an examination of morality.

Ethics, in turn, can be broken into three subareas:

1. Metaethics analyzes the meaning of moral language. What do the words you use signify?
2. Normative ethics considers the norms that act as principles of ethical behavior.
3. Applied ethics, or casuistry, applies normative theories to specific ethical dilemmas.

This book asks you to explore both normative ethics and the principles of your chosen profession. It then encourages you to do applied ethics, as defined above, with the book's cases. Please note that these true stories of young professionals concern media ethics, not media law. Sometimes a society's morality may be transformed into law; a connection can exist, but remember, the two are not the same. The law tells you how to act while ethics tells you what you should do.

Codes for the Media Professions

Henry Watterson (1840–1921), longtime editor of the admired Louisville-Courier Journal, lamented at the end of the 19th century that journalism had no code of ethics and that its "moral destination" seemed confused. This worried Watterson and other U.S. newspaper editors and publishers. Journalism was now a profession instead of a trade and those who worked in that profession faced a lot of criticism. At the beginning of the 20th century, other media professions—such as advertising, radio broadcasting and press agentry (public relations)—also began coming under scrutiny for their "morals." Slowly, all media began creating codes of ethics. Some of those codes are still used today, but updated, of course.

As you learn about your chosen profession, you'll want to read and understand that profession's codes of ethics. Web links for codes from different organizations—from the Society of Professional Journalists to the Public Relations Society of America—are listed in the appendix, and some authors also share links to codes within their chapters. In addition, some media organizations have written their own codes, so you should always ask which code your new employer follows. Also, for transparency's sake, an increasing number of media organizations post their codes online for the public to see.

Media ethics codes are guidelines, though, not rules or laws. Because media professionals are not licensed the way lawyers and doctors are, they cannot "lose their licenses," so to speak, for violating an ethics code. They can, however, be fired. Getting fired doesn't mean a media professional can never work in the field again, but it does make finding another job difficult. Most important, violating a code of ethics can hurt people and damage the reputation of your entire profession.

Although codes remain a good place to begin your understanding of media ethics, it's important to be able to move beyond codes by using thought and analysis when a dilemma arises. Ethicist Bob Steele, the Poynter Institute's values scholar, stresses media professionals must go beyond gut feelings and "rule obedience," trusting instead in reflection and reasoning.[1] In other words, you can turn to codes for initial guidance when making an ethical decision, but usually you'll need to go further in your deliberations if your situation is not blatantly black and white. Few ethical dilemmas are clear-cut.

PHILOSOPHICAL THEORIES

When you're working to resolve an ethical dilemma, don't discount those who came before you—way before you. The ethical theories of philosophers such as Aristotle and Immanuel Kant can help in your deliberations as can the ideas of contemporary ethics scholars. Sometimes a single theory or professional code will be enough to point you toward a solution; other times you'll need to combine various theories and tools. It depends on the dilemma. The important thing is to start building your resources now before you're facing an ethical question on deadline.

SOCRATES

We begin with Socrates. He taught Plato, who taught Aristotle. Socrates, the son of a stone mason, lived in Athens from 469 to 399 B.C. He believed in following one's principles and being independent in thought. Because Socrates did not write "lecture notes," Plato wrote many of Socrates' philosophical teachings into dialogues with Socrates as the main character. Socrates believed that he could best help Athenians by asking them to examine their moral lives. He has been quoted as saying, "The unexamined life is not worth living."[2]

Socrates tried to convince Athenians that each of them was responsible for his or her own moral actions and that unethical behavior came from ignorance or a lack of knowledge. Remember this as you read the cases in this book; often the young professionals encountering an ethical dilemma did not have the information they needed in order to make a

---

1. http://www.poynter.org/uncategorized/1758/the-ethical-decision-making-process/

2. Plato, *Five Dialogues: Euthyphro, Apology, Crito, Meno, Phaedo,* translated by G. M. A. Grube (Indianapolis, IN: Hackett, 1981), 41.

sound decision. Back in Athens, Socrates believed his calling was to correct this ignorance in citizens.

The government of Athens saw things differently. In 399 B.C., it imprisoned Socrates and sentenced him to death for allegedly corrupting Athens' youth with his ideas and introducing false gods. Plato explained Socrates' situation in the dialogue "Crito" in which Socrates' friend Crito tries to persuade Socrates to escape prison. Socrates refuses, explaining his reasons to Crito. In this dialogue, Plato emphasizes Socrates' principles: independence, justification for one's actions and social responsibility—all important principles upon which media professionals should agree.

Socrates explains to his friend that he has been a citizen of Athens all his life, so why would he want to break the law and escape? That would be both disrespectful and unlawful. Socrates asks Crito what kind of message he would be sending to the people of Athens if he escaped from jail. Could he truly teach virtuous behavior somewhere else, somewhere outside of Athens? He would be a hypocrite. He has two sons. What message would he be sending to them?

Socrates believes if he remains in prison and is executed, he would actually enhance Athens' morality. Socrates uses his own independent reasoning to come to this conclusion, and he justifies his decision, which he believes to be socially responsible. Crito now understands why Socrates will stay in prison; he says nothing else.

Plato was one of the Athenians who learned Socrates' technique for finding the truth, called the Socratic method today. The speaker or teacher asks respondents a series of questions that eventually shows them they need to do more reasoning and reflection about their beliefs and actions. At your place of employment or at your university, you may find a "go-to" person whose mind works in ways that complement yours and who is good at asking questions when an ethical dilemma arises.

PLATO

After Socrates was put to death, his student Plato (428/7–348/7 B.C.) became conflicted about Athens' political atmosphere. Plato had wanted a life in politics but decided instead to continue his philosophy studies, so he left Athens. During his 12 years away, he is thought to have spent time in Italy at the colony, or commune, created by the Greek philosopher Pythagoras, and he also spent time at an agricultural community in Egypt. Some scholars believe that Plato incorporated his travels into his work *The Republic* (360 B.C.), which describes a utopian world where philosophers have positions of power.

After returning to Athens, Plato started the Academy, often considered to be the first university. The subjects studied were the sciences, mathematics and philosophy, which included Plato's writings with Socrates as the narrator. Plato taught that the virtues of moderation, courage and wisdom combined to create the highest virtue: justice. *Justice* had a broader meaning than it does today; it meant "the good life" with morality as the final "good." In other words, to have a good life was to have a moral life.

Plato's book the "Republic," specifically the section titled Allegory of the Cave, can help beginning media professionals understand their position in the world and how to achieve "the good life."

After reading the "Republic," you will come to understand that Plato did not have much faith in humankind to act morally. He thought that if given the chance, and if they could get away with it, many people would act immorally. Plato believed that being ethical comes from using reason, and those who truly had a grasp of reason could be the philosopher king and the guardians in the "Republic."

In the book's short passage the Allegory of the Cave, Plato shows how the masses sometimes do not reason well. Because some believe the passage to be the most influential in Western philosophy, it's important to understand its symbolism.

To summarize, in Plato's cave, men have been chained by their necks and legs to a wall all their lives; they can only look straight ahead. Behind the prisoners, a fire burns, reflecting light above them. Between the fire and the wall is a passageway where "puppeteers" walk, holding artificial objects above their heads. These items make shadows on the wall above the prisoners, and for these prisoners, the shadows become their reality. However, one prisoner escapes from the cave. He sees the real world outside and returns to the cave to tell the other prisoners the truth—that the shadows they see are not reality. They do not believe him.

As a media professional, you could consider the prisoners to be a society composed of people who believe everything they see or hear such as rumors blasted through the internet. Consider the puppeteers to be the information manipulators, controlling what society sees and keeping it entertained. Outside of the cave sits reality or the truth. The prisoner who escapes is you, the media professional, returning to the cave to educate the other prisoners. In other words, if you become a member of the media, you need to educate society—but, first, you must educate yourself and have the courage to speak the truth.

ARISTOTLE'S VIRTUE ETHICS

Socrates and Plato both had an influence on the philosopher Aristotle (384–322 B.C.). Born in Macedonia, north of Ancient Greece, and the son of the doctor Nicomachus, Aristotle later created a decision-making tool, the Doctrine of the Mean, which can still be useful to us today. In 367 B.C., Aristotle moved to Athens and studied at Plato's Academy for 20 years. After Plato died, Aristotle left Athens for several years. He returned in 335 B.C. and created his own school, the Lyceum; Plato's nephew Speusippus had taken over the Academy after his uncle's death.

Although Aristotle died in his early 60s, he left many writings that read like lecture notes; scholars believe that what exists today is only about one third of his writings. His work differed from Plato's in that Aristotle used no comedy or irony as Plato sometimes did, and he studied diverse topics, which included biology and physics. Aristotle's writings on ethics include "Eudemian Ethics," edited by his student Eudemus, and "Nicomachean Ethics," edited by his son Nicomachus and thought to be the work written closest to his death and, therefore, to be the closest to his beliefs.

Aristotle believed that ethical decision making is a skill (a *tekhne*) and that ethical behavior cannot be an exact science; no formula fits every situation. Aristotle didn't give his decision-making tool a name, but many call it the Golden Mean or the Doctrine of the Mean. (The latter is preferable so as not to be confused with the Golden Rule.)

Although Aristotle believed no specific right action exists for any ethical situation, he did believe you should avoid the extremes. He saw virtue as a middle state between excess and deficiency. For instance, he said the virtue of courage, or being courageous, sits between two extremes—one being foolhardy and the other being cowardly. Finding the perfect point between these two extremes may be different from person to person or from case to case.

Examples of extremes follow:

Extravagance--Stinginess

Buffoonery--Boorishness

What is the most virtuous action between two extremes? To know what to choose, according to Aristotle, you must be working from the right character, which he said can't come just from reading. What's learned from a book, Aristotle called intellectual virtues; for instance, learning your profession's code of ethics by reading the code would be an intellectual virtue.

Aristotle believed you need to learn moral virtue through action, by actually practicing virtuous behavior. Moral virtues must be lived or be habits, he said. To use his Doctrine of the Mean, you must have the correct character. Aristotle would say that his mean can be understood and used by those who have grown up practicing the correct virtuous habits.

Character building should start with your parents and other adults involved in your early years. The people at your church might be included as well as your grade school and secondary school teachers. In college, university professors should be taking on the task. When you graduate and get a job, co-workers and supervisors should be mentors. Character building becomes an ongoing process. Adults should take on that responsibility, Aristotle said, and as you become older, he would ask that you do the same for the next generation.

To practice using his Doctrine of the Mean, let's say you work for a local news organization. The scanner announces a bad single-car accident in which a high school student has died. A photographer/videographer from your newsroom goes to the scene and takes a variety of shots—from gory images of the body to faraway shots showing just crime scene tape with authorities standing around. You and your colleagues need to choose a photo to use for the daily print product and to put online.

As in every such situation, additional information comes into play. In the past 30 days, four other high school students have died in automobile accidents in your community, and all of them involved underage drinking. The police say they suspect alcohol may be a factor in tonight's accident as well. People in the community have become increasingly concerned. Given this information, how could Aristotle's Doctrine of the Mean help you decide which photo to publish and whether video is appropriate? Crime scene tape photo? Gory photo? Those are the extremes, and you need to choose something in between. Would the recent cluster of accidents push you more toward the "gory" extreme because you'd reason the situation should not be sugar-coated?

Each person in each situation may come up with a different decision, a different point between extremes. The Doctrine of the Mean helps you and your colleagues make a choice after reflecting on the facts. Aristotle wrote in his "Nicomachean Ethics," "Virtuous behavior is to experience emotions at the right time, toward the right objects or people for the right reason in the right manner in accordance with the mean."[3] As you build character, finding the mean will become easier—and it will become "habit."

KANT'S DUTY-BASED ETHICS

We now move a few centuries ahead from Aristotle and Ancient Greece. Modern philosopher Immanuel Kant (1724–1804) was born in Konigsberg, East Prussia (now Kaliningrad, Russia), the son of a harness maker. At age 16, he began attending the University of Konigsberg, where many of his professors emphasized individual moral behavior. After his studies, Kant became a professor at the university, where he taught for most of his life.

Kant believed following a society's laws is necessary, so order can be maintained. However, he also believed all men are equal, and no one should be treated as a means to an end. Kant's duty-based categorical imperative asks us to act in a way that everyone would agree upon; thus, everyone, following laws, would live in a free and equal society. In his "Grounding for the Metaphysics of Morals,"[4] Kant writes that the

---

3. Aristotle, *The Nicomachean Ethics*, trans. David Ross, revised by J. L. Ackrill and J. O. Urmson (New York: Oxford University Press, 1998), 38.

4. Immanuel Kant, *Grounding for the Metaphysics of Morals*, trans. James W. Ellington (Indianapolis, IN: Hackett, 1981), G421. (Citations from Grounding are cited G with page number from the Prussian Academy edition; original work published in 1785.)

categorical imperative is the supreme principle everyone should follow in all areas of life.

Take note: For Kant, your will should be influenced only by reason; you can control your will, but you can't control the consequences of your actions. His "supreme" version of the CI states, "Act only on a maxim that you can at the same time will to become a universal law."[5] (A maxim is a principle upon which everyone can agree. "Do not plagiarize," for instance, could be considered a maxim to keep in the media professions; it should be universal.) Therefore, people should follow, or create, maxims that they trust all reasonable people would follow. Kant believed people have the capacity to reason, and reason should always come before desire. According to Kant, only a good will is moral, and a good will is determined by duty—not desire.

If you can't ask that everyone act on a maxim you have created, you should not act on that maxim yourself. For instance, if a public relations professional constantly lies to make his client look good, Kant would urge him to ask himself whether he would want all PR professionals to behave this way. Of course not. This is not a maxim to keep because it would cause people to believe, incorrectly, that all PR professionals lie and are not to be trusted.

Kant's second "formula"[6] of the CI, the formula of humanity, states, "Act so as to treat humanity in oneself and others only as an end in itself, and never merely as a means." You would certainly avoid treating others with whom you deal in your job in a way that you would not want to be treated yourself. Let's say a reporter from your news organization doesn't like the state's governor. In the story she's writing, the reporter wants to use only quotes that make the governor appear incompetent—although she has other quotes that make him sound intelligent. "Choose quotes to fit your agenda." Is that a maxim you'd like all reporters to keep? No. Should all reporters use quotes judiciously? Yes. That would be the maxim to keep.

Kant believed our responsibility includes following maxims that make us law-abiding members of society—which, for the purposes of this book, includes being a responsible media professional. As he wrote in

---

5. Ibid.

6. Ibid., G436.

another formulation of the categorical imperative, called the formula of legislation for a moral community, "Every rational being must act as if by his maxims he were at all times a legislative member of the universal kingdom of ends."[7]

Like Aristotle, Kant believed that if you don't have the appropriate moral education, you can't apply the categorical imperative. How do you learn which maxims to keep? Kant provides his opinion on moral education in his "Doctrine of Virtue: Part II of the Metaphysics of Morals" when he explains "the very concept of virtue implies that virtue must be acquired." For the media professional in training, university courses would be an appropriate place to begin. Kant believed in teaching his students using the case method as this book does, so they could learn to reason through ethical dilemmas already experienced by others.

UTILITARIANISM AND J. S. MILL'S PRINCIPLE OF UTILITY

The doctrine of basic utilitarianism says the best course of action is the one that creates the greatest benefit for everyone affected. The doctrine has been both expanded and refined over the years, and today it has many variations.

Today, utilitarians often describe benefits and harms in terms of the satisfactions of personal preferences or in economic terms. Although utilitarians differ, most believe in the general principle that morality depends on balancing the beneficial and harmful *consequences* of their conduct. This idea is familiar to many media professionals. For instance, let's say that a state's director of disability services is not doing his job correctly, and thus dozens of developmentally disabled adults are not receiving the services they need. If the director asks a journalist why she thinks it's important to report on him, she might answer, "Look at the good a story could do" or "Look at the harm a story could prevent." The journalist is weighing the harm to the reputation of the agency and its director against the good the story could do for society—warning people about a problem and furthering the beneficial work of the social service agency.

---

7. Ibid. G431.

Enter John Stuart Mill (1806–1873). Rigorously educated in London by his father, James, and Jeremy Bentham (considered to be the father of utilitarianism and "the greatest good for the greatest number"), Mill was tutored in classic utilitarianism as a youth. (He allegedly learned the Greek language at age 3.) In his early 20s, Mill had a nervous break-down from his intense schooling. After his illness, he re-explored Bentham's brand of utilitarianism and came to believe that merely using math (the calculus of felicity)[8] to decide the number of people who will benefit instead of the number who will be harmed was not enough when making a moral decision. Mill argued in the 19th century that "quality" was also essential to ethical decision making.

"It would be absurd that . . . the estimation of pleasure should be sup-posed to depend on quantity alone," Mill wrote in his "Utilitarianism."[9] For example, he said the act of reading poetry was better (quality-wise) than playing "push-pin," a silly game of the time, although lots of people played push-pin. Mill's theory goes beyond the catchphrase "the greatest good for the greatest number"; he believed quality should also be fac-tored into the calculation of the greatest amount of happiness.

Mill feared that a literal application of Bentham's version of utilitarian-ism could, over a number of generations, erode culture; he believed it is part of our human heritage to have desires higher than those that lend themselves to Bentham's kind of analysis.

To understand the importance of including "quality" in your decision making, think of the extremes media professionals might go to if they believed "the greatest good for the greatest number" is an abso-lute. What's to stop them from using lies, coercion and manipulation, or even breaking the law, as they gather information? They could argue that their reported information would help more people than it would hurt, then poof! They would have a justification for almost anything. Obviously, you will need to moderate these actions with a sense of perspective. You know that deception by media professionals

---

8. This is Bentham's mathematical formula to precisely chart the pleasure and happiness factors of any activity.

9. John Stuart Mill, *Utilitarianism,* edited by G. Sher (Indianapolis, IN: Hackett, 1979), 8.

is permissible only in rare situations, when no other route exists to accomplish your goal, a goal that must be of extreme importance to the public. After all, why should anyone believe the information you present is true if you lied to get it?

Let's say you're a TV reporter who wants to go undercover to expose a carpet cleaning company whose practices have been a source of viewer complaints. You and a colleague rent a house on your news organization's dime and pretend to be married. After setting up your "household," you call the carpet cleaning company and ask for the advertised special: three rooms of carpeting cleaned for only $99.

The cleaners show up and tell you that because of a number of factors peculiar to your house, the cost will be much higher. Your hidden camera gets everything on tape, and you air the tape and story the following week. Although you believe you have benefitted viewers and kept them from harm, were you thinking of quantity rather than quality?

A carpet cleaning scam is not a life-or-death situation for the public. Using deceit to find the truth is justified only when the situation you're exposing is of extreme importance to the public's well-being and then only when there's no other way to get the information you need. Hiding cameras would not be virtuous behavior, according to Mill, and he certainly wouldn't consider "sweeps month" when stations hype coverage in order to increase viewership and advertising rates, an argument in favor of deception.

Mill would ask the broadcast journalists who are about to set up their undercover investigation the following: "How would you use my principle of utility in this situation?" He would ask the journalists to choose their means wisely, and this is where he differs from Bentham. Do the journalists have other means available to them? What about interviewing people who have been scammed by the carpet cleaning company—with social media and the complaints the station has already received, the aggrieved parties shouldn't be tough to find—then asking the company to respond to the allegations? People who watch a segment done this way would be just as protected from harm as people who watch a hidden camera exposé. No deceit is needed.

Similar to Aristotle and Kant, Mill believed people need to cultivate a love of virtue before applying his principles, and he said that habit is the only thing that imparts certainty. A journalist, via habit, needs to rely on his or her own conduct when making ethical decisions. Therefore, merely following a quantitative approach to the greatest happiness, or greatest good, is no way to come to a reasoned decision. When decision making gets complex and you are on deadline, however, Mill said in "Utilitarianism"[10] that following the guidance of basic moral rules (for the media, think codes) can be appropriate. He called these the secondary moral principles.

ROSS' PRIMA FACIE AND ACTUAL DUTIES

Welcome to the 20th century and to philosophers who work from the ideas of earlier scholars. Scottish-born philosopher Sir William David Ross (1877–1971), a leading Aristotle scholar during his lifetime, translated many of Aristotle's works. He presented his own ideas on ethical decision making in his 1930 text "The Right and the Good." He was not a fan of utilitarianism (or consequentialism) and instead appealed to common sense or intuition.

Ross believed in prima facie duties—obligations that most people can understand and accept as important. Ross' prima facie duties include the following:

- Keeping promises (fidelity)
- Showing gratitude for favors
- Practicing justice
- Making others' lives better (beneficence)
- Avoiding harm
- Making amends when necessary (reparation)
- Improving yourself

Note that Ross didn't call these the only duties; he believed you could add to the list. In some ethical dilemmas, though, two or more of your duties will conflict. When this happens, Ross advises you to look at the

---

10. Ibid., 8.

duties on your list. Which one ranks highest for this particular situation? The duty that fits best is the one to choose. The prima facie duty that you choose is called the actual duty. Ross would say that moral principles are not absolute; principles, or codes, have exceptions. You should use your common sense.

For example, let's say that a PR professional has a client who is building a housing development on top of a former landfill. Environmental experts have determined that the site will pose no threat to future homeowners. The PR professional has promised her client, the developer, that she won't mention the landfill in press releases. After making this promise, however, she begins to weigh her duties again, and she decides that not mentioning the landfill to potential buyers will create more harm than good. The buyers might feel deceived. For this media professional in this particular case, the duty to avoid harm takes precedence over the duty to keep her promise to the client. The PR professional decides to tell her client that she can't keep the promise and to explain why.

Sometimes called an intuitionist, Ross believes our duties should be obvious or self-evident. Although we use reasoning about our duties, common sense ultimately becomes the basis of Ross' theory. He's been criticized for believing that intuition makes a decision self-evident, but some embrace this "common sense" approach.

JOHN RAWLS' VEIL OF IGNORANCE

John Rawls (1921–2002), a contemporary philosopher and Harvard professor, created a concept of justice that many students find especially helpful in making ethical decisions. Rawls' 1971 book, "A Theory of Justice," provides a theory of justice as fairness, addressing personal rights. When you work through an ethical dilemma, Rawls does not want you to think about your place in society. Instead, Rawls wants you to get into "the original position." Instead, he advocates putting yourself behind what he calls a "veil of ignorance."

When you're behind this veil, you must forget who you are; only then can you step into the shoes of others who are involved in the dilemma. Forgetting who you are means not considering your class status, religion, ethnicity or values. You consider the viewpoints and welfare of everyone involved because everyone is equal. When the veil lifts after the decision is made, you don't know what your identity will be; you could be master or slave, royalty or pauper.

Media ethics scholar Deni Elliott, the author of the next chapter, suggests taking the following steps when using Rawls' theory:[11]

- List all the people who will be affected by your decision, including yourself.

- Put yourself behind a veil of ignorance, giving up your identity, then assume one by one each of the identities of the people involved in the dilemma.

- Imagine a discussion taking place among the various players, with no one knowing what his or her ultimate identity will be when a decision is made.

Consider this situation: You work for an ad agency, and your supervisor has asked you to do a mockup for a print advertisement. In the ad photo and copy, he wants you to stereotype a certain ethnic group in a way that he thinks will be hilarious. You, however, do not see the humor; you believe the ad will cause harm.

Try working through this dilemma, preparing for a discussion with your boss about the inappropriateness of his idea, using the steps above. People to consider in this discussion are consumers; members of the ethnic group; your boss; you; and, finally, the client, who has hired the agency. Can you think of others?

Because all those involved are equal under Rawls' veil, "The principles of justice are the result of a fair agreement or bargain, and perhaps the question will be answered."[12] A discussion among equals leads to a "reflective equilibrium," he said. A consensus surfaces, a contract, and everyone's principles conform and everyone benefits.

For both Rawls and Kant (according to Kant's categorical imperative), an act is chosen because of a person's nature as "a free and equal rational

---

11. Deni Elliott. 2001. Handout from Association for Education in Journalism and Mass Communication Media Ethics Division workshop, Washington, D.C.

12. John Rawls, *A Theory of Justice* (Boston: Harvard University Press, 1971), 120.

being." The word Rawls stresses is equal. Society as a whole will be better off if we allow for equality. Rawls' view can help us raise our social awareness when we make ethical decisions.

SISSELA BOK'S TEST OF PUBLICITY

Contemporary philosopher Sissela Bok, author of the book "Lying: Moral Choices in Public and Private Life," believes in the importance of justifying our actions to others—which means not only do you need to think through your decisions before making them, but you should also be able to make your decision-making process public.

Although her model "the test of publicity" addresses the question, "When is it OK to lie?" it can be used with other ethical dilemmas in the media professions. Lying aims to mislead or deceive—and if a media professional encounters a situation where it seems that misleading or deceiving the public might be appropriate, it's time to reason through the dilemma.

Bok's ethical decision-making model is based on these two principles: We must have empathy for the people involved in our ethical decisions, and we must maintain social trust. Once you've acknowledged those two things, she advocates analyzing your ethical decision making in three steps:

1. Consult your own sense of right and wrong. How do you feel about the proposed course of action that is creating the dilemma? (What exactly is bothering you?)

2. Seek advice on alternatives. Is there another way to accomplish the same objective without raising ethical issues? You can ask colleagues or consult a philosopher's theory.

3. How will this action affect others? If possible, have a discussion with the parties involved. If impossible, conduct the discussion hypothetically, with colleagues in your workplace representing various points of view.

If you go through all three steps before making a decision, Bok says, you'll be able to justify that decision—in other words, it will stand the test of publicity.

Let's say you're an editor for a news website. Rioting broke out in your city's downtown area last night after a concert. If you decide to publish on your site the video your reporter shot—a video that shows graphic violence with police officers and citizens who are clearly identifiable—will you be ready to answer the public outcry that's likely to follow? Will you know how to justify your decision to the police officer shown clubbing a student or to the family of the student lying bloodied on the ground? Will you survive the test of publicity?

The acceptable justification is that the issue you're investigating is crucial to the safety of the public. Poynter's Bob Steele has a valuable checklist, available at Poynter.org, relating to one specific kind of deceit, the use of hidden cameras. Steele's first guideline states that hidden cameras should be used only when the issue being investigated is of extreme importance to society. "It must be of vital public interest, such as revealing great system failure at the top levels, or it must prevent profound harm to individuals." Even then, he lists five other criteria that must be satisfied before the deception can be justified.[13]

AN ETHICS OF CARE

Another area of contemporary ethics, known as the "ethics of care," is based on feminist theory and takes into account both self and other. In other words, this idea puts relationships at the center of ethical decision making. The ideas of two notable "ethics of care" advocates follow.

Carol Gilligan's book "In a Different Voice," first published in 1982, points out that women tend to uphold an ethics of care in which taking care of others becomes most important in deliberations. Gilligan believes that women have a unique morality: They speak in a different voice from men, she says, because they have been taught a "language" of care and responsibility since childhood. People who develop a morality of care go from caring only about themselves to including the care of themselves and others—and, thus, being careful that no one is harmed.

In Gilligan's view, male scholars, including psychologist Sigmund Freud and educational psychologist Lawrence Kohlberg, ignored the

---

13. http://www.poynter.org/uncategorized/744/deceptionhidden-cameras-check list/

differences between men and women; thus, she believes their studies and findings about moral development may not always apply to women. Although later research showed that moral reasoning does not always follow gender lines, Gilligan's work helped to create awareness of the concept of an ethics of care.

Nel Noddings, an educator who wrote the 1984 book "Caring: A Feminine Approach to Ethics and Moral Education," believes utilitarianism and duty-based ethics do not provide an understanding of the way women approach ethical dilemmas. For women, she says, ethics begins with a relationship. Real care requires actual encounters with specific individuals—it cannot be accomplished only through good intentions.

The first party in the relationship she calls the "one-caring," and the second person is the "cared-for." To complete the relationship, the cared-for must give in return. This could be through a verbal response or via the cared-for's personal growth, which is witnessed by the one-caring. In "Caring," Noddings writes that she believes the following as a teacher: "The student is infinitely more important than the subject."[14] For instance, you may have had instructors who not only taught you in class but also made clear that they cared about your overall well-being.

Noddings believes people grappling with a dilemma should see human care as their main responsibility. So, to apply her ideas to the media professions, when reporters interview a source for a magazine article, it would be caring behavior to spend time with that source, to listen carefully and to record statements correctly—and the interview would preferably be face-to-face. Of course, this behavior would not only demonstrate that you care about the people you interview; it would also make them more comfortable and willing to talk to you.

An ethics of care may not seem to apply as directly to media professions as it does to medicine, for instance. Given all the studies showing that the public sees the media as uncaring, however, it's clearly important to demonstrate care in your professional work, thus avoiding unnecessary harm.

---

14. Nel Noddings, *Caring: A Feminine Approach to Ethics and Moral Education* (Berkeley: University of California Press, 1984), 20.

Ethical Decision Making and Religion

Some of us begin our ethical training in Sunday school or catechism classes. As children, we start to learn right and wrong through religious teachings. Many Christians, Muslims, Hindus, Jews and others will contend ethics is not separate from their religions; a divine command theory exists. Yes, religion can be considered to be moral in some sense, but teachings are often interpreted in ways that can be confusing.

The English philosopher Anthony Garrad Newton Flew rebelled against religion as a teenager; his father was a Methodist minister. He became an atheist, but a few years before he died in 2010 at the age of 87, he said he believed that God did exist. However, during his lifetime he posed a question to the timeless dilemma: "Is conduct right because the gods command it, or do the gods command it because it is right?" There is no answer to this question that will please everyone.

Christianity's theory of agape can be described as selfless, unconditional love for humankind (and humankind for God). The concept of loving your neighbor has been around for centuries. It's "neighbor-love." Neighborly love is when one considers the interests of others and not simply his or her own. We have regard for others, in other words. So we must always love our neighbors—no matter what they have done or who they are. We can't describe your "neighbors" as superior or inferior—we can't prefer one neighbor to another. We cannot discriminate. And this is sometimes where Christians fall short. One ought to be "for" another, but this does not always happen.

Although the Judeo-Christian tradition is the most prominent in U.S. culture, one does not have to be a Christian to use aspects of agape or aspects of any religion that appeal to you. The concept of love in all religions should not be discounted. For instance, Muhammad the prophet, the founder of Islam, professed selfless relationships. Although many Muslims believe that the Quran is the word of God, Muhammad's sayings and actions are included in the book—and he is also called upon during the daily call to prayer. While the ethical teachings of Islam are rooted in the Quran, an example of excellent ethical character has always been Muhammad's.[15] He was very much like Jesus, living very simply, practicing spiritual poverty and devoting himself to the poor. Different sects of Islam have been created over the years—sects that interpret the Quran and its core values differently.

According to Mohammad A. Siddiqi, the author of "Muhammad: Honor-Centered Morality," Muhammad would promote a universal code of ethics to be followed by all communicators. "It would not allow the use of communication to support a particular nation or people," he says. "Rather, it would urge people to use communication for the benefit of all."[16]

Although this book focuses on Western philosophy, Eastern ethical theories from Asia could also be considered: Confucianism, Hinduism, Buddhism. For instance, born in 1869, Mahatma Gandhi, a Buddhist with roots in Hinduism, created principles that may be useful in decision making. Gandhi professed a nonviolent social order with the welfare of human beings being the ultimate consideration in ethical decision making; Confucius (born 551 B.C.) professed equality for every person and education for everyone without discrimination. This is socially responsible thinking.

Concluding Thoughts

Now that you've learned the basics of some theories and codes that help working professionals make ethical choices, the next chapter takes a look at moral development and how it affects the way you make those decisions. You should be able to identify the stages you have been through already. After that, you'll be ready to move from theory to practice.

The remaining chapters of the book are true stories about tough situations young people encountered while they were students or at their first jobs. In addition to the narrative of what happened, the authors of

---

15. http://www.britannica.com/biography/Muhammad/The-ethical-and-spiritual-character

16. Clifford G. Christians and John C. Merrill (eds.), *Ethical Communication: Moral Stances in Human Dialogue* (Columbia: University of Missouri Press, 2009), 143.

the chapters share their thoughts on theories, codes or other decision-making tools that might be helpful in resolving each dilemma. You may agree or disagree with the approaches they take, but now you have some tools to help you think and discuss. As Aristotle would say, let the character building begin!

Bibliography

Aristotle. *Introduction to Aristotle.* Translated by Richard McKeon. New York: Modern Library, 1947.

Aristotle. *The Nicomachean Ethics.* Translated by David Ross. New York: Oxford World's Classic, 1998.

Baron, Marcia, Pettit, Philip, and Slote, Michael. *Three Methods of Ethics.* Malden, MA: Blackwell Publishing, 1997.

Bok, Sissela. *Lying: Moral Choices in Public and Private Life.* New York: Pantheon Books, 1978.

Christians, Clifford G., and Merrill, John C., eds. *Ethical Communication.* Columbia: University of Missouri Press, 2009.

Gilligan, Carol. *In a Different Voice*, 29th ed. Boston: Harvard University Press, 1992.

Good, Howard, ed. *Desperately Seeking Ethics.* Lanham, MD: Scarecrow Press, 2003.

Good, Howard, ed. *Journalism Ethics Goes to the Movies.* Lanham, MD: Rowman & Littlefield, 2007.

Herman, Barbara. *The Practice of Moral Judgment.* Cambridge, MA: Harvard University Press, 1993.

Kant, Immanuel. *The Doctrine of Virtue: Part II of the Metaphysics of Morals.* Translated by Mary J. Gregor. New York: Harper & Row, 1964. (Original work published 1797)

Kant, Immanuel. *Ethical Philosophy.* Translated by James W. Ellington. Indianapolis, IN: Hackett, 1983.

Kant, Immanuel. *Grounding for the Metaphysics of Morals.* Translated by James W. Ellington. Indianapolis, IN: Hackett, 1981. (Original work published in 1785)

Mill, John S. *Utilitarianism.* Edited by George Sher. Indianapolis, IN: Hackett, 1979.

Noddings, Nel. *Caring: A Feminine Approach to Ethics and Moral Education.* Berkeley: University of California Press, 1984.

Plato. *Republic.* Translated by Robin Waterfield. Cary, N.C.: Oxford University Press, 1998.

Rawls, John. *A Theory of Justice.* Boston: Belknap Press of Harvard University Press, 2005.

Ross, W. D. *The Right and the Good.* Indianapolis, IN: Hackett, 1988. (Originally published 1930)

Steele, Bob. "When might it be appropriate to use deception/misrepresentation/hidden cameras in newsgathering?" Available at the Poynter Institute website, http://www.poynter.org/uncategorized/744/deceptionhidden-cameras-checklist/

Sullivan, Roger J. *Immanuel Kant's Moral Theory.* Cambridge, UK: Cambridge University Press, 1989.

Vaughn, Stephen, ed. *Encyclopedia of American Journalism.* New York: Routledge, 2007.

Wick, Warner A. "Introduction." In *Ethical Philosophy* (I. Kant). Indianapolis, IN: Hackett, 1995.

CHAPTER 2

The Morally Developed Media Professional

Deni Elliott

Some people think of ethics as a personality trait: You either have ethics or you don't; you learned the right thing to do from parents or church, or you didn't. In this view, there are bad guys and good guys, them and us. Choices are absolutely right or absolutely wrong. You shouldn't have to think much about how to behave; you just know.

In truth, making ethical choices is a skill that gets better with experience. It's a skill that we are all hardwired to have, just as we are hardwired as human beings to have the capacity to walk, talk and grow intellectually. In the same way that playing a sport well requires paying attention to your physical movements, making good ethical decisions requires paying attention to your motivations and choices. The more you understand, the more you practice, the better you get at considering all the important aspects of ethical decision making and the more honest you become in recognizing your own limitations and opportunities for moral development.

In this fast-changing digital age, when everyone with access to the internet can be both a publisher and consumer of mass communication, and many news organizations feel intense pressure to do whatever's necessary to attract audiences and money, it's more important than ever for media professionals to cultivate and exhibit high ethical standards.

This chapter takes you through the stages from early ethical decision making to moral sophistication. (The descriptions of psychological theories come from a variety of sources, which are listed in the footnotes.) Then you'll read the story of a young reporter who found herself in a clash between her own ethics and those of the profession, ultimately creating an opportunity for self-reflection and moral growth.

MORAL DEVELOPMENT IN THEORY

The best analogy for human moral development is how we learn to use our native language. Both processes are sequential, meaning that development happens in a consistent and predictable way. Both depend on environment; excellence may be fostered by those around you, or not.

Finally, moral sophistication, like having excellent communication abilities, describes what you're capable of, not what you actually do in every situation. This is the difference between capacity and achievement. For example, even if you're capable of speaking as eruditely as an Oxford professor, you don't (and shouldn't) talk that way when ordering breakfast at a diner. Even if you're capable of the most sophisticated moral reasoning, you don't sit in your car pondering the benefit to society when you see blue lights flashing behind you and pull over.

The sequential, predictable nature of moral development has led psychologists to identify important signs that indicate where people are in their progress through the stages toward sophisticated reasoning.

WHO'S WHO IN MORAL DEVELOPMENT THEORY

Research in moral development began in the early 20th century with the work of Swiss psychologist Jean Piaget. Studying the rules that children create in playing games, Piaget recognized that the way they governed their play grew more complex over time, as did their understanding of fairness and what one player owed another, or how one player should compensate for the limitations of another.

A psychologist who expanded the work of Piaget, Lawrence Kohlberg, is often called the father of moral development theory. Kohlberg was the first to indicate specific markers that revealed how people were reasoning about right and wrong. His theory, along with the work of moral psychologists William Perry and Carol Gilligan, provides a multidimensional view of the progression from externally oriented decision making to acting autonomously—making choices that reflect one's own careful reasoning.

Acting in an autonomous way is an essential aspect of moral development. True moral sophistication means not just making choices that avoid causing unjustified harm and promote the overall good, but also making those choices for the right reasons. In an analogous way, consider a student who does well on a math test. What's important is not just that she achieved a high score, which she might have done by looking over her neighbor's shoulder, but that she is demonstrating her ability to reason through the problems and find the correct answer. Just as students who truly understand math can reason about math concepts in an autonomous way, so too can morally developed media professionals choose to report accurately and fairly, whether working for editors in a traditional newsroom or working alone on a blog or hyperlocal site.

THE EARLY STAGE OF MORAL DEVELOPMENT

When they make choices about how to treat others, children reason in simple ways: They do what people in authority tell them. Gilligan, Kohlberg and Perry look at this strong external orientation from different angles but reach complementary conclusions.

Gilligan says a morally immature person perceives herself as powerless, working to protect herself from those who might cause her harm.[1] Kohlberg says a person in the early stages of moral development is motivated by the desire to reap reward and to escape punishment.[2] Perry describes learners in the early stages of ethical (as well as intellectual)

---

1. Carol Gilligan, *In a Different Voice* (Cambridge, MA: Harvard University Press, 1982).

2. Lawrence Kohlberg, *The Philosophy of Moral Development* (San Francisco, CA: Harper & Row, 1981).

development as being dogmatic and dependent on external authority for the perceived "correct" answer.[3]

No matter how morally sophisticated we might be, we all respond to authority sometimes, quite appropriately. For instance, we know that we must submit to (if not necessarily respect) authority when we allow ourselves and our bags to be screened at the airport. We show up to work on time because we don't want to get fired. Pragmatically, it would take too much time to agonize over every choice. It's natural to save our ethical energy for the tough decisions.

THE CONVENTIONAL STAGE OF MORAL DEVELOPMENT

The middle stage of moral development is called "conventional" because it's the level on which most people operate, most of the time. Gilligan describes people working from this level as recognizing that they do have power and that a "good" use of that power is in assisting others. Kohlberg says that the hallmark of conventional-level moral development is that people look to peers and to the rules/laws that govern a situation in deciding what is ethically right and wrong.

Perry adds the notion of relativism. While people thinking conventionally are willing to accept that no authority has all the answers, they are also likely to think that maybe there are no truly right answers at all. Rules and notions of right and wrong are thought to change with the situation, culture or group.

Gangs and middle school cliques provide many good examples of reasoning based on conventional morality as do college faculty, sports teams and dormitories. Any situation in which individuals are encouraged or coerced to adopt group norms is rich with elements of conventional morality. Consider the college classroom. When students speak, when the teacher speaks, whether students text their friends during class time—all these things are almost always controlled by unspoken, assumed conventions of behavior.

---

3. William G. Perry, *Form of Intellectual and Ethical Development in the College Years* (New York, NY: Holt, Rinehart and Winston, 1970).

The same is true of any office where you do an internship or get a job. You need to take the time to notice how the place functions—whether interactions are formal or casual, whether decisions are boss-directed or collaborative, and dozens of other variables—before you can be sure of the best way to behave and get your job done. As you'll see in the cases in this book, when young media professionals who are new to an organization encounter an ethical dilemma, their good impulses can be stymied by lack of knowledge of "the system" or fear of speaking out of turn. Learning the office culture is a key part of learning to make good decisions.

Competent adults make hundreds of choices every day about how to act in regards to other people. We don't trip people as they squeeze by on the bus. We don't yell in the library. We wait our turn in the check-out line. These choices don't take much conscious thought, nor should they. We make them to conform to what we have come to know as conventional morality.

THE LATER STAGE OF MORAL DEVELOPMENT

At some point in their development, people are faced with the need to make their own decisions. Authority figures do not seem to offer an answer that sits well. Going along with the crowd doesn't feel right. The realization that each person is responsible for his or her own decisions is an important step on the road to moral sophistication.

Morally sophisticated decision making is autonomous. The individual is able to reason beyond the reflex to do as he or she is told or to follow external rules. Instead, the person attempts to articulate the principle behind the rules and chooses behaviors that respect others. Morally sophisticated choices aim to contribute to the overall good of community. If someone is going to receive special consideration, it will be because the decision maker perceives that person as having special vulnerabilities. Yet the decision maker also considers her own needs in calculating the best choice. Moral sophistication includes the realization that no one needs to be left out or sacrificed for the overall good.

Morally sophisticated decision making takes time and effort. Most choices do not require this kind of careful calculation, but people who have matured to this level can recognize an ethically complex situation when they encounter it. They work to make sure that no one is hurt unless there is strong justification for causing that harm.

Ironically, recognizing one's fallibility is an important aspect of becoming morally sophisticated. It is a sign of moral maturity to recognize that you may be wrong. So while the morally sophisticated individual tries to make choices that express her values and take all affected others into account, she is open-minded about considering alternatives that may not have occurred to her.

Perry calls this open-mindedness "commitment with uncertainty." We make the best decisions we can, using our knowledge of the relevant facts; meanwhile, we remain open to taking in new information that may end up showing flaws in our previous reasoning. As you read the true stories in this book, you'll see that the young media professionals who consult with others when they face an ethical dilemma are more likely to move beyond their first response and thus more likely to make decisions that take into account all morally relevant aspects.

Morally sophisticated thinking requires being conscious of the decisions that we make and the justification that we use in making them. Doing this consistently and well takes practice.

Moral Development in Practice

Sara was an eager new journalist, having just completed her bachelor's degree. She was pleased to have landed a job as a reporter in a medium-market news organization; she loved the work and the interesting people she met on her reporting assignments. Sara arrived at work early and left late, intoxicated by the possibilities. She was moved by the plights of her story subjects and often found ways to help them. It made her feel strong, proud and ethical to be making a difference in her new community.

I met Sara when she took part in a newsroom ethics workshop that I facilitated; her name has been changed here to protect her privacy. Her editor had signed Sara up for the workshop, and she came with a dilemma to share.

ONE YOUNG REPORTER'S WAKE-UP CALL

Sara told us that her news organization did not appreciate her ethics. She didn't mind working long hours, she said; she had moved cross-country to take the reporting job and didn't know anyone yet. In high school and college, Sara had always been rewarded for her extra effort but not in the newsroom. The week before Sara came to the workshop, a union representative had told her that she could not work more than eight hours a day without claiming overtime. This policy surprised Sara and didn't seem fair. Because she was new to journalism, she was sure it took her longer to do each story than it would take a more experienced reporter, so she didn't want to point out her inexperience by asking for overtime pay.

The same day that the union representative told her to stick to the negotiated workday, the city editor set limits for Sara as well. "You're a great reporter," he said, "but when you are done reporting a story, its over." He told her it was not OK for her to check in on the pregnant drug addict she had interviewed. It was against newsroom policy for her to drop off a bag of groceries at the under-the-bridge cardboard shelter where the subject of her story on homelessness lived.

"You are a journalist," the editor said. "Your job is to tell the story. It's up to others in the community to take care of the problems. If the social workers or public agencies are not doing their jobs, then write about that. It is not your job to fix what's broken."

Both the union representative and the city editor told Sara that the other reporters had been complaining about her. "You're making those who have family responsibilities look bad," said the rep. "Being a missionary rather than a reporter is not a good way to make friends in the newsroom," the editor said.

Sara felt angry and hurt that her extra efforts were being criticized rather than appreciated. She thrived on the satisfaction she got from pursuing stories; she loved seeing her byline. How could any of this be wrong?

THE MORAL DEVELOPMENT PERSPECTIVE

As Sara shared her plight at the workshop, it was clear that she expected sympathy. Instead, the more seasoned journalists in the group patiently explained to her why they thought that the management perspective had some merit.

Over the lunch break that followed, I sat with Sara; I wanted to make sure she didn't feel beaten up by her peers. To my surprise, Sara said that she was not upset by the feedback she'd gotten; the others were right that she needed to think more about her choices and motivations. She didn't want to be a "lone ranger," but she did want to make a difference—and now she realized it was up to her to figure out how she could do good while working within the conventions of journalism and of her newsroom.

That was the last I saw of Sara. Her story has lived on for me, however, because I've discussed it with so many student journalists wondering about the challenges they'll face in their first jobs and with journalism ethics instructors who appreciate Sara's dilemma from a moral development point of view.

Here are some aspects of moral development that Sara's story illustrates:

1. No matter how morally sophisticated you are, most people when put in an unfamiliar environment tend to regress to the simplest form of ethical analysis. On some level, Sara knew the importance of building connections with her peers, and she knew that journalists had the power to change the world through their work. But, feeling isolated and inexperienced in her new job, she looked for approval in the ways that had worked for her before: She put in extra time, she tried to stretch every assignment into a front-page story, and she befriended her story subjects. She looked for others to reward her with gratitude or say that she'd done a good job, just as they always had in school.

2. Moral growth is best facilitated by exposure to people who are thinking in more morally developed ways. When Sara shared her dilemma, participants at the workshop encouraged her to consider what her peers might think about her choices and why they would question those choices. They let her know that her motivations and intuitions did not jibe with conventions of the newsroom.

3. Moral development is best understood by examining motivations rather than by looking only at the behavior. Helping others is a good act, but one may do so for any number of reasons. Doing something nice for her story subjects made Sara feel good and gave her some sense of control at a time when she often felt lost and powerless. When encouraged by the other journalists at the workshop, she was able to think about larger differences that she could make, even if it meant giving up a little immediate self-gratification. She was encouraged to move from a simplistic way of thinking about herself and her job to thinking about herself as a professional journalist.

BECOMING A MEDIA PROFESSIONAL

People change and grow through challenging experiences. In the realm of moral development, people can learn how to think more broadly about the situations in which they find themselves, ultimately resulting in what some moral philosophers have described as wisdom or moral sophistication. If Sara wanted to figure out what was reasonable for others to expect of her in her new job, the role-related responsibilities of journalism would provide a place for her to start.

Media theorists Bill Kovach and Tom Rosenstiel have provided a succinct description—"The primary purpose of journalism is to provide citizens with the information they need to be free and self-governing"[4]—that provides a way for journalists to balance the risks and benefits of a proposed action. Sometimes accurate reporting causes harm. The role-related responsibility of journalists to provide citizens with information helps determine when harm caused through publication is justified and when it is not.

For example, citizens need to know that an elected public official has been charged with misuse of public funds. This type of information helps people make important choices. But if the son of that public official was disciplined by his school for underage drinking, knowing this has no obvious benefit to the audience. The publication would cause

---

4. Bill Kovach and Tom Rosenstiel, *The Elements of Journalism* (New York, NY: Three Rivers Press, 2007), 12.

unjustified harm to the child involved. Even if you can legally publish such information, that doesn't make it ethical to do so.

In Sara's case, she was not causing any obvious harm; in fact, she was doing what she could to ease her subjects' burdens. Still, her city editor made a good point: If vulnerable people in the community are not receiving services that government should be providing, then that is the important story that needs to be told. Telling the story of one individual, without using it as a portal into a story about the larger issue, causes harm by diverting newsroom resources and public attention from the systemic problem.

Providing groceries to one homeless individual temporarily helps that person. Reporting a well-researched story that explains why people are homeless and looks at how other communities are handling the problem can help your audience advocate for better job opportunities, treatment for mental illnesses and housing to meet the needs of the disenfranchised.

RESOLVING SARA'S DILEMMA

We have no way of knowing what happened to the real-life Sara, but looking at her situation through the lens of moral development provides an idea of how Sara might have learned to better express her best self. If she had left the workshop and resolved to start thinking differently about the way she did her job, here's what might have happened:

Sara had chosen to become a journalist because she wanted to make a difference in the community. The comments from her editor and the union rep, and then from the professionals at the workshop, helped her realize that she would not be the most effective if she stuck to her lone ranger role. When Sara looked at the world solely from her own point of view and those of her story subjects, it was easy to meet the obvious need. When she included the perspectives of her newsroom colleagues and the community as a whole, the choices got more complicated.

She liked to write profiles of individuals, but she realized her editor was right: Stories about larger societal problems, using individuals' experiences to illustrate, could make a bigger difference. Somehow, it just hadn't registered before that her journalistic power gave her the ability to effect great change in the community rather than meeting individual needs here and there.

Because Sara still wanted to do something hands-on to make a difference, she began volunteering at a local women's shelter. Her volunteer work helped her make friends. With more things to do, she began leaving work as soon as she filed her assignments, at least on some days. Sara found herself thinking about how her stories could help readers recognize something new about their community. Sometimes she was successful, sometimes not, but she found that keeping this broader perspective gave life and relevance to her writing.

Sara stopped thinking of herself as competing with her peers; instead, she saw herself alongside them, working collaboratively. They were all journalists. They were community members. They were partners and friends and parents. And, through shared experiences and support, they worked to put together the puzzle pieces of becoming the best people that they could be.

EXERCISE YOUR OWN MORAL DEVELOPMENT

There are many good ways to stretch your moral decision-making abilities. Here are three that are easy to try:

1. Consider your recent ethical choices—in simplest terms, choices that promote good or avoid causing harm. Using the categories in this chapter, decide which level of moral development— simple, conventional or sophisticated—describes each choice. Practice explaining to yourself why you make which choice in difficult circumstances.

2. Appreciate your evolving moral sophistication. Think about how your reasoning has changed over time. Take a rule that you try to live by, such as "Don't lie" or "Respect other people's property." Think about when you first learned that rule and the reasons that you had for following it then.

   Usually, if the rule was implanted early in childhood, your memory of early motivations will be filled with parental messages of what would happen to you if you did or didn't follow the rule. You may then find yourself thinking about an experience in middle school and how a child who didn't follow these rules was ostracized by the group. Finally, your own contemporary reasoning is likely to include an understanding of how following that rule protects vulnerable individuals and how it helps the community to thrive. You still choose to be honest most of the time, but as an adult, you have different reasons for making that choice.

Now try the same exercise using rules you try to follow in a work environment.

3. Find a moral hero to interview. No, this doesn't have to be a present-day Gandhi. Look around for peers or managers who impress you with the way they treat others. Invite one of them to coffee and start with your observation, saying something like, "I've been watching you work, and I like how you always seem to consider other people." Everybody likes to be noticed for their positive attributes.

Then conduct a good profile interview: "Why do you do that? How did you learn that technique? When you were younger, did you behave differently? Why do you think that this is a good way to live?" The more that you can try on professional and personal styles that you admire, the more likely you can better develop these traits in yourself.

Now that you've grounded yourself in some theory and seen how that theory applies to one young journalist, and to yourself, you're ready to keep broadening your perspective. The chapters that follow tell the stories of young media professionals and the dilemmas they encountered early in their professional careers. Follow along with their choices, and think what you'd have done in their place, or what advice you might give them if you found yourself in a workshop hearing their stories.

BIBLIOGRAPHY

Elliott, Deni. *Ethics in the First Person.* Lanham, MD: Rowman & Littlefield, 2006.
Elliott, Deni. "Moral Development Theories and the Teaching of Ethics." *Journalism Educator*, Autumn (1991): 18–24.

Elliott, Deni. "Universal Values and Moral Development Theories." In *Communication Ethics and Universal Values,* edited by C. Christians and M. Traber, 68–83. Thousand Oaks, CA: Sage, 1997.

Gilligan, Carol. *In a Different Voice.* Cambridge, MA: Harvard University Press, 1982.

Kohlberg, Lawrence. *The Philosophy of Moral Development.* San Francisco, CA: Harper & Row, 1981.

Kovach, Bill, and Rosenstiel, Tom. *The Elements of Journalism.* New York, NY: Three Rivers Press, 2007.

Perry, William G. *Form of Intellectual and Ethical Development in the College Years.* New York, NY: Holt, Rinehart and Winston, 1970.

Piaget, Jean. *The Moral Judgment of the Child.* New York, NY: Free Press, 1948.

CHAPTER 3

Confronting Others' Violations

The Case of the Manipulated Photo

Donica Mensing

B eing mindful of your own ethical behavior is generally a full-time job. But what do you do when you encounter what appears to be unethical behavior by others? What responsibility do you have to confront or report other people's unethical actions?

A recent photojournalism graduate had to reason his way through these questions when he saw a professional freelance photographer manipulate photos of a major sporting event and then upload those photos for publication by a wire service. The young photojournalist had to decide whether he had a responsibility to report the violation of professional standards and, if so, when and how.

MORAL DEVELOPMENT IN THEORY

At age 25, David Calvert had been shooting photos for national wire services, newspapers and other clients for several years. An inspiring high school journalism teacher had turned him on to photojournalism, and it had become his passion. After college, he opened a freelance photography business, shooting everything from major news stories and national sporting events to marketing campaigns and weddings. He made a decent living and enjoyed the creative challenge and variety of assignments.

Through his school and work experiences, Calvert had been developing his own set of standards for doing his job ethically and professionally. He believed that any manipulation of news photos beyond cropping and making small lighting corrections was deceptive and wrong; numerous professional workshops, classes and mentors had reinforced that standard. Thus, what he witnessed one weekend in the press tent at a major sporting event took him by surprise.

Sitting behind an experienced freelance wire service photographer who was working on his computer, Calvert watched the photographer use Photoshop to manipulate an image of the event they were both covering.

"This was on Friday," Calvert said. "On Saturday, I saw that the image had been posted on the wire. Sunday, I sat behind him and saw him do it again. I couldn't believe he was doing it again. So I took out my phone and recorded him as he manipulated the image.

"I recorded it for a close friend. I didn't think about doing anything else with the video, just wanted to show her: 'Look what this guy did!'" However, Calvert was upset enough to check the wire the next day. He saw that the manipulated photo, in which a person had been removed from the background behind a player, had been posted. But that's not all he found.

While scanning his daily news links, Calvert noticed a link to a blog post by the photo editor of a major metropolitan newspaper. The photo editor had discovered the manipulated image by the freelance wire service photographer and had written about it on the newspaper's photography blog. The editor wrote that he'd been looking for an image of the sporting event for the next day's paper when he noticed two photos—one a medium-distance shot of a major sports figure, the other a much tighter shot that seemed to have been taken at the same moment.

Looking more closely, the editor realized the two photos had been taken by the same person and were identical with one exception: In the tight shot, a person behind the player had been removed, leaving the background clear and uncluttered. "If [that person] is not there, the image is somewhat better," the photo editor wrote in his column. "But at what cost?"

After having called the photo desk of the wire service and confirming that they, too, believed the image had been manipulated, the photo editor posted both images on his newspaper's blog and wrote a post about what he found.

Reading this, Calvert was relieved that the deception had been uncovered. According to the photo editor's blog, the wire service had issued a "kill notice" warning others not to publish the manipulated image. The wire service also announced that it was terminating the freelancer's contract. As far as Calvert was concerned, the problem had been solved. It was a stark lesson that reinforced the importance of maintaining professional standards.

TOOL FOR THOUGHT:
The Potter Box

The Potter Box provides simple guidelines for ethical decision making. Developed by Ralph Potter Jr., who was a professor of social ethics at Harvard Divinity School, it focuses on four dimensions of ethical reasoning: facts, values, principles and loyalties. To reason through an ethical dilemma, one should start with the facts, identify values, make principles explicit and then decide which loyalties are most important. This final step will lead to a potential way to resolve the dilemma. If necessary, the process can then be repeated until the facts, values, principles and loyalties align and a justified decision can be made.

1. Facts	4. Loyalties
2. Values	3. Principles

Facts. The analysis of any ethical question begins with

assessing all relevant facts. What do we know about the situation? In the situation in this chapter, it would have been a mistake for Calvert to say anything about the photographer based solely on what he saw in the press tent. If the photographer had not submitted the altered photograph for publication, no harm would have been done. Journalists always confirm facts.

Values. In this step, the decision maker identifies his or her most important values. For example, the values identified in the National Press Photographers Association Code of Ethics include truth, accuracy, comprehensiveness, respect and dignity. In this case, truthfulness was a key value because Calvert strongly believed that published news photographs should be accurate and that professionals should be truthful. Identifying truthfulness as a value required Calvert to address the issue in some way and not simply move on. Valuing dignity meant that he wouldn't take an action that would embarrass the photographer publicly. Being explicit about the importance of particular values gives the decision maker a concrete way to evaluate potential actions.

Principles. Looking at your values through the lens of different systems of ethics can help you develop a range of possible actions. These principles might include (among many others) Aristotle's Doctrine of the Mean, Kant's Categorical Imperative or Mill's Principle of Utility.

In Calvert's case, applying Aristotle's mean would help him identify extreme actions—doing nothing or, at the other extreme, posting the video on a website read by professional photographers—and develop a moderate action that would address the problem respectfully. Kant's Categorical Imperative, on the other hand, might suggest that Calvert contact the newspaper photo editor and let him know that he had been lied to. If we believe that no one should lie, then Kant's principle requires actions

(Continued)

(Continued)

that punish lying and promote honesty.

Mill's utilitarian principle requires choosing the alternative that factors in not just quantity but quality. In this case, the consequences of staying silent benefit only the photographer but harm the profession and the public, whereas the consequences of speaking up benefit the public and the profession and censure only the photographer who failed to practice professional standards.

Loyalties. At this point in the reasoning process, determining whom or what you are loyal to helps clarify thinking. In this case, Calvert could identify loyalties to himself, to his profession and to the public. He could ask himself whether loyalty to another photojournalist was more important than loyalty to his profession or to the public. Loyalty to both his profession and the public would require speaking up in some way to prevent the publication of manipulated photos. Once a decision is made to be loyal to the profession and the public, the direction is clear. All that remains is to determine the mechanics of how to carry out the decision respectfully and effectively.

THE CHALLENGE: SPEAK UP OR STAY SILENT?

The next morning, Calvert's sense of closure about the event was shattered. He found an update to the blog post by the newspaper photo editor. The editor reported that the freelance photographer had called and told him that he had uploaded the manipulated sports photo by mistake after creating it to show one of the players how easy it was to make someone disappear in a photo. The photographer said it was a moronic mistake, a one-time error that he deserved to be punished for. The newspaper editor accepted the photographer's apology and wrote about the conversation, explaining that it sounded like an innocent mistake.

Calvert was stunned. "When I read his quote about making an innocent mistake, I thought, 'You're lying!' That's when I felt I should let someone at the wire service know. There are a lot of amazing photographers at the wire service who don't deserve to be painted with the same brush as him."

Calvert's dilemma was obvious: Should he contact someone at the wire service? Write to the newspaper photo editor who'd written the columns? Should he post or send someone the video he'd taken of the photographer manipulating the image?

The Response: Seeking Counsel

Calvert debated the dilemma in his mind for two days. It was true the problem had been addressed by someone else, but only partially. The public resolution was not an accurate one. If other editors believed the "innocent mistake" explanation, the photographer who'd manipulated and lied might continue to get jobs and potentially deceive the public again. Calvert also discovered other photos in the wire service archive taken by this photographer that looked to him as if they'd been manipulated, including burned-out backgrounds and cloning inconsistencies.

As a member of a profession he cares about deeply, Calvert believed the standards of professionalism had meaning only to the extent they were upheld. If he knew about a violation and said nothing, he would be complicit in failing to uphold standards he considered vital to maintaining public confidence in photojournalism. He had a duty to defend standards he believed in and practiced.

"It was never my intention to play gotcha," Calvert said. "At that point, the photographer had already been punished by the wire service. What really bothered me was the lying. I felt saying something was important for the industry and for the professionals at the wire service."

For counsel, Calvert turned to his mentors: his journalism professors and two photographers he respected. One person validated his decision not to "out" the professional on his own blog, saying that action would forever identify Calvert as "the person who outed so and so." Others had a range of advice, including calling an editor at the wire service and reporting what he had seen.

After listening to all these pieces of advice, Calvert put several suggestions together and came up with a plan he believed he could live with and believed would have the desired result. He contacted a friend who knew a photo editor at the wire service where the photographer had worked. In an email and follow-up phone call, he explained to the friend what he had observed at the sporting event and told him that he had a video showing what the photographer had done. The note also mentioned that he believed other photos taken by the photographer and still available on the wire service may have been manipulated. He requested that the friend relay his message to the wire service editor if he thought the information was important to share.

After sending the message, Calvert felt relieved. He had resolved the situation to his own satisfaction, speaking up in a way that would honor the standards of the profession while avoiding a public confrontation.

■ ■ ■ TOOL FOR ACTION: NPPA Ethics Code

The code of ethics[1] of the National Press Photographers Association, an organization dedicated to the advancement of visual journalism, defines the standards and ideals of a professional visual journalist. The preamble to the code states, in part:

> Visual journalists operate as trustees of the public. Our primary role is to report visually on the significant events and varied viewpoints in our common world. Our primary goal is the faithful and comprehensive depiction of the subject at hand.

As visual journalists, we have the responsibility to document society and to preserve its history through images.

Photographic and video images can reveal great truths, expose wrongdoing and neglect, inspire hope and understanding and connect people around the globe through the language of visual understanding. Photographs can also cause great harm if they are callously intrusive or are manipulated.

The code itself is divided into two parts. The first half defines the standards that visual journalists should uphold in their daily work:

1. Be accurate and comprehensive in the representation of subjects.

2. Resist being manipulated by staged photo opportunities.

3. Be complete and provide context when photographing or recording subjects. Avoid stereotyping individuals and groups. Recognize and work to avoid presenting one's own biases in the work.

4. Treat all subjects with respect and dignity. Give special consideration to vulnerable subjects and compassion to victims of crime or tragedy. Intrude on private moments of grief only when the public has an overriding and justifiable need to see.

5. While photographing subjects do not intentionally contribute to, alter, or seek to alter or influence events.

6. Editing should maintain the integrity of the photographic images' content and context. Do not manipulate images or add or alter sound in any way that can mislead viewers or misrepresent subjects.

7. Do not pay sources or subjects or reward them materially for information or participation.

8. Do not accept gifts, favors, or compensation from those who might seek to influence coverage.

9. Do not intentionally sabotage the efforts of other journalists.

In addition to Standard No. 6 addressing manipulation, the NPPA website has numerous resources on digital manipulation, including an article[2] in which a photographer explains that even small changes in photos act cumulatively to gradually erode the credibility of the entire profession.

As was clear in the comments posted on the newspaper editor's blog about the manipulated image, some people don't see any harm in "cleaning up" a cluttered background and in fact assume

(Continued)

(Continued)

that photographers do so regularly. While photographers do accept cropping or changing exposure, neither practice changes the content of a photograph. The NPPA standard of maintaining the "integrity of the photographic images' content and context" must be interpreted by each photographer, as cropping and removing dust and other imperfections present plenty of opportunity for judgment. However, the removal of any person from the scene of a news event, for any reason, alters the reality of what was captured and contributes to making all photography more suspect.

_____

1. The National Press Photographers Code of Ethics can be found here: http://www.nppa.org/professional_development/business_practices/ethics.html

2. A report on ethics in the age of digital photography can be accessed here: http://www.nppa.org/professional_development/self-training_resources/eadp_report/

THE AFTERMATH: PROFESSIONAL STANDARDS DEFENDED

The photographer's contract with the wire service had already been terminated after the first blog post by the newspaper photo editor. In addition, the wire service later removed all archived photographs taken by the freelancer. While Calvert doesn't know whether expunging the archives is standard practice or was the result of his email, the fact that the wire service purged its records of everything the photographer had produced for them was evidence that the editors took the infraction seriously and dealt with it fully. Calvert believed he had defended his profession's standards in a way that was honest, respectful and effective.

"I believe people like this will always be the exception," Calvert said. "I did not get any satisfaction out of doing this, but I felt that it was important for the wire service to know that one of their photographers was violating their ethical guidelines. I did not want any credit for it; I just wanted people to know what was happening."

Thinking It Through

1. Suppose the photo editor at the newspaper had not discovered the manipulated photos and instead had published them. Would that have changed Calvert's obligations and his decision-making process?

2. Imagine that Calvert had uploaded to the web the video he took of the photographer manipulating the images. What consequences do you think would most likely have resulted from that action? What might have been the implications for Calvert? Would it matter what sort of site he posted the video on?

3. Many people place great emphasis on loyalty to one's friends and family and look down on "snitches" or "rats." Was Calvert being a snitch? Do you think standards for professional ethical violations should be different from standards for violations of personal ethics?

4. Some people argue that removing extraneous clutter from the background of an image doesn't change the "truth" of the image. What do you think? What guidelines would you recommend be used in governing the manipulation of news photographs?

5. As photo-editing software has made image manipulation more common in advertising and art, people begin to assume that all images may be altered. What impacts does this view have on photojournalism? Does this mean photojournalists should tighten or loosen their standards for how much manipulation is allowable?

6. The list of web links at the end of this chapter includes a Dartmouth College site that shows manipulated photographs in the last century. As you look at the examples, choose one to analyze using the NPPA Code of Ethics or the Potter Box. Think through what you would have done had you been in the situation of the photographer/editor. What questions might you have asked before the manipulation was done to the photo? What standards of publication might you develop to avoid the types of problems shown in these examples?

What If?

You are a reporter for a local television station. You've read the code of ethics for the Radio Television Digital News Association[1] as well as the ethics policies of your news station. It's clear in the policies that staging photos, manipulating images and using deceptive video editing are unethical and are grounds for discipline or termination.

As you get to know your colleagues, however, you discover that they have developed their own standards for what's acceptable. You realize that if you spoke up about everything you believed was ethically questionable, you'd have a difficult time in the newsroom. You decide to remain quiet as you get to know your job. After three months, however, you are increasingly concerned about the range of unethical behavior you have witnessed, including the following:

- A cameraman who asked the subjects of a story to reenact the first five minutes of a public speech, so he could get better sound and multiple vantage points.

- A reporter who did a very positive story about the opening of a new business owned by her husband's friends.

- A reporter who accepted a free annual membership to a fitness gym after he profiled the gym for a health segment.

- A producer who had a long conversation with the mayor then asked a videographer to remove all mention of a controversial issue from a story about a recent city council vote.

- A reporter who called in sick for three days because she was in another state interviewing for a job.

- A secretary who took supplies from the news station to supplement her home office.

---

1. http://www.rtdna.org/pages/best-practices.php

- A weekend producer who ran a video news release from the local hospital as if it were a news story.

- A reporter who appeared to be having a romantic relationship with a key source on his or her beat.

Use the Potter Box to think through the facts in the context of your values, principles and loyalties in each case. As an employee of the station, would you speak up about any of these instances of misconduct? If so, which ones and why? Whom would you approach to air your concerns, and what might you say? What consequences can you imagine resulting from your decision to speak, or to not speak, about these behaviors?

Travis Linn, a former bureau chief for CBS News, often counseled students to develop a "go-to-hell" fund. His idea is that if you save enough money to afford a period of unemployment, you will feel freer to speak up when you see an ethical problem. Can you imagine a circumstance in which you'd consider quitting because of an ethical conflict in your workplace?

Suppose you wanted to avoid accepting a job at an organization that tolerated unethical behavior. What interview questions might you ask to find out about an organization's standards? Outline the steps you could go through to evaluate the ethical reputation of a workplace before you accepted a job. Keep in mind that many job interviews at media organizations involve no talk of ethics, so it may be up to you to broach the subject and do some research.

Go Online for More

NPPA resources on "Ethics in the Age of Digital Photography":
http://www.nppa.org/professional_development/self-training_
    resources/eadp_report/ethics.html

The Associated Press, the world's largest newsgathering organization, has a "statement of news values and principles" that includes several sections on images and digital manipulation:
http://www.ap.org/company/News-Values

This site contains an excellent collection of manipulated photographs over the past century:
http://www.fourandsix.com/photo-tampering-history/

While journalists value the integrity of unaltered photographs, artists celebrate the aesthetics of manipulated images. Consider some of the images on this and similar websites:
http://www.instantshift.com/2009/07/20/80-excellent-examples-of-photo-manipulation-art/

This essay, "The Ethics of Digital Manipulation," is a thoughtful follow-up to the comparison of documentary photos with artistic images. The author, a sports journalist who also takes astronomy photos, carefully considers the question, "What is ethical in the digital manipulation and enhancement of a photo?"
http://www.astropix.com/html/j_digit/ethics.htm

CHAPTER 4

Political Espionage or Politics as Usual?

The Case of Political Campaign Tactics

Lucinda Austin

As a college sophomore and first-time intern, Nicole Miller felt honored to be selected as an intern for the most closely followed political campaign of the year. Being new to interning and new to politics, Miller believed she should do what was asked of her without asking questions. Initially, she did not question "strategic thinking" and other so-called clever ways to win the political campaign. However, as she was given more responsibility and asked to do tasks she found ethically questionable, she began to wonder if she should question what she was being directed to do. How could she support a candidate whom she believed in, still play what she believed to be the "political game" and follow directions from her supervisor while maintaining her own values?

Because the political candidate Miller represented is still involved in politics, and Miller works for a strategic communications firm that represents public affairs as an area of interest, the name of the candidate has been omitted from this case and Miller's name has been changed to a pseudonym.

The Situation:
A High-Profile Political Campaign

As a strategic communications major at Elon University, Nicole Miller was headed into her first internship to support a political candidate in a presidential primary. Miller had already been dedicating her time outside of school to support the candidate, so she was eager to play an active role in the campaign while fulfilling her internship requirement.

At the time, Miller had not been exposed to the world of politics and wasn't sure what to expect, so she thought she would experience it through the internship. Each day presented Miller with new opportunities to interact with the press, community members and surrogates who spoke on behalf of the political candidate. Although Miller said this internship was the most exciting one she had during college and that it made her a better writer and strategic thinker, it also convinced her that she did not want a career in politics.

Ethics came into play as the political party Miller represented came into contact with the opposing party on a regular basis. Campaign events were well attended by supporters of Miller's candidate; however, the supporters of the opposing candidate also came in force. She didn't understand why an event kept secret until hours before it happened was filled with people her team sought to avoid.

She quickly figured out the "game," though; both sides played it very well. An inquiry to her campaign manager revealed the many strategies used: strategically placed supporters with signs opposing the competition, fake social media accounts to follow key influencers on the competition's side and inaccurate media advisories to keep the competition away.

The Challenge:
Misrepresentation and Diversion

Now able to recognize the decoys used by both sides of the campaign, Miller began to question how ethical it was for her to contribute to the situation. While doing her work as an intern, she was asked to assist with "strategically" placing protesters at competitor events and follow and interact with the competition via "dummy" social media accounts.

She was asked to equip her party's supporters with signs of opposition and to ward off the "follows" from the opposing parties' fake social media accounts. She had to sift through decoy press that made their way to the campaign office and send out media advisories that purposely miscommunicated information about events to "throw off" the competition.

For example, Miller had to coordinate protesters outside a local restaurant where an opposing candidate was having lunch with small business owners. She took signs that questioned various aspects of the candidate's agenda to the restaurant and distributed them to the staged protesters outside.

The fake social media accounts she managed for her campaign were designed to follow the competition, not comment; however, she did have access to accounts used to oppose tweets made by the competition. These Twitter accounts with their fake personas responded to challenges made to her candidate's recent statements.

Miller also saw these "fake" accounts being created by the opposing party. As Miller said, "We identified these accounts from the other side by researching the name used to see if they were even a registered voter in the state. I'm sure the other party did the same because not all tweets were responded to."

The misleading media advisories she created were brief announcements about upcoming events, appearances or speaking engagements. Sometimes she produced multiple versions. Some had the correct event information, but some were misleading about the time and place of the event, and those went to individuals from the opposing party who might attend.

Miller believed she was at a crossroads: Should she support her party and her employer or follow her sense of ethics? The two paths were consistently obscured by her learning curve of the political area and her own moral compass.

"This situation was tough for me. I fully supported the candidate and the overall morale of the team and campaign, which made it difficult to question anything that my moral compass flagged as potentially unethical," Miller explained. "I often ignored the red flags or disregarded them simply because I saw the 'other side' doing the same things."

Political experts state that "dishonest campaigns" are commonplace with "little distinction between fact and fiction."[1] Scholars such as Dulio, Medvic and Nelson[2] suggest that "campaign ethics is an oxymoron" as practices become increasingly questionable with each new political campaign. Political ethics and ethical expectations are often defined based on organizational codes of ethics. As Medvic states, these professional codes create moral obligations or ethical expectations for individuals entering into roles as agents in order to advance their own interests or those of their clients.[3]

"The situation regarding social media was somehow easier to disregard," Miller said. "I found myself more conflicted with situations that required me to interact with people. When I was sent to provide supporters with signs of opposition, I felt that I was unnaturally interrupting individuals' rights to support their candidate of choice." In these situations, Miller believed she had to put herself in the shoes of individuals wanting to represent their candidate—just as she wanted to represent hers.

However, she explained: "In addition to being completely annoyed that protesters were placed at an event, I worked hard to organize for the candidate I was supporting; I would feel that my rights to support my candidate of choice were being violated." Miller believed strongly in individuals' rights of free speech and their right to have a say in the political process.

"Although our choice in candidate differed, we shared a longing to support our candidate uninterrupted," she said. Efforts that interfered with this part of the political process made Miller stop and think a bit more

---

1. C. Jaffe-Pickett, "Ethical Issues for Political Candidates," Markkula Center for Applied Ethics, http://www.scu.edu/ethics/practicing/focusareas/government_ethics/roundtable/elections.html.

2. D. A. Dulio, S. K. Medvic, and C. J. Nelson, *Shades of Gray: Perspectives on Campaign Ethics* (Washington, DC: Brookings Institute, 2002).

3. D. E. Miller and S. K. Medvic, "Civic Responsibility or Self-Interest? In *Shades of Gray: Perspectives on Campaign Ethics*, eds. D. A. Dulio, S. K. Medvic, and C. J. Nelson (Washington, DC: Brookings Institute, 2002), 18–38.

about what she was being asked to do. "I didn't think it was right," she said. "I didn't think it was necessary."

THE RESPONSE: STICKING TO "MY MORAL COMPASS"

When faced with these situations, Miller said she had to "stick to my moral compass." As a sophomore, Miller had not yet taken her university's communications law and ethics course or many of the courses specializing in her major. She had focused on ethics more minimally in her curriculum to that point. As such, she relied more heavily on her own values,[4] but she was somewhat familiar with codes of ethics such as those of the Public Relations Society of America.[5]

"Honestly, my own moral compass did a lot of the guiding in this situation; however, I was consistently forced to balance advocacy with honesty," Miller said. "I was extremely loyal to the candidate, campaign and my team and sometimes felt that questioning the ethics of the situation didn't make me a 'team player.'"

Although she hadn't taken a law and/or ethics course yet, Miller was able to identify the various factors at play and how they related to the PRSA ethics code. Miller approached her supervisor and let him know that she was uncomfortable with some of the tasks she was being asked to perform.

"My supervisor admired my taking a stand on what I was not willing to do," she said.

Bruce Weinstein, also known as "The Ethics Guy" and a contributor to Business Week and CNN, proposes a code of ethics for politicians

---

4. L. Austin and Y. Jin, "Approaching Ethical Crisis Communication With Accuracy and Sensitivity: Exploring Common Ground and Gaps Between Journalism and Public Relations," *Public Relations Journal* 9, no. 1 (2015). http://www.prsa.org/Intelligence/PRJournal/Vol9/No1.

5. Public Relations Society of America (PRSA), "Member Code of Ethics." https://www.prsa.org/aboutprsa/ethics/codeenglish.

TOOL FOR THOUGHT:
PRSA'S Code of Ethics

PRSA's code of ethics lists professional values as advocacy, honesty, expertise, independence, loyalty and fairness. The professional value of advocacy states that professionals serve the public interest through acting as responsible advocates for clients or organizations. For the value of honesty, representatives should show accuracy and truthfulness while advancing interests of the party they represent. Also, for example, loyalty stresses the need to be "faithful to those we represent, while honoring our obligation to serve the public interest."[1] Lastly, fairness stresses the right to respect all opinions and to support free expression.

In this case, Miller was trying to balance advocacy for a cause in which she believed with honesty and fairness. Honesty was one of the more obvious ethical quandaries in her case; some of the tasks Miller was asked to do were not reflecting complete accuracy and truthfulness while she tried to advance the interests of her candidate.

In her case, these decisions became even more muddled at times because she strongly believed in her candidate and that person's ability to make a difference. As such, she also believed helping this candidate get elected was serving a greater public interest. Ultimately, however, fairness came into play because she wanted to support free expression and support the rights of the opposition to share their opinions and support their candidate while having the same rights to support her candidate.

---

1. Public Relations Society of America (PRSA), "Member Code of Ethics." https://www.prsa.org/aboutprsa/ethics/codeenglish.

rooted in honesty, responsibility, staying focused on the issues and the goal of the campaign, avoiding personal attacks, listening, keeping promises and spending fairly, among other values.[6] The American Association of Political Consultants has put forward a similar but more detailed code of professional ethics including the following: treating colleagues and clients with respect, respecting confidence of clients, avoiding discrimination in appealing to voters, promoting equal rights and privileges, refraining from false or misleading attacks, fully documenting criticisms of opponents, honesty in interactions with media, and appropriate use of funds.[7]

"Generally speaking, I strayed away from any tasks that made me feel like I was deceiving the public/voters," Miller said. "I refused to distribute any messaging that was inaccurate or that I felt defamed the competition." Miller was unwilling to spread messaging that might tarnish the reputation of the other candidate in the eyes of the voters when she was not sure if the message was based on factual information. Her experiences going through this process made Miller more cautious and more thorough in examining sources and information.

THE AFTERMATH: POLITICALLY AWARE

Once Miller expressed how uneasy she was about going into these situations, she was not put in the same position again. She continued to monitor the competition's posts via social media, as instructed, because she viewed these posts as public information and believed she was gathering information that would eventually steer strategic thinking for her candidate's campaign.

"My supervisor was very understanding and let me know that politics was a different arena and took some time to get adjusted to," she said. "He did his best to explain why they did these things and how much was at stake."

---

6. B. Weinstein, "A Code of Ethics for Politicians," *Anderson Cooper 360*, CNN. http://ac360.blogs.cnn.com/2008/06/10/a-code-of-ethics-for-politicians.

7. American Association of Political Consultants, "AAPC Code of Professional Ethics," http://theaapc.org/member-center/code-of-ethics.

Although Miller did not believe the arena of politics as described by her supervisor was something she wanted to "get adjusted to," she tried to make the best of her internship without compromising her sense of ethics.

"I learned that there is a very thin and blurred line between strategic and unethical thinking," she said. "I concluded that because everything we dealt with was public, it wasn't unethical. The campaign simply came up with strategic ways to access the information."

Thinking It Through

1. In Miller's case, her campaign was performing the same kinds of deceptive practices the other side was. What could Miller have done to follow her ethical principles but still give her candidate—a candidate she believed in and wanted to win—a fair chance?

2. In this situation, Miller felt comfortable with the fake social media accounts if they were used to monitor information that was public about candidates and not used to post information under a false identity. Are there situations in which a fake social media account could be appropriate, and, if so, what are these?

3. Although Miller was able to remove herself from personally performing acts she believed were ethically questionable, the campaign was still performing these acts while Miller was interning. Does this present an ethical dilemma, and, if so, how should it have been resolved?

4. What would Miller's options have been if her campaign supervisor was not willing to take her off the tasks with which she felt uncomfortable? What should she have done?

What If?

In Miller's situation, she was being asked to utilize fake social media accounts to follow accounts for the opposing candidate—accounts that shared information publicly to followers and supporters. What if Miller had been asked to create fake social media accounts, posing as an average citizen supporting the campaign with the intention of posting positive comments about her candidate and posting negative remarks about the opposition on various comment threads and pages?

Consider the following scenario. You've been hired to work as a representative on a political campaign for a candidate running for state governor. You believe in this candidate and her mission, so you want to see her become the next governor of your state. Your responsibilities include writing online about the candidate via blogs and social media.

Recently, a statement your candidate said was taken out of context. Your campaign manager has asked you, as an official representative of the campaign, to make several fake Facebook accounts with fake pictures, job descriptions and educational backgrounds, so you can go into discussion forums and comment threads related to news stories on this controversy. Once there, you need to defend the candidate, stating the candidate's statement had merely been taken out of context.

So, in essence, your campaign manager has asked you to falsely represent your identity in these forums to help correct public misperception about your candidate.

Would you agree to create the fake Facebook accounts and post comments about your candidate? Why or why not? What factors would make you more likely to consider it, and what factors would make you less likely to do so? If this scenario is ethically troubling for you, what could you suggest instead to your campaign manager that would still help to correct public misperception about your candidate?

Let's take this scenario a bit further. If you were asked to use these fake Facebook accounts to go onto discussion forums and comment threads to comment negatively about the opposing candidate, would you do this? Why or why not, and, if so, under what circumstances?

Go Online for More

The Arthur W. Page Society, an association of educators and senior public relations executives:
http://www.awpagesociety.com

Association of Government Relations Professionals code of ethics:
http://grprofessionals.org/join/code-of-ethics/

International Association of Business Communicators code of ethics:
https://www.iabc.com/about-us/leaders-and-staff/code-of-ethics

Public Relations Society of America policy on reporting ethical violations:
http://www.prsa.org/AboutPRSA/Ethics/AboutEnforcement

Public Relations Society of America advisory on deceptive online practices:
http://www.prsa.org/AboutPRSA/Ethics/ProfessionalStandards
    Advisories/PSA-08.pdf

Society of Professional Journalists, Ethics Committee Position Paper on Political Involvement:
http://www.spj.org/ethics-papers-politics.asp

United States Office of Government Ethics, code of ethics:
http://www.oge.gov/Education/Education-Resources-for-Ethics-
    Officials/Resources/Code-of-Ethics

Word of Mouth Marketing Association ethics code:
http://womma.org/ethics

CHAPTER 5

Focus Group Dilemma

The Case of the Compromised Tagline

Nancy Furlow

A nonprofit organization decided to "rebrand" and scheduled a series of focus groups to test new taglines. The newly hired vice president of communications came up with her own idea for a tagline and wanted it to be part of the focus groups. Then, when the first focus group didn't reach the conclusion she wanted, she took steps to predetermine the outcome.

Having inside knowledge of what the vice president was doing put a young professional in a difficult position. She believed her boss was pushing the nonprofit in the wrong direction—but what would she risk if she confronted the boss or reported that the boss was manipulating the market research? Because of the sensitivity of this issue, and to protect an organization whose mission she still supports, the young professional asked that the names in this story be changed.

THE SITUATION: REBRANDING A NONPROFIT

In two years of working in the communications department of an environmental nonprofit organization headquartered in Washington, D.C., Jessica Shelby had found her job exciting and rewarding. Still, she sometimes felt left out of big decisions; she believed she had more to offer than was being asked of her.

So, when she was selected to be part of the small group that would lead a rebranding effort—designing a new integrated marketing strategy for the organization—she looked forward to the challenge and was thrilled that she would be able to put her knowledge to good use. She thought the rebranding was a good idea because the organization was facing competition from other environmental groups, and she liked the creative ideas that an advertising agency had already proposed.

It was an exciting time at the nonprofit but also a tumultuous one. Her department had been feeling pressure to get more media coverage of the group so that more people would be aware of its work. In her two years there, Shelby had seen many staff members quit, mostly to go to other organizations in the area—even groups that were deemed as the "competition."

Shelby's department had experienced so much turnover that she was working for her third boss. The new vice president of communications, Joanna Gilbert, was full of energy and enthusiasm—just what the department needed, Shelby thought. When Gilbert took over, morale in the department received a much-needed boost. "I really thought I was going to learn a lot from our new VP," Shelby said. "She was very approachable and easy to get along with. I was really looking forward to working with her."

THE CHALLENGE: THE BOSS IS MANIPULATING THE CAMPAIGN

The rebranding group's first meeting focused on laying out a strategy and defining the steps needed to make the rebranding campaign a success. Team members decided that a series of focus groups would be conducted in three major metropolitan areas to test communication messages and a series of taglines—slogans highlighting the group's mission—that an advertising agency had developed for the campaign. Everyone, including Shelby, was pleased with the progress the group was making and left the meeting in good spirits, tasks in hand.

At the next meeting, Gilbert surprised the group by announcing that she had come up with her own great idea for a tagline. The atmosphere in the room changed, and everyone squirmed nervously as Gilbert said she wanted her idea considered by the focus groups along with the taglines developed by the ad agency. After a little hesitation, everyone agreed that her tagline was good and should be included. No one expressed any other view.

Although she went along with the idea in the meeting, Shelby was uncomfortable with the way that Gilbert had made a decision before asking the other group members for their views. Shelby did think Gilbert's tagline was clever, but she also thought it seemed a bit negative and didn't fit with the rebranding strategy that the organization and the ad agency had developed. "We had already decided that our strategy was to be positive and not to project the organization as a bunch of doomsayers," Shelby said. "The work that the agency had done was very different from what Gilbert was recommending. It just wasn't a good fit."

Although Shelby didn't feel as enthusiastic about her boss's idea as everyone else seemed to, she supported it publicly because she wanted to be a good employee and a team player. "I was afraid that I would be kicked off the team if I didn't go along with it," she said later.

At a great expense, the nonprofit hired an outside research firm to conduct an initial focus group in Chicago, to be followed by groups in Boston and Los Angeles. The report from the Chicago focus group was shared with the team, and the results did not make Gilbert happy. The focus group had not completely dismissed Gilbert's proposed tagline, but neither had it chosen hers as the best.

Shelby felt secretly vindicated that the focus group had preferred the more positive ideas; she was sure the next two groups would come back with the same results. Then she overheard Gilbert on a conference call: Her boss was telling the consultant to make sure that the next two focus groups came back with her idea as the selected phrase. At first, Shelby thought she must have misunderstood what Gilbert was saying. "I thought maybe I was jumping to the wrong conclusion," she said. But later in the day, Gilbert told Shelby directly that she was sure her idea would be the one selected by the remaining focus groups.

Upset by the situation and what she had overheard, Shelby considered confronting her boss. But fearing retaliation, she hesitated, and the more time went by, the more action began to seem impossible. Alone with her dilemma, she began to doubt herself. "I actually thought that maybe this is just the way things worked in 'real life' and that I was very naïve," she said.

THE RESPONSE: SILENCE BECOMES DREAD

Over the next week, focus groups were conducted in Boston and Los Angeles. Gilbert never distributed the results or discussed them with the rest of the rebranding team; she simply proceeded as if her own tagline had emerged the clear winner. As far as Shelby could see, the other members of the team didn't question her statements or wonder why Gilbert hadn't followed procedure in showing them the research results.

Shelby was caught in a bind. It seemed that everyone else on the team agreed with the new strategy, but she wasn't convinced it was best for the organization. She believed she and her colleagues had been manipulated in a way that not only ignored their experience and the stated purpose of the rebranding team, but also wasted money that donors had contributed to help the cause. Above all, she thought Gilbert's actions were unprofessional.

"No one questioned the fact that we didn't get a report about the other two focus groups," Shelby said. "I couldn't believe it. I was beginning to think it was a conspiracy or something, and I didn't trust anyone."

Upset about what was happening, Shelby began to dread going to work. She felt she should do something, but whom could she turn to? How could she discuss the situation without being seen as a traitor? What would she be risking if she tried?

The rebranding campaign moved forward using Gilbert's idea. Shelby continued to work on the project but lost interest—and it showed. She put forth minimal effort on the rebranding campaign and instead found other projects to work on. When a co-worker who had long been a mentor to Shelby asked her what was wrong, Shelby told her in confidence what she knew about the focus groups.

"I couldn't take it anymore and had to tell someone," Shelby said. Her co-worker seemed upset but shrugged it off. "She said that she had been with the organization for 15 years, and nothing surprised her anymore." The way this person saw it, exposing Gilbert wouldn't do much good. "Besides, she had a family that she had to take care of and was getting paid pretty well since she had been there so long. She really didn't want to make waves." Shelby left the conversation feeling completely alone.

At the same time the rebranding campaign was being developed, the nonprofit was undergoing major restructuring and downsizing. Everyone was nervous about job security, especially the newer members of the team, including Shelby. She had begun searching for another position just in case things didn't work out, so when she was offered a new job at a different organization, she jumped at the opportunity. She no longer wanted to work for a vice president who she believed put her own ego ahead of the organization's best interest.

TOOL FOR THOUGHT: Two Codes of Marketing Research Standards

Codes established by professional groups address ethical standards in general terms. It's up to you to decide how these provisions fit with your personal moral code and how you want to apply them in the workplace. The codes of the Marketing Research Association and the Qualitative Research Consultants Association might have been useful in helping Shelby decide what to do about her boss's actions.

(Continued)

(Continued)

The MRA Code of Marketing Research Standards asserts that association members "will never falsify or omit data for any reason at any phase of a research study or project. Falsifying data of any kind for any reason, or omitting data that do not conform to preconceived notions, will not be tolerated."[1]

The code continues to say that researchers will "present the results understandably and fairly, including any results that may seem contradictory or unfavorable." Given Shelby's evidence that Gilbert was omitting research results she didn't like, the code makes clear that Gilbert's actions were unethical. Although neither Gilbert nor Shelby was a member of the association, the standards set forth in the code would have given Shelby something to rely on, other than her gut feeling that her boss's behavior was wrong.

Most organizations today work with outside consultants and agencies when developing marketing communications strategies. Consultants bring objectivity, expertise and a network of contacts to the process that many companies believe it's harder to achieve in-house. Although the client–consultant relationship can at times be difficult, it is vital to the success of an overall communications strategy.

Many professional associations address ethics, but none is more explicit about the client-consultant relationship than the Qualitative Research Consultants Association. The group's Guidelines to Professional Qualitative Research Practices states, "The client should not alter a consultant's report, either for internal or external distribution, without the consultant's express consent or without providing an opportunity for the consultant to disclaim authorship."[2]

Shelby could have used this rule to make it clear to Gilbert that what she was asking the consultant to do went against the profession's standards. In fact, the QRCA encourages consultants to use the guidelines document to clarify project issues with clients. By simply sharing the document with her, Shelby would have had a tool to make Gilbert aware of the awkward situation she was creating for the consultant hired by her nonprofit.

———————

1. Marketing Research Association, *The Code of Marketing Research Standards*. http://www.mra-net .org/resources/documents/ CodeMRStandards.pdf.

2. Qualitative Research Consultants Association. *QRCA Guidelines to Professional Qualitative Research Practices*. http://www .qrca.org/associations/6379/ files/Guidelines1-29-07.pdf.

THE AFTERMATH: LEARNING HOW TO SPEAK UP

A few months after leaving the environmental group and starting her new job, Shelby saw a public service announcement for her former employer, an ad that was part of the new campaign the nonprofit had developed. It had turned out better than she'd expected, but she still felt that the message wasn't quite right for the organization. Not long after that, a former colleague called to tell her that the group was changing the campaign and that Gilbert was no longer with the organization. The rebranding campaign ended up costing the organization much more than had been budgeted.

When she heard Gilbert was gone, "my first reaction was that I wanted my old job back," Shelby said. "I missed the friends that I had made there, but more importantly, I missed being a part of what the organization was doing. I really did believe in their mission."

Looking back, Shelby regrets not telling anyone except her co-worker about what Gilbert had done. Had she spoken up, not only would she have saved the organization money, but she might have been able to stay there and keep working for a cause that she supported.

Three years after switching jobs, Shelby believes she should have confronted Gilbert about her control of the focus groups. At the time, she saw the dilemma as simply whether to speak up or go along. Now, with more experience, she realizes the issue was really that a supervisor was violating key ethics of her profession. Shelby did not even think at the time of taking several steps that would be second nature if she encountered a similar situation now. For instance, talking to her former professors and consulting professional ethics codes would have let her move beyond gut feelings and find a concrete basis for her views, so she wouldn't feel the dilemma was all in her mind.

It didn't occur to Shelby until later that Gilbert's ethics weren't the only issue. She realized that if she'd used a professional code of ethics as a way to construct the discussion, she could have pointed out to Gilbert that not only was she being unethical, but she was also putting the consultant in a bad position by asking him to violate his professional standards. In fact, where she once thought of the issue as a tainted focus group, she now realizes that everyone else involved may have acted perfectly honorably, and then Gilbert subverted the process by choosing not to pass along legitimate research results that didn't suit her purposes.

"You know, since we didn't actually get the results of the other two focus groups, I'm guessing that the consultants told Gilbert that they wouldn't adjust the results to accommodate her idea," Shelby said. "I'm not 100 percent sure, but I have a feeling that they stood up to her. I wish I had, too."

Thinking It Through

1. If you had been in Shelby's place and decided to speak up, who would you have talked to first, Gilbert or Gilbert's boss? Do you think Shelby had enough evidence to tell the boss that Gilbert was manipulating the rebranding campaign? What do you think would have happened if Shelby had done that? Can you think of other options she might have tried, other than losing interest in her work and eventually quitting?

2. On the website of the Qualitative Research Consultants Association (www.qrca.org), read the Code of Member Ethics and the Guide to Professional Qualitative Research Practices. Are you surprised by any of the guidelines for their members? Which provisions do you think would have been useful to Shelby if she'd known about them?

3. Think about what it takes to accomplish rebranding, and why a company would want to rebrand itself or one of its products. Check out the gallery of winners of the global rebranding awards (www.rebrand.com/winners-showcase). Select an example that you think is excellent and explain why. Now find one that you think is poor and explain why you think so.

4. With the rise of social media, it is possible to conduct a virtual focus group using Facebook or Twitter. In what ways do you think this method would be more or less effective than in-person focus groups? Would use of social media make it easier to manipulate research?

5. See if you can find some focus groups taking place right now using social media. Check out https://www.facebook.com/find paidfocusgroups/ or other marketing research communities to see if you can find a focus group that you can participate in from the convenience of your own home—and maybe even get paid. What does this experience tell you about using technology for research?

What If?

You were hunting for a part-time job and have found a good one: A company has put you in charge of building enthusiasm for a new energy drink on your campus. They're paying you to set up focus groups and report back on what you find. Excited about the opportunity to do some market research, you set out to facilitate the groups. Think about how you would go about performing the research. Here are some links to help you prepare:

- Lehigh University: http://www.cse.lehigh.edu/~glennb/ mm/Focus Groups.htm

- Free Management Library, Carter McNamara, Basics of Conducting Focus Groups: http://managementhelp.org/ evaluatn/focusgrp.htm

- University of Kansas, Community Tool Box: http://ctb .ku.edu/en/table contents/sub_section_main_1018.aspx

Before you set up your groups, you have many questions to consider: Who will do the research—you alone, or will you have a note taker? Will the sessions be recorded? What type of release will you need from the participants?

Where will you do the research? If on campus, what sort of permissions will you need? Will you provide refreshments (other than the energy drink)? Do you have a budget to pay the participants?

Who are the participants? How many will there be? How will you determine the "target market" in terms of age, gender and specific sub-cultures? How will you invite people to join?

Develop a list of questions to guide your group research. You want the discussion to flow, so avoid yes or no questions. Here are some things to keep in mind: What is the purpose of the focus group? How will you keep the participants on track? How will you handle participants who dominate the discussion, or others who never say a word?

Let's say you've conducted your research and are ready to let the energy drink company know your findings. Should you write up a report or just hand over your notes? Perhaps you've been instructed simply to tell the local representative about your experience. At this point, any number of "what if" scenarios might develop. Consider these:

What if the company tells you it really isn't interested in the results of the focus group; it's just been using the guise of "research" as a way of making sure people on campus learn about the energy drink. Would this be an example of unethical research practices, or is it clever public relations? If you think you've been used unethically, what recourse do you have?

What if everyone in your focus group took only a couple sips and declared the drink to be gross? How would you present these findings to the company? Since you're being paid to conduct the research, do you have an obligation to tell them something positive?

What if the company tells you to hide the fact that the drink contains 200 calories per serving and that the bottle, whose size would lead most people to see it as a single serving, actually contains what they're calling three servings? What would you do with this information when conducting the focus group? What about the idea that "energy drink," in this case, actually means a drink loaded with caffeine? The calories and ingredients are listed in small print on the label. Do you have any obligation to point them out if your focus group participants haven't noticed? What should you do if they ask?

Go Online for More

Websites of professional organizations that provide ethics codes and other resources on marketing and public relations follow:
Marketing Research Association, http://www.mra-net.org
Qualitative Research Consultants Association, http://www.qrca.org
American Marketing Association, http://www.marketingpower.com
Public Relations Society of America, http://www.prsa.org/

Links about how to conduct research through social media follow:
http://amabaltimore.org/1939/social-media-the-new-focus-group/
http://www.socialmediatoday.com/content/how-use-social-media-
    market-research
https://www.ama.org/publications/eNewsletters/MarketingInsights
    Newsletter/Pages/working-hand-in-hand-qualitative-mr-and-so-
    cial-media-research.aspx
http://boss.blogs.nytimes.com/2012/01/05/turning-facebook-followers-
    into-online-focus-groups/?_r=0

CHAPTER 6

OMG! This Band Is SOOO GR8!

The Case of the Phony Teenager

Richard D. Waters

Working for an international public relations firm, Jennie Quinn was excited to be assigned to the promotional campaign for a new musical artist. Helping design a major creative campaign was a fascinating challenge, and Quinn was really enjoying herself—until she discovered that part of the plan for building "buzz" about the musician called for her to go online and pretend to be someone she wasn't.

Everyone else at her agency seemed fine with this plan, but to Quinn, it just felt wrong. She loved the rest of the work and didn't want to lose the project, nor did she want to risk her agency losing this big account. Could she find a way to serve her own standards—the standards of the profession as she understood them—while meeting her employer's and client's goals?

Quinn did manage to navigate her way to a solution. Because the promotional campaign is still debated within the company, she asked that the names in this chapter be changed.

The Situation: "You Want Me to Do What?"

The PR agency where Quinn worked as an assistant account executive had just won the account of an up-and-coming hip-hop artist who was being marketed to the tween and early teenage demographic. The artist's record label had chosen the first single from the new CD and wanted the PR firm's help developing a plan to launch the artist into superstardom. Executives from the record label were aiming for one giant hit that they hoped would kick off a string of future hits.

The PR firm began developing a multifaceted campaign to introduce the world to the hip-hop musician. First, Quinn and a group of staffers prepared a traditional public relations campaign with media kits, news releases and special events tied to the CD release. Once industry buzz began, the campaign called for a media tour, with the artist giving interviews to outlets ranging from popular magazines and industry publications to satellite radio and commercial music stations around the country.

Ten years earlier, this level of public relations campaigning would have sufficed for most agencies and their clients; however, the rise of the internet and social media meant the campaign needed a strong virtual public relations effort as well. The PR firm created a website to furnish information about the artist's life, musical influences and upcoming appearances; to give the audience an opportunity to upload pictures and videos; and to provide an outlet for the artist's journal as well as chat rooms where fans could share information. The campaign also included a Facebook page for the artist and a microsite that allowed free downloads of an MP3 file of the first single, as well as videos of the new song that the record label hoped would go viral.

The campaign was well designed and reflected many of the principles taught in public relations textbooks. Quinn was proud of its thoroughness, and all was going well until she heard about the next steps. The client asked the agency to work on a buzz marketing effort before implementing the official campaign. Specifically, the music company wanted the PR agency to target virtual chat rooms and post messages on social networking sites with positive comments about the musician and links to the MP3 for downloading.

Many organizations hire employees to monitor social media and participate in online chats; those have become fairly standard promotional efforts. In this case, however, Quinn had a problem: The bosses told her and other employees to pretend to be members of the targeted demographic. In other words, Quinn said, still not quite able to believe it, "They wanted me to pretend to be a 12-year-old and promote [the musician] in chat rooms."

THE CHALLENGE: SERVING THE CLIENT WHILE STAYING HONEST

Ethical communication requires open and honest participation by all parties, and Quinn's public relations agency was asking her to lie to the campaign's target audience. Moreover, the agency was asking adults to lie to children and teenagers. Quinn felt fine about working on the campaign as an adult and letting online audiences know that a new hip-hop artist was releasing a single. The client's reps, however, did not want the appearance of an orchestrated campaign; they wanted people to see buzz about the artist growing online in what seemed a natural way.

With the growth of social media, public relations professionals constantly discuss how best to hold virtual conversations to represent clients—whether the comments are posted in monitored chat rooms, on message boards linked to blogs or community forums, or on sites like Facebook or Google+. At first, practitioners were skeptical of using chat rooms to carry out campaigns at all.[1] Gradually, some began to see chat rooms as a way to have conversations with targeted audiences, a virtual focus group where they could find out what consumers thought.[2]

Researcher J. M. Lace found that while practitioners often enjoyed these virtual conversations with stakeholders, they also questioned

---

1.   S. R. Thomsen, "@Work in Cyberspace: Exploring Practitioner Use of the PR Forum," *Public Relations Review,* 22, no. 2 (1996): 115–132; Tracey Cooley, "Interactive Communication—Public Relations on the Web," *PRQ,* 44, No. 2 (1999, Summer): 41–42.

2.   P. Hurme, "Online PR: Emerging Organisational Practice," *Corporate Communications: An International Journal,* 6, No. 2 (2001): 71–75.

whether the tactic was effective.[3] Some expressed discomfort with using a screen name that did not identify them individually but rather as the organization itself (e.g., one practitioner writing as "OrganizationX" rather than "GW@OrganizationX"). Hiding behind an organization name was quickly identified as a strategy best avoided in virtual public relations efforts.

Public relations professional Susan Kohl maintains that individuals should identify themselves in all public relations efforts online, for example, by using their initials in their chat room user names. The openness allows users to feel a personal connection to an individual rather than interacting with a faceless organization.[4] While this strategy certainly benefits the organization, it also reinforces larger industry ethics practices.

THE RESPONSE: REFUSING TO LIE

After thinking hard and reviewing various decision-making models she'd studied in college, Quinn found her choice to be relatively simple. She kept thinking back to the definition she'd learned in class: "Public relations is the management function that establishes and maintains mutually beneficial relationships between an organization and the publics on whom its success or failure depends."[5] With this definition in mind, she questioned why public relations practitioners would knowingly engage in behavior that could ruin a relationship with stakeholders. In her view, deceiving tweens and teenagers online about her identity ultimately could lead to the failure of the promotional campaign for the hip-hop artist.

It wasn't easy for Quinn to speak up: She was a young assistant account executive at a large global public relations firm where no one else

---

3. J. M. Lace, "At the Crossroads of Marketing Communications and the Internet: Experiences of UK Advertisers," *Internet Research*, 14, No. 3 (2004): 236–244.

4. Susan Koh, "The Nasty Truth About High-Tech Public Relations," *Public Relations Strategist*, 6, No. 2 (2000, Summer): 27–30.

5. S. M. Cutlip, A. H. Center and G. M. Broom, *Effective Public Relations* (Englewood Cliffs, NJ: Prentice-Hall, 1994).

TOOL FOR THOUGHT:
The Potter Box and
the Navran Model

When Jennie Quinn's bosses asked her and others at the agency to engage in online deception in order to promote a singer, their plan violated two parts of the Public Relations Society of America ethics code: being honest and accurate in all communications, and revealing sponsors for represented causes and interests. By pretending to be teenagers and by not disclosing that the messages were part of an organized campaign, people working on this aspect of the account would be engaging in unethical behavior.

In addition to the ethics code, Quinn turned for guidance to two other models, the Potter Box[1] and the Navran Model,[2] both of which outline steps that a practitioner should follow to resolve an ethical dilemma. The Potter Box (see also Chapter 3) asks practitioners to define the situation; identify the key values that must be reflected in the decision; select the guiding principles of the entity making the decision; and, ultimately, choose personal loyalties to determine what decision needs to be made.

The benefit of the Potter Box is that it forces the practitioner to prioritize the values and stakeholders that are most important in a particular situation. As was true for Quinn, PR professionals juggle multiple relationships (employer, clients, consumers, online audience); they can't afford to overlook any of those relationships when making decisions.

The Navran Model presents a simple step-by-step process for making ethical decisions in business. It asks professionals to consider their decisions in light of their organizations, the law and their own standards. These are the steps in the model:

1. Define the problem. Look at all aspects of the organization and its stakeholders, the interactions among the parties and the situation causing the problem.

2. Identify available solutions. Brainstorm a range of possible courses of action.

3. Evaluate the solutions. Consider short-term and long-term ramifications of each and their impact on all stakeholders involved.

4. Make the decision. Public relations strives to develop mutually beneficial relationships between an organization and stakeholders. It's possible for a one-sided solution to be ethical, but consider the future of the relationship after that decision is made.

5. Implement the decision. Once the decision is made, you have an obligation to your client and employer to carry out that decision in a timely and cost-effective manner.

6. Evaluate the decision. Did you properly assess the situation? What other actions might be needed to ensure the best resolution?

In evaluating possible solutions and your eventual decision, the Navran Model calls for applying filters that it abbreviates as PLUS: P for policies of your organization; L for the law; U for universal values; and S for self, your own definition of what's right.

Although the Potter Box and the Navran Model provide useful systems for analysis in decision making, professor Shannon Bowen of Syracuse University notes that these models do not truly apply universal ethics, because they allow the decision maker to define the principles he or she is considering.[3] For example, Quinn hypothetically might have concluded that participating in a chat room conversation disguised as a teenager could be ethical, given that it was consistent with the practice and guidelines of her organization, and that talking with tweens and teenagers online about music is not illegal.

---

1. M. P. McElreath, *Managing Systematic and Ethical Public Relations Campaigns*, 2nd ed. (New York: Brown and Benchmark, 1996). See also in this book, Donica Mensing's

(Continued)

(Continued)

chapter, "Confronting Others' Violations: The Case of the Manipulated Photo" for more details on using the Potter Box.

2. F. Navran, "12 Steps to Building a Best-Practices Ethics Program," *Workforce*, 76, No. 9 (1997):117-122.

3. S. A. Bowen, "Expansion of Ethics as the Tenth Generic Principle of Public Relations Excellence: A Kantian Theory and Model for Managing Ethical Issues," *Journal of Public Relations Research*, 16, No. 1 (2004): 65-92.

seemed bothered by the plan for fake online identities. She stood her ground, however, and told the senior account executive and account coordinator that she would not participate in the deceptive online component of the campaign. She stressed that she would like to work on the traditional campaign because she believed in the singer's future, but she could not in good conscience pretend to be a 12-year-old online. As a PRSA member, she also said that she would feel obligated to point out the potential ethical violation to the association's Board of Ethics and Professional Standards.

Quinn had been nervous about making her views known—especially about mentioning filing an ethical grievance with the industry's governing body. As things turned out, however, she was not fired; she was not even dismissed from the campaign. Instead, the senior account executive asked how she would create buzz about the hip-hop artist's new single if she didn't want to follow the plan of masquerading as someone younger.

In response, Quinn proposed using legitimate means of web communication—strategically placed online promotions and YouTube videos to drive traffic to the microsite that was offering free downloads of the song. Members of the account's management team were concerned that this approach wouldn't work in the limited amount of time they had; they were supposed to create internet buzz before the special events surrounding the official release of the CD.

Nevertheless, the agency's management supported the decision to abandon the unethical practices. Instead, the agency carried out a legitimate social media campaign that used the singer's own social media pages to spread information about the upcoming release.

The Aftermath: Honor Upheld, Business Lost

With this strategy, it took longer to build the buzz the record company expected, though attention did rise to the desired level by the end of the campaign. The record label executives had mixed reactions to the campaign's results. While they were pleased with the successful launch of the hip-hop artist's single and album, they were dissatisfied that the agency hadn't followed their wishes. When the agency bid to continue representing the music company, it lost the contract.

Quinn felt responsible for this loss of business, and she apologized to the account team and agency management. One member of the team told Quinn that she had felt similarly uneasy about using deception to build online buzz, but she'd been too intimidated to speak out. Others didn't talk to Quinn about the change in strategy, but they also didn't act as if losing the account was a crisis.

Only one member of the management team told Quinn that he still supported the idea of masquerading as teenagers in chat rooms in order to get the message out quickly. He believed that hitting the chat rooms for two or three days, at strategic times when tweens and teens were most likely to be online, would be the best use of the agency's resources to meet the client's goal. When asked about the ethical dimension, he reiterated an objection that some professionals had been citing since the PRSA's code of ethics was created: A public relations practitioner who behaves in an unethical way may have his or her membership revoked, but that person can continue to practice public relations.

In all likelihood, the agency could have carried out the online deceit and not faced any industry repercussions. Both scholarly approaches and professional standards can help a practitioner reach a decision, and Quinn used both as she thought about the questions she faced. Ultimately, however, an individual's personal ethics guide her professional behavior. Facing an ethical dilemma, Quinn returned to her basic sense of right and wrong, and to the basic definition of public relations she'd learned in school. She realized that if she wanted to keep long-term, mutually beneficial relationships as a viable goal for her client, her course was clear: She had to stand on principle and refuse to participate in unethical behavior, no matter what might happen as a result.

Thinking It Through

1. Can you think of any situation in which it would be OK for a professional to assume a false identity online? For example, the police do it to catch pedophiles. Why are media professionals different? If you believe this type of deception is not permissible for public relations campaigns, then what about for undercover reporting for a news organization?

2. If you were asked to develop an online promotional campaign to build buzz for a new CD, what elements would you include? Look online for effective campaigns for already famous or previously little-known artists, and describe the elements that work or don't work for you. What other promotional ideas do you have that no one seems to have tried yet?

3. What do you think about Quinn's statement to her bosses that if the agency went forward with the online deception, she would have to report the violation to the PRSA? Do you think that mixing her objections with the wider professional context was appropriate for that meeting?

4. Imagine that her boss had allowed Quinn to withdraw from the deceptive part of the campaign or had moved her off the hip-hop artist campaign entirely. If other agency employees did pretend to be teenagers in chat rooms but Quinn was not involved in that behavior, would the ethical question be settled? Why or why not?

5. Do you think Quinn should feel any responsibility for her agency losing the music account? Why or why not?

What If?

In 2009, when President Barack Obama had 2.7 million followers on Twitter, he surprised many of those followers by telling an audience in China that he did not tweet.

Though most people realize that major public figures do not personally type each 140-character dispatch that goes out on their Twitter accounts, this was the first time people had heard that the president in fact did not write any tweets at all. Instead, a variety of communications team members used the @BarackObama account to send information.

Defenders of this practice say it's simply the high-tech version of ghost-writing. It's long been accepted, they say, that presidents and other prominent people in government, business and the arts do not write their own speeches or opinion columns, even if no other writer is credited. With social media still in its infancy, however, it's not at all clear what the public understands about the origins of what they see.

Let's say you've landed your dream job in Washington in the public information office of one of your state's U.S. senators. In addition to the tasks you expected, such as talking to reporters and writing news releases, you're told that part of your job is to write updates on the senator's Facebook page, where her "friends" will see the updates under her name, just as they'd appear if she were writing them. When people post notes to the senator on the page, you will be the one responding.

You ask around and hear that this is fairly standard procedure on other senators' staffs. Still, you feel uncomfortable about it; it seems you're being asked to masquerade as someone else, plus you worry that you might accidentally write something that could damage the senator's reputation.

Would you keep quiet and write the Facebook posts? Or would you raise your objections with your boss? If the latter, what would you say? Check the PRSA ethics code and the code of the Word of Mouth Marketing Association for provisions to buttress your argument.

Think about what compromises you might be willing to make. For example, would you feel comfortable writing the Facebook updates if the senator read and approved them before they were posted? How about if her chief of staff approved them? Would it be enough to have a conversation with the senator in which she tells you what she does and doesn't want on her Facebook page? Can you think of a way to present the updates on the page so they seemed more honest to you?

As you think about these issues, some tips from the book "Ethics in Human Communication" by Richard L. Johannesen might help. Johannesen proposes asking five questions when dealing with potentially deceptive communication practices:

1. What is the client's and communicator's intent, and what is the audience's degree of awareness that the parties are working together?

2. Does the client use others, including ghostwriters and deceptive communicators, to make the client appear to possess qualities that he or she does not have?

3. What are the surrounding circumstances of the communicator's job that make deceptive communication necessary?

4. To what extent do clients actively participate in the writing of their own communication materials online?

5. Do clients accept responsibility for messages that are presented on their behalf, or does the responsibility fall on the unnamed writers?[6]

Go Online for More

The Arthur W. Page Society, an association of senior public relations executives:
http://www.awpagesociety.com/

Word of Mouth Marketing Association ethics code:
http://womma.org/ethics/

---

6. R. L. Johanneson, *Ethics in Human Communication* (Prospect Heights, IL: Waveland, 2000).

Public Relations Society of America policy on reporting ethical violations, with a form for submitting a report:
http://www.prsa.org/AboutPRSA/Ethics/AboutEnforcement

Public Relations Society of America advisory on deceptive online practices:
http://www.prsa.org/AboutPRSA/Ethics/ProfessionalStandards
    Advisories/PSA-08.pdf

New York Times story about efforts to redefine public relations in the social media age:
http://www.nytimes.com/2011/11/21/business/media/redefining-
    public-relations-in-the-age-of-social-media.html

At press time, the PRSA redefinition effort was just beginning. Learn more about it here:
http://prdefinition.prsa.org/

CHAPTER 7

Identifying Suspects
The Case of the Waco Shooting
Ray Niekamp

The most basic tenet of journalism is to seek the truth and report it. While that sounds easy, in practice it often is not. When nine people were killed in a gunfight, local media were under pressure to report the names of the victims—but one young reporter felt it would be better to wait.

THE SITUATION: MOTORCYCLE GANGS, POLICE WITH GUNS AND A SHOOTOUT

Sunday, May 17, 2015, was a bright, sunny day in Waco, Texas. At the Twin Peaks restaurant in a shopping center on the south side of the city, the staff was preparing for a gathering of motorcyclists who were in town for a meeting of a statewide biker coalition. The group would talk about political issues involving bikers. But the gathering also raised the possibility of a renewal of a turf war between two rival motorcycle gangs, the Bandidos and the Cossacks. The Bandidos, based in Houston, consider Texas their territory. The Cossacks dispute that claim. Police took up positions around the parking lot of the Twin Peaks.

When the Bandidos arrived, they found the Cossacks had already occupied most of the outdoor seating around the restaurant. They gathered at the periphery of the seating area, but there was no trouble until a Bandidos motorcycle rolled over the foot of a Cossack during a dispute over a parking spot. Both sides started throwing punches, then produced knives, chains and guns. Gunfire broke out. Police fired into the crowd. When it was all over, nine people lay dead in the parking lot, 20 more were wounded, and police arrested 177 bikers, charged them with engaging in organized crime, and jailed each of them on $1 million bail. The justice of the peace who set the bail said it was to "send a message" because most of the bikers were from out of town.

The Challenge: To Report the Names—or not?

It was a big story nationally on an easy-going Sunday in spring, and it led national newscasts that evening. It was a huge story for the Waco television stations. At a disadvantage against large market stations and network crews, the smaller Waco stations were under pressure to be the first to break new information. One reporter, Janet Wheeler (not her real name), found herself scrambling for information on the story as well, setting aside coverage of her usual beat. One of the stories she was chasing was trying to find the identities of the dead bikers. They would be important to have for any news story, but the Waco media were interested in whether the bikers were from the area or if they were from other parts of the state.

"Were they from so-called 'biker gangs'?" she wanted to know. "Were they local bikers?"

The Waco police weren't releasing the names, though, because they were not able to get in touch with all of the next of kin. A police department spokesman, Sgt. Patrick Swanton, told reporters some people hadn't been cooperating with police, which delayed getting in touch with relatives even more. He said as soon as all the relatives had been contacted, police would release the names of the dead.

But two days after the melee, one of the other Waco stations had the names of the victims on its noon newscast and its website. "Immediately the newsroom starts making calls to see if our station can get the names," Wheeler said. It turned out the competing station had gotten the names not from police but from a local justice of the peace who released preliminary autopsy reports. Waco police still would not release the names.

THE RESPONSE: USE THE NAMES

That touched off a debate in Wheeler's newsroom. "I and a few others felt we should wait until the police released the names," she said. "There had to be a reason they didn't release them just yet." She said Sgt. Swanton was usually "pretty good" about releasing information. But the majority of newsroom personnel, including managers, wanted the names reported right away. Wheeler said their attitude was that since the names were already out there, it no longer mattered why the police were holding back.

Wheeler found herself in the uncomfortable position of reporting the names in the station's 5 p.m. and 6 p.m. newscasts. Also troubling to her was her boss's insistence that she comb through social media to find out if the victims belonged to biker gangs, and if so, which ones. Two of the nine dead turned out to be from Waco; the others were from other cities in Texas. One was a Bandido, seven were Cossacks, and one was not a member of any biker gang.

"At one point I was asked to Facebook message the wife of one the bikers, so we could try and get sound," Wheeler said. "Mind you, this is a time where Waco police were warning that these biker groups were threatening to target law enforcement, and I have my boss telling me to try and message the loved ones of the deceased through social media."

Meanwhile, a third Waco affiliate held off on reporting the names until Waco police released them the next day. "Many of their Facebook viewers praised them for doing so," Wheeler said.

The Aftermath: When Competitive Pressures Drive Newsroom Decisions

After the incident, Wheeler wished there had been more discussion of the pros and cons of releasing the names before the police had done so. For her, the ethics question was the risk that people would learn of the death of one of their family through the news media and not from authorities.

"I found it disappointing and disheartening that the majority of my newsroom and leaders found nothing wrong with releasing the names before Waco PD announced them," Wheeler said. "It was as if there was no question about it, like it wasn't even an issue to be questioned."

She said the shooting story was "overwhelming" in a market the size of Waco. Once the names were public, the general feeling in the newsroom was that there was no longer a problem. "Just as there was little to no discussion on releasing the names, there was no discussion about it after it had been done," she said. "It literally was treated like it was nothing at all, and that is alarming to me."

Wheeler said she understands the need to be first, but asks, at what cost? "Social media has created that monster," she said. "It's more of a, 'post the information now, double-check later.' Ethics tend to go out the window and come second when there's big information to release."

TOOL FOR THOUGHT:
Minimize Harm

The third element in the Society of Professional Journalists Code of Ethics is Minimize Harm. It's an old notion, even an ancient one, stemming from the Golden Rule's admonition to treat others as you would wish to be treated. This means you would be expected to put yourself in the shoes of the stakeholders—in this case, the relatives of

(Continued)

(Continued)

the shooting victims. As in most ethics situations, having a discussion with colleagues and asking key questions will help determine what course of action to take.

Past SPJ President Fred Brown, in a commentary on the "Minimize Harm" section of the ethics code,[1] offers several questions for discussion:

Who gets hurt if we tell this story? Not only in the Waco case, but in any case, the relatives—especially the immediate family—of the deceased would be caught by surprise. The information coming from the media instead of an authority could cause emotional trauma. Brown says compassion is the key. Imagine yourself in the relatives' situation, and treat them as they would wish to be treated.

Does the benefit to the public of knowing that truth outweigh that harm? The question the reporters wanted answered was whether the victims were local or not. The victims were not public figures. Two turned out to be from Waco, so odds are they would be known by more people there than the other victims would be. So, the public benefit of learning the names is arguably more applicable to Waco than to the rest of the state.

What does the public need to know? The names of the shooting victims were basic information needed to follow up on the original story. However, is it important to get those names reported as quickly as possible, or to wait until it is certain that the next of kin has been notified?

_____

1. F. Brown, *Journalism Ethics: A Casebook of Professional Conduct for the News Media* (Portland, OR: Marion Street Press, 2011).

Wheeler's concern was complicated by the fact that a competitor had aired the names. Since the names were now in the public realm, her news managers decided their station needed to air them, too. Since the names had already been broadcast, it could be argued that any harm had already been done. But that presumes the family members had seen the one broadcast that used the names. That's quite a presumption. Midday newscasts have fewer viewers than evening newscasts, to start out with, and the probability that relatives would be tuned in at that time was slim—maybe. It could also be argued that other relatives (not necessarily immediate family) of the bikers would be consuming local media to stay on top of any information as the story developed, and they could be in a position of being surprised by the release of the names. The anguish they would feel could outweigh the need to report the names.

But is it in the public interest to know the names even before the family finds out? Most ethics commentators say there are always exceptions. After all, the SPJ standard is to "minimize harm," not to "avoid harm." One exception would be based on the prominence of the deceased, and if knowing the identity is crucial to the public. For example, if the mayor of a city is gunned down, most news organizations would report the name. The bikers in no way approached that kind of prominent status. Maybe a middle ground could be staked out: Report that two of the nine dead were from Waco, without using the names until police released them. Dr. Ronald Rogers of the University of Florida points out that police do not have to release anything until the case is complete—and they would argue it is not complete until kin are notified.[1]

Thinking It Through

1. Of the four main tenets in the Society of Professional Journalists' code of ethics (Seek Truth and Report It, Minimize Harm, Act Independently, Be Accountable and Transparent), does one carry more weight than the others? If you were to rank their importance, which would you put at the top? How would that affect the way you handle the information in your story?

2. In your own experience, how much importance do you give to beating the competition? Is being first with information your

---

1. R. Rodgers, R. "Pending Notification of Next of Kin," *Editingmonks blog*, http://editingmonks.blogspot.com/2010/02/pending-notification-of-next-of-kin.html.

primary goal? Can you see any problems that might arise by rushing to get information reported first?

3. What could the newsroom have done to deal with the view held by Wheeler and some other reporters that reporting the names before the police released them would be unethical?

Now Try This

Reporting vs. withholding: Another tragic situation

You're on duty in your radio station's newsroom on a Saturday in summer. Things are quiet. But then, the police scanners erupt in chatter. A helicopter has crashed. You're stuck at the radio station because you have to anchor a short newscast every hour, so you can't drive out to the scene of the crash. You rely on the telephone and social media to get the latest information.

Phone calls to addresses near the crash site finally turn up a witness who describes first responder activity. The helicopter was owned by a local real estate company. It's generally known that it was used to fly prospective customers to vacation properties in the area to avoid long drives on gravel roads. The witness speculates that the helicopter clipped some power lines and crashed into a wooded area next to a lake.

Police confirm that the helicopter belonged to the real estate company, but they don't have the names of the crash victims. You go on the air with what information you do have: "Police say both the pilot and his passenger are dead at the scene."

You didn't name the victims. You reported what information you had at the time. You've observed the SPJ Code of Ethics—or have you?

Consider the stakeholders in this case. Put yourself in their shoes. Once you think the situation through, would you have handled the story the same way, or differently? Remember the questions Fred Brown suggests, and see if the answers help you make a different decision.

CHAPTER 8

Solo Judgment Calls

The Case of the One-Person "TV Crew"

George L. Daniels

O nce upon a time in television news, large stations went out to cover stories with full crews—a reporter, camera operator and sometimes an audio person. Smaller stations sent out one-man bands, journalists who did both shooting and reporting.

Today, with the shrinking size of both news budgets and video equipment, the differences between small and large broadcast news operations have nearly disappeared. Big-city TV stations, and even the networks, are almost as likely as small operations to send out a one-man or one-woman band—also known as a VJ (video journalist) or sojo (solo journalist). Solo coverage is becoming more the norm than the exception in local television news.[1]

Going solo presents challenges for anyone, and even more for young broadcast journalists in their first jobs. Because reporting, writing, editing

---

1. Deborah Halpern Wenger and Deborah Potter, *Advancing the Story: Broadcast Journalism in a Multimedia World,* 2nd ed. (Washington, DC: CQ Press, 2012), 80–81.

and presenting the news are complex skills that can require years to learn, it can be tempting for a new journalist to take a video shortcut in order to create more time for all the other tasks that solo coverage requires. When a solo journalist wonders what's ethical, there's no one nearby to ask.

Is it OK to use video handout material from a publicist? Can you rearrange people for a better shot? Can you ask them to re-create a moment you missed? Out on his own, a young video journalist in Alabama found that even a simple-sounding story can present multiple questions like these.

THE SITUATION: A TORNADO AND ITS AFTERMATH

On April 27, 2011, an EF-4 tornado (EF-5 being the strongest) destroyed several neighborhoods in Tuscaloosa, the home of the University of Alabama and of WVUA-TV, which the university owns and operates. The Tuscaloosa storm killed 43 people, and dozens more died in tornadoes in other counties. Every journalist at WVUA was busy keeping up with the rising death toll, the impact of the storm on the university and multiple communities' efforts to provide aid and begin the cleanup.

Daniel Sparkman, a journalism student at the University of Alabama and a full-time anchor/reporter at WVUA-TV, was part of the weather team that provided on-air updates at the height of the storm. In the days and weeks that followed, the team traveled to communities devastated by the twister to report stories of survival and of community members helping neighbors in need. One of those follow-up stories involved heavyweight boxer Deontay Wilder, a hometown hero who graduated from Tuscaloosa's Central High School and went on to become the only American boxer to win a medal at the 2008 Summer Olympics.

Six weeks after the tornado, the undefeated Wilder fought in a Tuscaloosa event called Rumble on the River. Free tickets to the bout had been distributed a few days in advance in Alberta City, an area where the storm had leveled an elementary school and swept away entire neighborhoods. At one of the Rumble events, a raffle to help raise money for tornado survivors awarded a prize: "Dinner with Deontay." Sparkman was assigned to cover the dinner, a week after Wilder's fight, where proceeds from the raffle would be presented.

Sparkman would cover the dinner on his own as a one-man band. He would need to shoot the video then write and report the story that night for WVUA's 10 p.m. newscast. The producer was expecting a one- to two-minute story on the dinner with footage of Wilder and the raffle winner.

Static events like dinners and check presentations rarely make for thrilling television, but Sparkman was glad to be heading out to cover such a well-known athlete, a local celebrity in Tuscaloosa. Though he realized that Wilder's promoter had proposed the story mostly to enhance the boxer's reputation, he thought it still had news value. Heartwarming stories had been in short supply since the storm, and Sparkman wanted to show how a resilient community was recovering and how Wilder was a playing a role.

Like most of the reporters at WVUA, Sparkman was accustomed to one-man-band assignments, so he wasn't worried as he left the station. He knew from his producer that someone had won the raffle the previous week and that the dinner was going to take place at the local Red Lobster restaurant. After he arrived, he learned that the raffle winner was Mrs. Louisa Dunn of Alberta City.

As is often the case in news, however, what sounded like an easy assignment turned out to be less straightforward. By the time Sparkman arrived at the Red Lobster with his camera and tripod, Dunn had already been presented with the check for her raffle winnings. Worse still, Deontay Wilder had not arrived. Several expected elements of Sparkman's story were in jeopardy as his deadline for the 10 p.m. newscast approached.

THE CHALLENGE:
TO RE-CREATE OR NOT TO RE-CREATE

Sparkman faced three dilemmas. First, he needed video of Wilder, but Wilder wasn't there. Second, he needed video of the raffle winner receiving her check, but that had happened informally, before he arrived.

Third, he also needed general footage of Louisa Dunn, the raffle winner, but even that was tough to come by because Dunn's pastor, who was not related to the story, was prominent in every shot that Sparkman could get.

Each of those challenges presented ethical questions. If he couldn't see the raffle winner from where he was standing, should he ask other people to move out of the way, changing the "natural" setting in which Louisa Dunn was having dinner? Should he ask Dunn to step away from the scene for a separate interview? If there was no official check presentation planned, how could he visually depict for viewers that Dunn had received the proceeds from the raffle? Should he ask someone to re-create a check presentation so he could show the moment on camera?

Finally, if he couldn't interview or even show the supposed star of the evening, Deontay Wilder, what would happen to the story's news value? Though the story had other newsworthy elements, the celebrity was the draw, the reason that viewers would tune in. Sparkman could always use file video of Wilder fighting, but that would not make the connections he considered important to the story.

■ ■ ■ TOOL FOR ACTION:
Using File Footage and VNRs

Video journalists frequently encounter the problem of what to do about nonstandard footage—video shot by an outsider or file footage from their news organization's archives. Using video that does not come from that day's journalistic news gathering requires informing the viewers truthfully about what they're watching.

VNRs, video news releases, are video pieces that businesses, public relations firms and government agencies provide in hopes that overworked reporters at a station or website will simply run the piece as a story, thus allowing the businesses and agencies to control the content. In other words, VNRs are a video version of a press release.

In theory, no reputable news organization would run an entire story furnished by an outsider. Doing so makes little sense competitively: Other news organizations will have the same video news release that yours has, so your stories will look identical. Using a VNR makes little sense journalistically, too: You have no idea whether anything in the piece is accurate or what the maker's motives were.

In practice, however, using at least part of a VNR can be tempting—for cover video ("b-roll") or for times when you don't have access to a faraway building or person who's essential to your story. Video journalists have to ask, when is it OK to use any part of a provided video, whether it is old footage from the station's own archives, a VNR or captured footage from an online site such as YouTube?

Daniel Sparkman points to times when a law enforcement agency makes a major drug bust or confiscates a large number of weapons. Usually, the police will present the drugs or weapons during a news conference, so the media can get pictures and video. But in one situation Sparkman covered, the police did not show what they had confiscated. He had to resort to using file video from a network news feed.

This is the one part of the issue that's easy: When you use file footage—any video not gathered that day or as the story was breaking—you put the word File onscreen, so viewers know what they're seeing. This is station policy at WVUA and at many stations. In the case of the drugs and weapons, it was also essential that the narration explain that the drugs and weapons shown were not the ones confiscated locally but instead were an example of a similar haul from elsewhere. Explanatory notes and narration are crucial for an ethical presentation of news.

For a thorough explanation on the ethical use of VNRs and other file footage, explore the Radio Television Digital News Association News Director's Guide to Video News Releases, in the links at the end of this chapter. The organization recommends that, like file footage, VNRs be clearly labeled for viewers, and that journalists do their best to find out the purpose for which the VNR was shot and the standards used in producing it.

The Response:
Reality, with a Tweak

In addition to his role as a reporter at WVUA, Sparkman was the treasurer of the campus chapter of the Society of Professional Journalists, so thinking about journalistic standards and ethics wasn't new territory for him. He'd reported enough stories as a one-man band to be familiar with the use of b-roll, or "cover video," that plays while a reporter narrates the story. The best cover video would show the principal players in the story—Deontay Wilder and Louisa Dunn—doing the activity that was newsworthy, the dinner and the check presentation.

"A lot of times there are stories that have an ample amount of b-roll, especially with all that's been going on here in Tuscaloosa," Sparkman said. "If you're shooting a tornado story like a clothing drive, there's a lot of video. But if you're shooting a story like a press conference where there is minimal cover video, you have to find file video from other sources." On this particular night, the story was the dinner for Louisa Dunn, who was supposed to have a chance to eat with a championship boxer.

As Sparkman was trying to figure out how to do the story without Wilder, the Olympic medalist arrived 45 minutes late, and Sparkman had his camera rolling. He shot Wilder arriving, shaking hands and signing autographs, and he already had video of people talking around the table. For video of the check presentation, however, Sparkman needed to improvise.

"There is definitely a fine line between staging video and just making events happen when you need them to happen," he said. "As a photographer and news crew on the scene, you're kind of in charge of what's going on. If you ask them, most of the time people are willing to help you."

As soon as Wilder arrived and Sparkman got his shots, he asked Wilder to formally present the check that Dunn already had received casually. Such check or award presentation shots, commonly called "grip and grins," are no journalist's favorite scene to record. In this case, however, Sparkman considered the shot essential to complete his story. He described the scene this way: "They didn't have a time frame. They were having dinner with each other and doing whatever, whenever they felt like it." It seemed easy to make the request that the check be formally presented, and everyone readily complied.

Following is a transcript of Sparkman's 80-second story as it aired, with Sparkman's narration in ALL CAPS. Dunn had lost her best friend, Yvonne Mayes, in the April 27 tornado. Like most residents of Alberta City even six weeks after the storm, Dunn was still reeling from the chain of events that destroyed everything around her and took the life of her friend. The story opened with her talking about the impact of the tornado on her neighborhood, including the death of a child.

Mrs. Dunn: And then, your friend gone and the baby gone. It just like you're in another world. It's not Alberta City no more. To me it ain't.

Sparkman: THOSE ARE THE THOUGHTS OF A STORM SURVIVOR WHOSE FRIEND DIED IN THE APRIL 27TH STORM. THANKS TO THE HELP OF BOXER DEONTAY WILDER'S RUMBLE ON THE RIVER, SHE'S GETTING HELP REBUILDING HER LIFE.

J. D./Boxing Promoter: One of them was a "Dinner with Deontay" contest and what it is, what we did was we put it out there, everybody made a donation. This is the culmination of that. We got the winner of the contest, gonna eat with us here tonight. And the proceeds from the Dinner with Deontay contest. Miss Dunn, we're gonna present a check to her. The amount came up to a little over 500 dollars.

Sparkman: PROMOTER J. D. SAYS HE'S GLAD IT [the money] HELPED AT LEAST ONE PERSON AFFECTED BY THE TORNADO.

J. D.: We knew that it just being raffle-type contest, that we weren't going to be able to help an entire city, but we knew we could help one person. And that's what we're here to do, and I think it's going to be a good thing for her.

Dunn:	I thank him and I pray for him [Wilder] and his family to be strong so they can get through like me. And get through the storm.
Sparkman:	DUNN SAYS SHE WILL USE THE MONEY TO HELP BUY NEW HOME FURNISHINGS. IN TUSCALOOSA, DANIEL SPARKMAN, WVUA NEWS.

THE AFTERMATH: MORE STORIES, MORE LESSONS

Even before the Dinner with Deontay story, Sparkman knew that understanding ethics in theory and locating an ethical line while out on assignment alone can be very different matters. When it comes to making ethical decisions, he says, "It depends on what type of story you're shooting." From the questions he faced about orchestrating video in this particular story, he learned, "I need to be very careful about staging video and make sure that I am doing my due diligence."

Sparkman is glad that Wilder did eventually show up at the dinner, and doesn't regret asking him to present the check. The organizers of the event had discussed having a presentation at some point during the evening, he said. If he were faced today with the same set of circumstances and same need for the shot, he'd act the same way. The story confirmed what he considers a basic tenet of journalism: "If I am making the subject of the story do something that he or she would not naturally do, it's not news. It's acting. That's entertainment." Because the point of the dinner was to reward Dunn, having Wilder hand her the check seemed natural.

Since the tornado, Sparkman has faced similar questions again and still hasn't found them easy. Like most journalists in every medium, he encounters some kind of ethical judgment call on almost every assignment. He doesn't think he faces more issues because he's a video journalist, or because he works alone; in his experience, videographers and reporters who work together face the same sorts of situations as one-man bands.

Thinking It Through

1. As a journalist, can you think of a circumstance in which you'd feel comfortable having people reenact something you missed, or do something that they weren't going to do on their own? Would it matter whether the reenactment was for a photo or video or for a written story? Do you agree with Sparkman that asking Wilder to present the check was OK, that it was just a case of "making events happen when you need them to happen"? If something is done regularly by your own news organization and others, should that be a consideration as you weigh your options?

2. Let's say you work for a TV station and were watching its newscast last night when you noticed that some file video shown during a story was not labeled as file. Because of the way the video was used in the piece, it appeared to have been shot the same day as the rest of the story. What should you do? Is this an ethical offense worth bringing to the attention of your producer? If you do that and he or she does not seem concerned, should you drop the matter or take it to someone higher up?

3. Television is a visual medium, but many stories are not visual. Consider the world financial crisis, for instance. If you don't have good video for a story that you consider important, and if you know that the story will be downplayed because of its lack of visuals, what can you do? Are there stories that simply should be told with minimal video elements? Should a TV station have different kinds of stories on its website from those it puts on the air?

4. Here's an exercise for starting to get a sense of what's involved in video journalism. Look online for a story done by a solo journalist; one good place to look is among the winners of contests, like the Solo Video Contest run quarterly and yearly by the National Press Photographers Association. Watch your chosen piece multiple times so that you can make a list of each person the journalist talked to; each place he or she had to go; and all the other tasks, such as writing and performing narration, that the journalist had to do.

5. On a news site online, find a video story or an audio slideshow in which you think music and sound effects enhance the storytelling. Now find one in which you think the sound risks misleading the audience, as warned about in the Radio Television Digital News Association guidelines (see the list of the links at the end of the chapter).

TOOL FOR THOUGHT: Guidelines for Ethical Video and Audio Editing[1]

Long after you've forgotten the facts contained in a video news story you saw on TV or online, you're likely to remember one sound or one image from the piece. The power of visuals is the reason broadcast journalists need to take such care in their use. As the Radio Television Digital News Association, the world's largest organization exclusively serving the electronic news profession, puts it, "Photojournalists and editors should exercise the same level of ethical professionalism and accuracy in editing sounds and images as reporters and producers are expected to exercise in their choice of words, sound bites and facts."[2]

The ethics codes of both the RTDNA and the National Press Photographers Association address reenactment and manipulation of images. RTDNA wanted to go further by helping journalists think about their responsibilities and how best to act on them. An ethics partnership with the Poynter Institute resulted in a set of editing guidelines, a portion of which appears below. (For the full text, see the list of links at the end of the chapter.)

1. **Do not reconstitute the truth.** Don't add sounds that did not exist, unless it is clear to the audience that they have been added in the edit room. Don't add sounds that you obtained at another scene or from another time or place if adding the sounds might mislead the audience. Do not add

something to a story that didn't happen.

2. **Be judicious in your use of music and special sound effects.** Music can send complex and profound editorial messages. If the journalist records music that occurred at the scene of his or her story, then that is ambient sound that might ethically be edited into the story. However, if the music is a soundtrack audio recording, then journalists must ask themselves whether the music adds an editorial tone to the story that would not be present without the music.

3. **Use photographic and editing special effects sparingly and carefully.** Slow motion, slow dissolves, tight cropping and framing, dramatic lighting and unusual angles can all send subtle or even overt messages to the viewer about a person's perceived guilt, power or authority.

4. **Apply the same careful editing ethics standards to your newscast teases, promotions and headlines that you do for your news stories.** If it is unethical to add sounds or production techniques to a news story, then it is just as harmful to use those techniques during a promotion for that news story.

---

1. RTDNA Guidelines for Ethical Video and Audio Editing, http://www.rtdna.org/content/guidelines_for_ethical_video_and_audio_editing.

2. Ibid.

What If?

You were recently hired as a television reporter in the market where you went to college. Your schedule requires that you work Christmas Day, and your news director suggests that for the 7 p.m. newscast, you find a "feel-good story" about people helping others.

You've had only a few assignments so far, so you want to do it correctly. Right away you have an idea: Members of the sorority in which you were active as a student are planning to volunteer on Christmas at a local homeless shelter, preparing and serving dinner to people who have nowhere else to go. You told your sorority sisters that you couldn't participate because you have to work, but now you think the meal sounds like a good way to fulfill your assignment. You already know someone you can interview from the sorority, plus you can help out and shoot video at the same time.

When you arrive at the shelter at 2:15 p.m. on Christmas Day for the meal that's supposed to begin at 2:30, you learn that most of the people who normally come to the shelter have already had a 1 p.m. Christmas dinner at a large church nearby. You and your sorority sisters sit for nearly two hours, and not one person comes to the shelter. Finally, at 4 p.m., one of the sorority sisters calls her family to come to the shelter and eat, so that all the food doesn't go to waste.

Your deadline for the 7 p.m. newscast is rapidly approaching, and you don't have a story. What do you do? Can you really shoot a sorority sister's family eating the dinner meant for the homeless? If not, what could you do that would be ethical and fill the airtime with something worthwhile? Is there some way to "save" the story at the shelter? Can you think of a story you might be able to get elsewhere, and fast?

Let's say you call your boss and he tells you to drive quickly to a restaurant on State Street that's serving Christmas Dinner free to anyone who wants it. You arrive and are relieved to see people eating. Several of them are willing to talk on camera about why they need help this Christmas. So you're feeling pretty good about your story when you start to interview the restaurant owner.

First, the owner says he won't talk to you unless you pitch in and serve some food yourself. Then he tells you to put on an elf costume to fit in with the other servers, all of whom are in Christmas dress. Then, as you're debating whether to participate in the story, he refers to your boss as "Uncle Joe." That's how you discover that the news director has sent you to do a story on his nephew's restaurant.

You're alone on the assignment. You know the station has only a skeleton staff working for the holiday, so your boss isn't likely to have another story to use if you send him nothing. You don't want your first month on the job to be your last. You stand there with an elf hat in your hand, thinking, Now what?

Go Online for More

RTDNA Code of Ethics:
http://www.rtdna.org/content/rtdna_code_of_ethics

Guidelines for Ethical Video and Audio Editing:
http://www.rtdna.org/content/guidelines_for_ethical_video_
and_audio_editing

More thoughts and guidelines of the use of VNRs:

BBC policy on use of video and audio news releases:
http://downloads.bbc.co.uk/guidelines/editorialguidelines/pdfs/video-
news-releases.pdf

RTDNA Guidelines for Use of Non-Editorial Video and Audio:
http://www.rtnda.org/pages/media_items/guidelines-for-use-of-non-
editorial-video-and-audio250.php

RTDNA story on the VNR issue:
http://www.rtnda.org/pages/media_items/full-disclosure817.php

NPR story on use of VNRs in local TV news:
http://www.npr.org/templates/story/story.php?storyId=5327152

CHAPTER 9

Seeking Answers for Students

The Case of the Undercover Reporter

Joe Mirando

A student frustrated by her university's policies on transfer credit reported on the subject for a journalism class. She collected the experiences of transfer students but still needed to find out exactly how university officials decided which courses to accept for credit. When the usual reporting methods produced no results, she considered going undercover.

Is it ever OK to lie in pursuit of truth? And if lying did enable her to get the information, should she submit the resulting story as a class assignment? Should she also try to get the story published in the student newspaper—and if so, what should she tell the editors and her audience about her methods?

Here is how this student faced up to those questions. Because rules on transfer credit are still being debated, and because some of the people in this chapter have continuing relationships with the university officials involved, the names of people and of the college have been changed.

The Situation: Inconsistent Rules on Transfer Credit

Lauren Sagona, a sophomore at Central State University, was perturbed when she switched her major to journalism and discovered that a math course she'd taken would no longer count as a core requirement. When she complained to other students, they told her about their own difficulties with transfer credit. The problems seemed far worse for students transferring from other schools than for Central State students who, like Sagona, were simply changing majors.

Sagona talked to transfer students who said that Central State had given them no credit for as many as 10 courses they had taken at the two-year Kilpatrick Community College. As a result, some students who thought they were entering Central State as juniors had arrived to discover that they were actually classified as freshmen. In addition, when transfer students compared their records, they found that Central had given some of them credit for certain courses but had denied credit to other students for the very same courses. Students also found inconsistencies in Central's decisions about which courses counted for major or core requirements as opposed to simply being counted as electives.

Sagona wanted to know more. She began her reporting with simple Google searches that turned up useful articles from The Chronicle of Higher Education, Education Week and Community College Journal. Through the LexisNexis database, she gained access to scholarly analyses in Current Issues in Education and Community College Review. These sources established that no federal laws exist on how transfer students' situations should be handled; colleges can accept or refuse transfer credits based on any criteria they choose. In some cases, schools are governed by state policies that complicate matters for students transferring from out of state or transferring from private to public schools.

The Challenge: Gathering Information from Difficult Sources

Next, Sagona interviewed academic counselors at Central State and Kilpatrick Community College and spoke with transfer students again to double-check their information. She found that the two schools, like most colleges in America, assigned staff workers to handle each transfer student's situation on a case-by-case basis.

All colleges have different systems of numbering and naming courses. For example, one college may list a course as EN 312 with the title Explorations in Modern Literature, while another offers a course with nearly identical content that is listed as ENGL 159 and called American Writers. Some courses at two-year colleges have names and content similar to courses that four-year colleges offer only to third- or fourth-year students. Given all these complications, Central State counselors said they always warned prospective transfer students that the information they provide about courses is purely advisory; the evaluation of transfer credit does not become official until the student is fully enrolled.

In the professional literature she read, Sagona saw references to a "course equivalency table," a database listing classes by prefix, number and name from one college that might be considered equivalent to specific courses at another college. When she asked counselors at Central State if she could see their course equivalency table, each referred her to the registrar.

At the registrar's office, Sagona identified herself as a journalism student working on a news story. The secretary told her that no course equivalency table could be provided to her. She asked to speak to the registrar who told her the same thing.

The next day, it occurred to Sagona that neither the secretary nor the registrar had clarified whether a course equivalency table actually existed; they'd simply said they couldn't give her one. She considered calling the registrar's office again and asking the question, "Is there such a thing as a course equivalency table?" She decided, however, that she was unlikely to get a response other than "No comment."

Then Sagona began to wonder, was identifying herself as a reporter the reason no one was willing to elaborate on the rules? If so, what could she do about it? She started to brainstorm about using some form of deception as a route to the information she needed.

■ ■ TOOL FOR ACTION: Rules of Engagement for Deception

The Society of Professional Journalists suggests that reporters consider lying or engaging in other deceptive techniques only when the following are true[1]:

- The information being sought is of profound importance.

- All other ways of gathering the information have been exhausted.

- The reporter will acknowledge the deception and explain the reasons for it to his or her audience.

- The harm that could be prevented by public knowledge of the information outweighs any harm caused by the deception.

- The journalists involved have fully examined their own motivations, the potential consequences of their actions and possible impact on the profession's credibility as well as their own and that of their news organization.

---

1. Jay Black, Bob Steele and Ralph Barney, *Doing Ethics in Journalism* (Greencastle, IN: Sigma Delta Chi Foundation, Society of Professional Journalists, 1993): 112-113.

THE RESPONSE: PRETENDING TO BE SOMEONE ELSE

From class, Sagona knew that some journalists who misrepresent themselves in reporting end up being honored for breaking important news. Textbooks and trade journals have documented the work of journalists who pose as hospital patients, bartenders, prison inmates, prostitutes, police officers and supermarket workers. They do so in order to expose dangers or inequities—for instance, mistreatment of the mentally ill, or discrimination minorities face in applying for jobs or buying a home—so that citizens can work to change things for the better.

She knew that lying would be risky. The journalistic deceptions she'd heard about were very deliberately planned in order to reach a specific goal, confining dishonest behavior to as few instances as possible. She would have to be ready to acknowledge the deception later and to accept any consequences. Above all, she would have to contend with the fact that this was not just a case of telling a harmless little fib to get a story done; it involved a series of actions that violated honesty, the most basic tenet of journalism. If she got the information and put together an effective story, some fellow students would be helped and possibly a whole institution's policy could be improved. Along the way, however, her actions were likely to make some individuals look bad and make the whole university appear less than trustworthy.

Sagona decided to call the registrar's office and disguise her voice so that the secretary would not recognize her from their previous conversation. She would say she was a Kilpatrick Community College student considering transferring to Central State and she wanted to know which courses from her school would receive credit at Central. This was the only way, she thought, that she'd have a chance of finding out whether a course equivalency table existed, and if so, what it said.

She was prepared to provide a fake name, but it turned out that she didn't need to. She simply introduced herself as a community college student and said she planned to transfer to Central State within one year. "I want to know what I should take here at Kilpatrick that will definitely transfer to Central State," she told the secretary. "If I tell you which courses I'm going to register for, will you tell me if I will receive credit for them?"

This secretary put her on hold, then came back and said, "OK, I have my 'cheat sheet' ready. Tell me which courses you plan to take, and I'll look on my list here to see if we will accept them."

Sagona gave her the names and numbers of five Kilpatrick courses. The secretary said two of the five would "likely" transfer. The secretary was careful to say that this information was unofficial and the courses would not be officially accepted until after the student enrolled. Sagona asked about three more courses and was told that one would "likely" transfer but there was no guarantee. Generally, the courses that were not acceptable were upper-level courses more specific to a major curriculum.

Sagona decided not to ask whether the "cheat sheet" was the course equivalency table. The secretary had said the information was unofficial, and Sagona did not want to make her suspicious since she'd asked about the equivalency table before. She did, however, ask whether the secretary would provide information on other specific courses to other Kilpatrick students if they called. The secretary said that would depend on several factors, including the time of day they called and how complete her list of courses was, because, she said, the list changed constantly. Sagona thanked the secretary and hung up.

TOOL FOR THOUGHT: Mill and Avoiding Rationalization

Journalists who consider going undercover—and thus violating the profession's core value of honesty—can easily fall back on self-serving rationalizations to justify what they want to do. John Stuart Mill's Principle of Utility asks you to consider the quality of your work, not just the quantity.

In her reporting, Lauren Sagona believed she was doing the greatest good (quantity) by using deception to expose inconsistent university policies. But what about the consequences of her actions? Would future sources on campus trust her? How might her deception affect the reputation of student reporters as a group? Mill would encourage her to consider this broader perspective and also to make sure she'd explored all the alternatives before resorting to deception.

Asking the registrar for the document she wanted didn't work, but what else could Sagona have tried? What about using social media to collect information from students willing to go on the record with their stories about transfer credit problems? Then what might have happened if she took that information—say, records showing that five students got transfer credit for a particular course while five others did not—back to the registrar, or to the registrar's boss, and asked how those decisions were made? Might those questions have resulted in someone producing the document that Sagona sought?

(Continued)

(Continued)

The Society of Professional Journalists cautions journalists not even to consider going undercover unless the information being sought is of utmost importance to the public. From Mill's perspective, one reason for this caution would be that using deception on any story leads to the erosion of media credibility in the public's eyes. Why would you risk that large an impact for a small story?

Recognizing some of the most common rationalizations that journalists use in decisions about undercover reporting can help ensure that your goals are sound and your reasoning legitimate. Only then can your work achieve the quality you desire.

- **It's only a "white lie," and it's done all the time.** The desire to entertain, make money or attract ratings during TV sweeps week doesn't justify lying. Keep in mind that "gotcha" shows such as "To Catch a Predator" are sharply criticized by professional journalists.

- **It will make the story even better.** Importance, relevance and impact on the audience are what make news stories worthwhile. Undercover reporting does not add news value to a story that does not already have it.

- **Everybody is going to want to read or see this.** Sure, but "everybody" will likely be noticing what the reporter did to get the information, rather than appreciating the information itself.

- **The government and big corporations lie all the time.** Journalism aims for truth. If government officials or business executives are acting dishonestly, journalists should be informing the public of that behavior, not joining in by acting dishonestly themselves.

- **We're on deadline, and we need to fill the space or airtime.** This rationalization is a key sign of unprofessional behavior. Deception should never be a last-minute way to get something finished.

The Aftermath:
Publication and Policy Changes

As Sagona wrote her story, she resisted the temptation to use a sensational tabloid-style lead like "An undercover investigation has turned up a scandal right here on campus." Instead, she stressed the impact: Transfer students at Central State were experiencing problems, and the university was using apparently inconsistent criteria to evaluate transfer credit.

She could not be sure whether the "cheat sheet" the secretary had used was an official course equivalency table or just unofficial handwritten notes, but the fact that a knowledgeable employee was looking to a document for answers to specific transfer questions was evidence of a policy being followed. Here is her lead:

> Transfer students from Kilpatrick Community College say some of their courses are not accepted here at Central State, and the registrar's office will not officially confirm or deny this information. A Central State student posing as a Kilpatrick student called the registrar's office and was unofficially given the names of three courses that would likely be accepted and the names of five other courses that would likely not be accepted by Executive Assistant Judy Edwards.

The rest of the 20-inch story provided details on why the process is difficult. Sagona limited the negative quotes to statements by students she had checked back with, to ensure they knew they were talking on the record.

When Sagona's journalism professor graded the story, he asked her why she had misrepresented herself as a prospective transfer student. Sagona explained her thinking and the actions she had taken, and the professor was satisfied that her motives were sound. He did say that Sagona should have checked whether the transfer students she spoke with actually did receive credit for the specific courses the secretary had identified.

The professor's policy was not to edit stories that a student was submitting to the campus newspaper. Instead, he provided the newspaper with an untouched copy on the same day that the student submitted it for class. Class handouts made clear that neither the student newspaper's decisions about whether to publish a story nor any changes the editors made to the story before publication would affect the professor's evaluation of the student's work for class.

A faculty adviser had encouraged the editor of the student newspaper, The Reporter, to check the accuracy of stories by calling sources to verify the information. However, no one was in the registrar's office at press time, and calls to Sagona using the phone number listed in the student directory went unanswered. The editor called the professor at home on a deadline, and the professor assured him that he had consulted with Sagona and trusted that she had not made up the story.

About five days after Sagona's undercover interview with the registrar's secretary, her story was published in The Reporter. It appeared on Page 3, where journalism class stories often ran. The lead was intact, and the editor had made few changes in the story.

Sagona had worried that her deception might result in a charge of violating the campus code of student conduct, which forbids withholding the truth from college officials. But that did not happen nor did campus officials ever contact Sagona. The story did, however, generate spirited class discussion of her decision to lie.

Some of her classmates agreed with Sagona that she'd taken the best action possible and that she was justified in her deception. Others, however, said she should have not done the story at all because it could damage the school's image or lead people to suspect dishonesty in other media reports, or it might encourage other student reporters to practice deception without considering the serious ethical questions involved.

In subsequent months, no other stories based on undercover reporting appeared in The Reporter. Although it's impossible to tell whether Sagona's story had a direct impact on university policies, several things did happen. Students who had transferred from Kilpatrick wrote letters to the editor criticizing the process of deciding transfer credit. A month later, Central State's Public Information Office put out a press release describing a cooperative effort by the administrations of Central and Kilpatrick Community College to promote a "seamless" transfer process. The local town newspaper covered this development.

Today, Central State posts its course equivalency table on its website. The table lists more than 200 courses offered by Kilpatrick Community College and shows whether they will be accepted for credit if a student transfers to Central State. The university posts similar information about course offerings from other two-year schools as well.

Thinking It Through

1. Do you think that Sagona exhausted all her reporting options before resorting to deception? If not, what other ways of obtaining information could she have tried? For example, might it have worked to recruit current or former Kilpatrick students to ask the registrar's office for the transfer credit information?

2. When Sagona lied about being a community college student, the secretary seemed willing to help her, though she had not been willing when Sagona asked questions as a reporter. If you were the reporter in this case, would the secretary's change in approach have seemed important to the story? Would you have worried about the impact on the secretary after the story with her name in it came out?

3. In professional newsrooms, journalists do not go undercover without permission from their bosses. Because Sagona was doing the story for a class and because she wanted to submit it to the student newspaper, should she have consulted her teacher or the editors before lying about her identity? The teacher and editors are all part of the same university whose policies her story would be exposing. Should that fact be a consideration in your decision?

4. If you were in the registrar's office reporting this story, and the secretary walked off and left the "cheat sheet" on her desk, would you have taken it? Or photographed it with your smartphone? If you did either of those things, would you have run the whole document in the paper or online, or quoted from it? For purposes of these questions, does it matter whether you had told the secretary you were a reporter or had said you were a prospective transfer student?

What If?

In November 1992, the ABC newsmagazine show "Primetime Live" aired a report about unsanitary conditions at the Food Lion supermarket chain that became one of the most hotly debated news stories of its time. Reporters for "Primetime Live" had lied about their experience to get jobs at two Food Lion stores and used hidden cameras to report on what their coworkers were doing. The show alleged that the stores used numerous unsavory methods to pass off old or spoiled food as fresh; after it aired, the company's stock value plummeted.

In the controversy that followed, Food Lion's owners did not dispute the information that ABC had uncovered. Instead, the company took issue with the network's deceptive techniques and sued for fraud, seeking more than $2 billion in damages. A jury awarded Food Lion $5.5 million; eventually, seven years after the report aired, a federal appeals court threw out all but $2 of those damages.

Take yourself back to the 1990s. You're a producer for "Primetime Live." You've heard many reports of unsafe practices at Food Lion—for example, bleaching spoiled meat to remove the smell. Is the story worth pursuing? Why? You know that Food Lion has been waging a nasty battle with a union that wants to represent its employees. If some of the people giving you negative information about the company are involved with the union, should that influence your decision? What reporting methods would you try in order to find out what's really happening behind the scenes at Food Lion stores?

If those methods don't work, what arguments would you make to your boss about why going undercover is your best option? You know that many viewers and critics view hidden-camera reporting as a ratings stunt. How will you justify it as essential in this case? In order to get jobs at Food Lion, your reporters will have to lie about their experience on their applications. How will you justify those lies in a profession whose first goal is truth?

Once you have the footage showing unsafe food handling, what kinds of questions will you want to ask the undercover reporters about how they obtained the footage? Should you provide your information to the authorities so that they can enforce public health codes, or is your first loyalty to your audience? You're fairly sure the practices that ABC employees witnessed will continue during the weeks or months it takes for your report to be edited. If you really think food from the store is dangerous, is it OK not to alert the public until your report is ready?

Go Online for More

Poynter Institute checklist on when hidden cameras might be appropriate:
http://www.poynter.org/uncategorized/744/deceptionhidden-cameras-checklist/

National Public Radio podcasts on the ethics of undercover reporting:
http://www.tedconover.com/2010/01/the-ethics-of-undercover-reporting/

Columbia Journalism Review analysis of the ethical dilemmas associated with going undercover:
http://cjr.org/campaign_desk/the_ethics_of_undercover_journalism.php?page=all

Many individual news organizations' ethics codes address the issue of undercover reporting. For example, here are the BBC's guidelines on secret recording:
http://www.bbc.co.uk/editorialguidelines/guidelines/privacy/secret-recording

More information on the Food Lion case:

A Poynter Institute analysis that separates the ethical and legal issues:
http://www.poynter.org/uncategorized/2125/abc-and-food-lion-the-ethics-questions/

An Accuracy in Media report based on a review of court documents and video:
http://www.aim.org/publications/special_reports/foodlion.html

A C-SPAN video covering a range of investigative reporting cases:
http://www.c-spanvideo.org/program/79835-1

CHAPTER 10

Prior Restraint

The Case of "See Below the Fold"

John H. Kennedy

Vinny Vella

S ome college journalists face a thicket of restrictions imposed on them by private schools that fund student media. Thus, administrators at these schools sometimes believe they're entitled to control content via prepublication censorship. So, how should student journalists respond when they get an exclusive story but are forced to sit on their hands as other news organizations publish and broadcast the same story?

That was the situation for staff members of The Collegian at La Salle University in Philadelphia. Editors at the student newspaper ultimately chose a unique response to protest those press restrictions—and to reclaim some of their journalistic dignity.

THE SITUATION: CLASSROOM ENCOUNTERS OF AN UNUSUAL KIND

In late March 2011, Editor-in-Chief Vinny Vella at La Salle University's weekly student newspaper got an interesting tip: Tenured business professor Jack Rappaport, while conducting an extra-credit seminar for students at a satellite campus, featured exotic dancers during one of the sessions. The story would quicken the competitive pulse of any journalist and raise readers' eyebrows—especially at La Salle, a Catholic institution.

Vella, a junior, assigned Luke Harold, the paper's news editor, to check out the tip, and his reporting yielded a story ready for publication April 7. But first, any such sensitive story had to be approved by the dean of students before it could be published—and the dean slammed on the brakes. Vella was told the story could not run until the university's lawyers had finished their investigation of the incident. Vella, managing editor Kevin Smith and Harold said they begged, argued and debated with the dean.

"I think we realized that if the administration was not going to acknowledge that this is a problem, we needed to acknowledge that this is a problem," Smith said. "Because without our coverage, this issue, a professor bringing exotic dancers to a classroom setting, was going to get ignored or washed over."

The paper had talked to several students in the seminar, and they agreed to go on the record. However, the answer from administrators was still "wait." "Eventually," they could publish the story, Vella said, but they weren't told when. Of course, "eventually" in the news business is a vague, often unsatisfactory response to journalists who operate in a hypercompetitive field. As it turned out, the student editors' fears were confirmed.

On April 8, the day after the Collegian appeared but without its exclusive, Philadelphia's City Paper, an alt-weekly,[1] published a version of the

---

1. The newspaper stopped publication in October 2015.

story written by an intern who was also a La Salle student. Her story went viral as national news organizations linked to the City Paper website and local news organizations rushed to do their own stories. Adding insult to injury, Collegian staffers had to sit by and watch as local TV outlets parked their trucks outside university buildings and interviewed students on camera.

Smith, who has since left journalism, felt disenfranchised, especially by the approach other media took in covering the story.

"The fact that City Paper scooped us led every other news outlet to campus with a camera and a microphone and no direction," Smith said. "They were stopping random people on the street and saying, 'Hey, did you hear about this?'"

It didn't help, Smith said, that the administration declined to comment in nearly every story or broadcast segment about the infamous seminar. Without that input, most media reprinted what the City Paper had reported: accounts of the seminar provided by students who spoke off the record.

And those accounts were not exactly what other attendees, ones willing to have their names appear in the Collegian, had told Harold. Most notably, the anonymous attendees quoted in the City Paper version said "lap dances were administered to willing students—and even Rappaport—while he lectured."

This clashed with the numerous, on-the-record accounts that Harold uncovered in his reporting, which was that the dancers touched no one during their visit to Rappaport's class.

"Instead of being open with it, La Salle basically forced all of these half-truths to be the focus of the stories," Smith said. "It had no basis in fact and only served to make La Salle look bad."

Vella felt defeated as he watched other journalists pursue a story his staff had been following since Day 1. A story they should have broken.

"It was very frustrating," Vella said. "It was disheartening. It was confusing. We were taught to be diligent, to pursue stories that needed to be told, and then when we presumably do what we were taught to do and still couldn't publish it, it made me sort of disillusioned. I didn't know what to do."

The Rappaport incident was the latest in a series of controversial stories the Collegian fought to publish during that academic year. The previous fall, a university official had been charged with stealing millions of dollars from La Salle's food service operations, but editors were initially told to wait on that story. In January, a student was arrested on charges she killed her boyfriend back home in New Jersey. The editors were told they could only publish vague details in their first story and not to identify the student even though she had been arrested.

Administration officials said they had reason to be cautious. Over the years, the newspaper had published student columns and cartoons considered gratuitously offensive and embarrassing. But the students who toiled every week to produce the paper didn't see it that way.

"The administration was hypersensitive and for no good reason," Smith said. "They handled it in such a way that seemed like we were idiots, like they never took us seriously and were just waiting for our next colossal screw-up."

So, along came the exotic-dancers-in-the-classroom story. The editors found themselves questioning their own status as journalists especially in contrast with the lessons they had learned in the classroom and as interns at professional media outlets in the area. "We felt betrayed, sort of along the lines of 'why are we taught one thing when we can't actually do what we've been told we could do—or should be doing?'" Vella said.

THE CHALLENGE: JOURNALISTS OR NOT JOURNALISTS?

The student journalists went back to the dean of students and argued again about publishing the story. The answer was still "not yet," Vella said, and they were told it had nothing to do with the university's upcoming Open House weekend when prospective students and their families visited campus.

A few hours after the meeting, though, the dean called the students and told them they could publish the story April 14, but only after the story was cleared by the university's lawyers. Vella asked whether it could lead the paper, above the fold—typically, the space reserved in newspapers for the most important stories.

In the past, the university had mandated that other stories be played below the fold, including those involving a mugging on campus and the embezzlement case. To Vella, the answer this time was predictable: it must be placed below the fold. The student editors didn't know what to do.

THE RESPONSE: WHAT SHOULD THEY DO NOW?

Smith and Harold, who had reported the story and even knocked on Rappaport's apartment door seeking comment, had an immediate, visceral reaction.

"We were pissed," Smith said. "Luke and I just wanted to defy the dean, to just say 'screw it' and run a banner headline."

But cooler heads prevailed. They realized that such insubordination would likely have negative effects on the Collegian itself, and the two didn't want the paper to be a casualty of their feud with the administration. So, they sought some advice from professors in the university's small journalism program. They entered Assistant Professor John H. Kennedy's office, closed the door behind them and sat down to vent their frustrations. What could they do now? What should they do now?

Kennedy said his role was to help them explore their options, not push for one position over another. The decision should be made by the students who ultimately would be living with the consequences.

In Kennedy's view, the choices were pretty straightforward: comply with the wishes of the administration; defy the administration and publish the story above the fold; or consider some third option. Almost as an afterthought, he said they might entertain publishing the story below the fold—but publish nothing above the fold.

Smith and Harold looked at each other. It was a moment of clarity.

"It became such an immediate understanding that that's what was going to happen," Smith said.

The two left the office moments later.

The Collegian appeared as it always did on Thursday morning. That morning, Vella was at his internship at The Philadelphia Inquirer, the region's dominant broadsheet newspaper. He was nervous about the Collegian editors' decision. Had they done the right thing? "This is the day we lay it all on the line," he texted his managing editor. "Yup," Smith texted back.

As it turned out, this issue of the Collegian would cause a stir on campus and make headlines around the city, the region and beyond, and not because of the Rappaport story co-authored by Harold and Justin Walters, another Collegian reporter, but because of how it was featured in the paper.

The staff had decided that the top half of the paper would be entirely blank, save for four words in small type: "See below the fold." In the lower right-hand corner was the Rappaport story, and inside the paper was an editorial explaining the decision to feature it there as well as the chronology leading up to publication. In Vella's view, the blank top half of the paper, while almost devoid of any words or images, spoke volumes about what he and his staff had to confront.

Sharon Gekoski-Kimmel, The Philadelphia Inquirer

■ ■ ■ TOOL FOR ACTION: Seeking Truth and (Some) Independence

How should college journalists deal with censorship, especially at private schools that don't have the same First Amendment protections available to those at public colleges and universities? The most widely consulted media ethics code is published by the Society for Professional Journalists, and it offers four main tenets: "Seek Truth and Report It"; "Minimize Harm"; "Act Independently"; and "Be Accountable and Transparent." While the code is essentially silent on ethical responses to censorship, the La Salle student journalists believed they were acting under at least three of those general principles: seeking truth and acting independently as well as being prepared to be held responsible for their decisions. Advice about handling censorship that student journalists anticipate follows:

1. **Nail down the story before you push for publication.** This is generally true for any story, controversial or not, but especially if you're fighting the administration to go public. "If you're unprepared or underprepared, if the story has holes in it, then that just increases the legitimacy of the argument against you," Vella says. "So first and foremost, make sure you have a complete story ready to go."

2. **Be fair and be firm.** Give administration officials the opportunity to respond. Have a conversation and assess their objections. "If they say no, why are they saying no?" Vella says. Is it because they believe the story is inaccurate—or they just don't want the bad publicity? For The Collegian, this wasn't the first time the students had acceded to the administration's wishes about a controversial story. "It was the last straw. I think that makes it a different conversation as opposed to they are saying no to you for first time. That makes you look petulant: 'They're saying no? We'll show you.'"

3. **Enlist your faculty adviser.** Advisers can be powerful advocates, especially if they have seen all the care

you've put into the story and they're willing to stake their reputations on publication.

4. **Prepare to educate administrators.** Just as professional journalists often have to educate their editors about the importance of stories, students need to go the extra mile to deal with reluctant college officials. Be prepared to detail the work you've done and argue for the importance of the story, especially if there's a public service component. Explain the ethical imperatives that guide your thinking.

5. **Appeal to their nobler instincts.** The Student Press Law Center (splc.org), a Washington, D.C.-based nonprofit that advocates for student journalists, argues that just because colleges can censor doesn't mean they should—especially in an educational setting where students are encouraged to apply principles learned in the classroom. A free press on campus is an important part of the democratic process, and undermining it can be downright un-American. Also, the First Amendment should have special resonance at schools with religious affiliations; the constitutional right to freedom of religion is just a clause or two away from the free-press right. "It would seem incumbent upon religious schools to advocate the guarantees that protect journalists as much as themselves," according to the SPLC.

6. **Take Your Case Outside the Institution.** Enlist the support of prominent alums in journalism and media who will see it your way. They can exert some powerful pressure on your behalf. And, finally, as a last option, student journalists should consider airing their grievances to other news outlets if the story is important enough. Like any other institutions, colleges often respond to bad publicity. "Administrators have been known to have a change of heart when it appears that their decision to censor student expression might have a negative impact on next year's enrollment figures or fund-raising totals," according to the SPLC.

The Aftermath:
"Part of Something Greater"

The decision was not popular with everyone. The paper's adviser, a public relations instructor, was not included in the decision, and he believed he had been blindsided by what he considered to be the lack of professional courtesy. Vella said he deliberately kept the adviser in the dark, fearful he would tip off the administration. Smith, while recognizing that probability, regrets not giving him some notice.

"In some ways, we threw him under the bus," Smith said. "And it's a shame because our relationship was always congenial—he acted as a great buffer between the administration and the paper."

Meanwhile, the dean of students never discussed the decision with Vella—it was the last issue of the academic year. (That administrator declined to comment for this chapter except to say he had been deceived by Vella.)

Vella was front and center in all the news stories about the decision to run the blank half-front page. He admits that his prominence in those stories didn't hurt his professional prospects—one newspaper editor offered him a job on the spot not knowing he had another year of college. But he also believed by becoming the focus of the publicity, the newspaper's staff could move on without him and even point the finger of blame his way. For his senior year, Vella planned to pursue internships as Smith assumed the helm of the paper.

"The decision we made and the manner in which we carried it out was the best possible solution," Vella says today. (After graduation, Vella became a police reporter at the Philadelphia Daily News and now works at the Hartford Courant.) "It might have angered the administration, it may have frustrated them, but it didn't have any repercussions on the staff or the newspaper. The last thing I wanted to happen was to have them turn around and say, 'OK, there's no more Collegian.'"

Summer came not long after the incident, and Smith as editor-in-chief initiated a rebranding campaign, reducing the size of the publication by "trimming the fat"— sections he felt weren't widely read and bogged down production.

"That, I think, helped calm the university and made them think times were changing and the Rappaport 'debacle' wouldn't happen again," Smith said.

He described his relationship with the administration as benign—something he attributes as much to a quiet year for news as to a change of editors at the top of the masthead.

"A big part of that [improved relationship] was the simple result of there not being any conspicuous scandals like there were the previous year," Smith said. "But that's the way journalism works sometimes."

At the end of his senior year, Smith received a personal email from La Salle's president, in which he congratulated the outgoing editor on doing "a really great job." The paper's adviser told Smith it was the first time the president had extended such a gesture.

Speaking now, Smith looks back fondly at the "See below the fold" decision.

"I don't know that I would do anything differently," he says, recalling the palpable excitement that coursed through the paper's staff after the issue ran.

"The newsroom was electric," Smith says. "It's one of those things that you can look back on and say, 'That's what being a journalist is all about—being a part of something greater.'"

Thinking It Through

1. Did you agree with the students' decision to publish the story below the fold and have a blank space above the fold? Why or why not? How would you have done it differently and still justified it to the administration?

2. Was it deceptive of the journalists to run the story below the fold with the small-type "see below the fold" printed above? Neither the dean nor the paper's adviser was told beforehand of the decision to treat the story this way. If it was deception, was it justified? Why or why not?

3. During the academic year, the editors at The Collegian faced other episodes in which they were instructed to either play down a story or hold off publication of some details. In your view, what could the student journalists have done to change

the conversation about the administration's philosophy toward student media? (For the record, the newspaper's adviser and the dean responsible for student media were offered the opportunity to discuss the case, but they declined to participate.)

4. On occasion, students frustrated with a college's or university's interference or censorship have launched an independent newspaper or news organization with its own financial model that relies on no college subsidies or student fees. What would be the advantages and disadvantages of such a decision?

5. This particular issue of The Collegian was the last of the academic year with a different editor taking over in the fall. If you were the incoming editor, how would you approach the new academic year?

What If?

A professor at a private college is conducting a Modern Sexuality seminar that has only one female attendee. No exotic dancers came to class, but this time the professor asks the lone female student to help him illustrate a point in class. The professor calls her to the front of the classroom and asks her to perform a suggestive dance with him, during which he does some groping, all to make a point about miscommunication between the sexes. Humiliated, violated and embarrassed, she goes to the administration to complain.

Days later, the campus newspaper, which is funded by the school's administration, hears about this from a male student who himself was embarrassed about the shocking events and feels guilty for not speaking up at the time.

The administration tells you, the editor of the paper, that you can't run the story. And the kicker is that the administrators produce the female student, who says she doesn't want the story out either because she is so embarrassed and traumatized. Publicity about the class would force her to re-live the trauma, she says. The professor has been fired and that closes the case, the administration reports.

Meanwhile, students ask why the class has been canceled as have students in the professor's other classes, which have also been canceled. He can't be found on campus.

On the one hand, you are sensitive to the woman's plight (although not so much the administration's), but you also feel an obligation to inform students and reveal this egregious behavior. This is a case where the administration says absolutely not to publish. What do you do?

Go Online for More

The Student Press Law Center offers support, advocacy and resources for high school and college journalists, including valuable advice for students who encounter censorship on campus. Here is its set of guidelines for college media:
http://www.splc.org/article/2009/02/splc-college-student-media-model-guidelines

The College Media Association serves college media programs and their advisers. The organization provides training and support, and on occasion has censured programs for punishing advisers who support students' First Amendment rights or for advocating or teaching student press rights. Its code of ethics for advisers can be accessed here:
http://www.collegemedia.org/about_cma/code_of_ethics/

Read about Chelsea Boozer, a former editor of The Daily Helmsman at the University of Memphis, and her efforts to report about rape on campus, including the campus police department's failure to promptly alert students. Boozer ran into opposition from a college administration that resisted records requests and attempted to discredit her and cut the budget of the paper. This is from the American Journalism Review:
http://ajrarchive.org/Article.asp?id=5444

Legislatures in some states have passed their own laws to afford protections to college journalists beyond what courts have interpreted through federal or state constitutions. In 2006, for example, California lawmakers extended the same protections to journalists at private colleges as those at public universities. Here is a description of the law from the First Amendment Center:
http://www.firstamendmentcenter.org/calif-expands-freedoms-for-college-press

CHAPTER 11

Face to Face with the Facts

The Case of the Disagreeing Sources

Cailin Brown

L earning how to weigh facts and serve the audience when your story takes unexpected turns can be a careful balancing act. How do you best represent the truth when you are faced with conflicting messages about what that truth is?

When a student journalist set out to write a light enterprise feature about a children's swimming program, she discovered additional angles to the story from those she had first imagined. The young reporter considered all of the information she had collected and then wrestled with how best to present the story fairly and accurately without causing harm.

THE SITUATION: DROWNING IN FACTS

Becky Wisniewski was a graduating senior and had been writing news stories for a while when she faced a dilemma. Wisniewski wrote for the student newspaper, The Chronicle, and The Pine Hills blog, a site for journalism students' work hosted on timesunion.com, the website of the most widely circulated paper in the state's capital city, Albany, New York. The public regularly reads the stories on the blog and often responds with posted comments.

During her undergraduate studies, Wisniewski swam for the college team, and she also taught swimming lessons. When it came time to research and write an enterprise story for a class assignment, she reported on a local elementary school swimming program.

However, when Wisniewski sat down at her computer with her notes, her photographs and her thoughts, she was stumped. "I am in a predicament, and I am confused on how to write the story," she emailed her editor-teacher. "I don't want to jeopardize the relation-ship" between the news outlets and the sources, she wrote, "but I also feel it is important for people to know what taxpayers' money is going toward."

This swimming program did not resemble the one with which she was familiar. The children came from a very different demographic. She was not prepared for the dueling opinions sources shared with her about the program's strengths and weaknesses.

Also, because her personal experiences with swimming lessons deviated so much from the program she was writing about, she struggled with reconciling those separate fact sets and with detaching from her first-hand understanding.

"I expected a little more structure in the lessons and more swimming time," Wisniewski said. "It just wasn't as much practice."

The goal of her story, she said, was to educate and inform the public about the existence of this unpublicized program at the local, inner-city high school where second graders learn to swim. She wrote about the bus trips to and from lessons, the once-a-week frequency of the lessons and the numbers of students who participated.

She further contextualized the local story by including national data generated by the Centers for Disease Control that revealed that the incidence of drowning for young African-Americans is substantially higher than for whites or Hispanics.

The high school athletic director was a willing source. She contributed time and energy to help Wisniewski understand the program. The A.D. connected her with other relevant sources and provided her access to the high school pool facility during the school day while the lessons were in session. Over time, Wisniewski developed a positive rapport with the A.D., and she was well aware of and sensitive to the value of that positive and productive relationship.

THE CHALLENGE: INCLUDE EVERYTHING OR JUST SOME THINGS?

The published story included multiple relevant sources who spoke about their experiences with the swimming program. Wisniewski interviewed program directors, parents, teachers and children. Wisniewski eventually decided that her notes and the information she had gathered told a full and thorough story, and enabled her to include varying viewpoints. She recognized a fair story would reveal program shortfalls to the audience, but she wanted to avoid including unsubstantiated or unwarranted criticism.

"It just wasn't right for me to do that. I didn't feel like it was my place," Wisniewski said. "It didn't seem right. It was my gut instinct."

During the interviews for the story her sources were generous with their time and forthcoming about their thoughts and opinions. In her preliminary research, the program director made the lessons sound "amazing." Wisniewski's one-day observational visit revealed a different view, and it wasn't amazing. So, she omitted that characterization from the story. She chose not to proffer some teacher criticisms about the program because, she said, "It just felt wrong. The city is paying them money to do this job, and they dissed their employer. If you put the teachers' names on the story, it would hurt their reputations and the district," she said later. "I wouldn't want my name attached to saying anything bad about my employer."

■ ■ TOOLS FOR ACTION: SPJ's Mandate to Minimize Harm and Sissela Bok's Test

The Society of Professional Journalists, which supports a free press where journalists aspire to high standards and ethical behavior, includes in its code of ethics a segment not unlike the Hippocratic oath taken by physicians—*do no harm*. For journalists, the oath is similar—*minimize harm*. In the code, SPJ includes a passage that states "ethical journalism treats sources, subjects, colleagues and members of the public as human beings deserving of respect."

To adhere to that guideline, the code states that journalists should:

1. Balance the public's need for information against potential harm or discomfort. Pursuit of the news is not a license for arrogance or undue intrusiveness.

2. Show compassion for those who may be affected by news coverage. Use heightened sensitivity when dealing with juveniles, victims of sex crimes and sources or subjects who are inexperienced or unable to give consent. Consider cultural differences in approach and treatment.

3. Recognize that legal access to information differs from an ethical justification to publish or broadcast.

4. Realize that private people have a greater right to control information about themselves than public figures and others who seek power, influence or attention. Weigh the consequences of publishing or broadcasting personal information.

5. Consider the long-term implications of the extended reach and permanence of publication. Provide updated and more complete information as appropriate.

(Continued)

(Continued)

The Society of Professional Journalists website offers readers a variety of resources to learn more about questions around ethics. The site includes access to case studies, as well as an ethics committee blog and position papers. An Ethics Toolbox article posted in the society's August 2015 magazine, The Quill, noted that "editors, producers, news directors and other managers can provide valuable insights into what people may find overly intrusive."

In Wisniewski's case, she reviewed all of the information she had gathered in the process of interviewing and researching her story. She took time to anticipate the potential fallout based on considering the "what if" question—what if she included or excluded certain information. She adhered to the ethics code when she weighed the consequences of publication of information that could be construed as negative.

Wisniewski also relied on philosopher Sissela Bok's ethical decision-making process, the Test of Publicity, in which she asked herself about the "rightness of her actions." The student reporter then sought advice from an expert in order to weigh the alternatives. She recommitted to her original approach in telling the story while maintaining her allegiance to the tenets of journalism and adhering to ethical conventions to try to minimize harm. Would she be willing to make her choices public?

Wisniewski collected the information and interpreted it through the prism of her own conscience, thus enabling her to deliver a story that served citizens and enabled the audience to use the information to make informed decisions about the topic.

THE RESPONSE: WHAT SHOULD I DO?

Wisniewski took the job seriously. She wanted to uphold the tenets of journalism and still maintain a loyalty to the public, to the profession and to her sources. She talked to her roommate about it and after they considered the various sides of the issue, she contacted her editor-professor and explained the quandary. She decided to seek more information and clarify what she had already assembled. She opted for a "nuts and bolts" approach and described for her audience how the program works and that the swimming lessons are often the first time these children have exposure to a pool.

When one child wasn't interested in actually immersing herself in the water, preferring to watch cautiously from the pool deck, Wisniewski told it that way. Not every participant was gung ho. She described for the reader what she witnessed—show, don't tell, and let the reader decide.

"I did some thinking and put myself in the teachers' shoes and realized the story was not worth burning a bridge over," Wisniewski said. "It wasn't honestly worth it. I delivered a good story that was truthful and didn't have to burn any bridges."

The Aftermath: Readers Respond

Like many mainstream newspapers, timesunion.com has a location for readers to respond to story posts, including Wisniewski's post on The Pine Hill blog, a student-produced neighborhood news outlet that has delivered about 500 online stories since 2010.

The very same day the article was put online, a reader posted a comment about the story. The class regularly considers the benefits and drawbacks of reader comments. Wisniewski and the class chose to publish the comment, and she later said it was valuable to approve the feedback because that first commenter provided an important perspective.

The commenter wrote this:

> Shouldn't this be an after or before school program? Between the transportation to and from the swimming pool, the time to change in and out of bathing suits and the actual time for swim lessons, at least half a day must be used. This amounts to about 10 percent of total weekly instructional time. And of course we'll penalize teachers if the students don't do well on their standardized assessments due to reduced instruction time.

A few days after that, another commenter responded to the original posted comment, and the class again approved the post:

John, this is a vital, limited-weeks program that teaches safety as well as swimming, which is vital to reduce the drowning deaths that we see in this population. From the CDC: "The disparity is greatest among those [aged] 11–12 years, where African Americans drown in swimming pools at rates 10 times those of whites." Offering inner city 8- and 9-year-olds the opportunity to learn to swim is wonderful. I wish they could continue this program in later years!

For Wisniewski, the published back and forth from the public provided further insight for the reader. "I think that was really good. She had a different opinion about it. It definitely contributes to the story because it shows the other side of the other guy's opinion."

TOOL FOR THOUGHT: The Veil of Ignorance

John Rawls' "A Theory of Justice" provides a valuable tutorial for making ethical decisions in a circumstance such as the one faced by this student-reporter. In Rawls' scenario, a group of individuals operate behind a "veil of ignorance," and all start out equally when they are presented with the circumstances of a case.

So, on equal footing, Wisniewski might not have worked as a swimming instructor nor would she have had familiarity with other swimming lesson programs. None of the players knows his or her position in Rawls' situation. The individuals vet the details of the case, and in this instance they would consider the facts, both the positive and negative comments learned in the interviewing process, then determine which information would be included and which would be omitted and why. With Rawls' theory, when decisions are made, both "individual liberty can be maximized," and "weaker parties can be protected."

When gatekeepers such as reporters and editors make choices about which information gets included in a story and which is omitted, they anticipate audience response and make decisions about how to frame stories in a way that minimizes harm, as outlined in the SPJ Code of Ethics.

In weighing the facts of this story, editors and reporters would share with the audience the details of this swimming program for second graders and the framework under which it operates. The reporter fulfills her obligation to provide her audience with the details of this swimming program and its purpose—to help children, some of whom are at risk, to learn safety techniques around water and to eventually learn how to swim.

Readers gleaned from this story the existence and implementation of a taxpayer-funded program and that its intent is to serve as a primer to introduce youngsters to the water. While the program did not resemble the one with which Wisniewski had personal experience, she decided the comparison was unfair and clouded her judgment about the story she was writing. She put aside her first-person experience as a swimming lesson teacher and instead concentrated on what she had learned, then presented a story about a program for children with very different backgrounds than those she herself had taught.

By stepping away from her own bias, her particular point of view as a swimming instructor and instead focusing on the facts, she could deliver a more balanced accounting of the circumstances of her story. This approach helped her to recognize that the few criticisms she heard aligned with her own personal assessment of what she witnessed in comparison with her own experience, but she knew that including those criticisms would only echo her own opinion, which was not part of the story.

Wisniewski consciously tried to minimize her bias borne of her particular viewpoint as an expert swimmer and swimming teacher. She implemented Rawls' "reflective equilibrium" when she acknowledged she had preconceived expectations about what the program

(Continued)

(Continued)

should do and what it did. All swimmers were not fully engaged, and all participants were not ready cheerleaders.

Wisniewski still told those stories by managing the information she had in a way that adhered to the truth and reduced the chance that participants would be harmed. She determined that the "rash," unfounded criticisms of some teachers did not improve the story. The beneficiaries of the swimming program—the children and their families—could have been damaged by a story filled with unsupported criticisms about the imperfections of the program. A damaging story about the program could ultimately result in the end of the program—that result would mean no swimming lessons for a group of children who are at risk of drowning. It turns out this seemingly simple feature story was built on a high-stakes subject—life or death.

Wisniewski considered how the story she was writing fit into the codes of ethics upheld in journalism. She avoided the stereotyping that may have come from her own personal experiences. She considered the public's need for information and provided the story accordingly. She carefully weighed the possible consequences of the information that she had collected, and she considered the long-term consequences of the publication of her story.

Thinking It Through

1. Good reporters usually collect more information than they need. In this instance, if the reporter included unsubstantiated criticisms from school district employees, how would the story have changed? What possible outcomes might have resulted from publishing teacher criticisms of the program?

2. Reporters should try to anticipate possible responses to stories, but it's nearly impossible to consider the varied ways in which

the public might respond. How might the school district have reacted to criticisms from sources employed by the district?

3. What possible consequences might result for the swim program if Wisniewski pursued additional story angles? How might her reorganization of the story—a change in the focus—possibly have affected reader response?

4. Reporters often develop reliable and credible sources over time. Would unfounded criticisms in the story have damaged relationships between the reporter and her sources? Would that damage have been justified or not?

5. What obligations do journalists have when they choose to include dissenting voices or sources in a story? How does the reporter determine when it is valid to include critics or to exclude critics from a story?

6. Sometimes story sources do not consider the repercussions of the comments they make to the press. If you reported this feature story about children's swimming lessons, how would you respond to sources who criticized the program, possibly putting both their own jobs and the swimming program in jeopardy?

7. Reporters make decisions every day about which information to include and which to exclude. Would a particular formula ease or improve the process of this decision-making function?

What If?

Reporters conduct all types of interviews—face-to-face, telephone, Skype and sometimes via email or text message. The more practice you get, the more exposure you will have to sources who may "overshare," mostly because they are not versed in the dynamic and do not anticipate the possible outcome of a story. Politicians make for savvy sources, but inexperienced sources may say more than they intend and not anticipate the possible outcome of a story.

If you are working as a full-time reporter for a local newspaper and start covering crime, heartache and other news, you are bound to end up hearing details that could cause pain if the information were published. Hearing certain details could have you questioning how to minimize harm when piecing together a story. Or, in the course of living your daily life, you might find stories in unexpected places from unknowing sources. If a source reveals some useful information, but that information might jeopardize his or her position or reputation, how would you respond to the following?

- A longtime state employee who has been a source for years tells you he has retired to collect his pension, but then was rehired so he could continue working at a lesser salary.

- Your favorite jerk chicken bodega takes only cash and the proprietor explains this arrangement helps limit his tax liability.

- A parent reveals that his son's DWI will be expunged from his record because the judge is a personal friend.

- An acquaintance who works as a public affairs specialist shares in a non-work setting that he "sanitized" state records before fulfilling a request for information under the state's freedom of information law.

- A teacher in a socioeconomically disadvantaged district describes an instance when a student pointed his hand at her in the classroom as if he were holding a gun.

How would you determine which information in these examples could or should be used to tell a story? How might you apply John Rawls' "reflective equilibrium" to evaluate the value of sharing the information you have learned in a published story for your employer and the audience?

Would you approach an editor to help decide what to do with the information you had just learned? How might you describe what you had learned, especially in an instance when the information was not shared in an interview? If some of the individuals who revealed these details were both a source and now a friend, where would your allegiance lie, and why?

Journalists often characterize themselves as "always on the job." They see stories everywhere—not necessarily because they are looking but because that is how they perceive the world. So many stories, too little time. How will you weigh the news you collect daily and determine which stories are publishable and why, and what information is necessary and which is not?

Go Online for More

The reliability of sources is often a point of concern for reporters, and the national media watch group Fairness and Accuracy in Reporting pursued the question of sourcing immediately after Hurricane Katrina, in this article: http://fair.org/extra-online-articles/suspect-sources/

An article titled False Sources and Misleading Information featured in the Nieman Reports provides insight for reporters trying to make decisions about their sources: http://niemanreports.org/articles/false-sources-and-misleading-information/

CHAPTER 12

Sensitivity and Social Media

The Case of the Student Death

Frances Parrish

Guy S. Reel

A nytime a serious story or stories break, editors and reporters should use caution when seeking sources or confirmation of the events. One editor at The Johnsonian, the student newspaper at Winthrop University in Rock Hill, South Carolina, learned some valuable lessons when news of a student's death began circulating through social media.

THE SITUATION: CROWDSOURCING A DEATH

During fall semester 2013, Frances Parrish, editor-in-chief at The Johnsonian, received a call near midnight from her managing editor informing her of social media reports about the death of a student. Abby Carroll died Oct. 31, 2013, in her hometown of Walhalla, South

Carolina, after being on medical leave for the semester. She allegedly had planned to return the following semester.

The weekly newspaper for Winthrop University, which also is available on the web, had just printed that week's issue, but the story was important enough to be reported online as soon as possible.

More information needed to be gathered because the editors gained much of their initial knowledge about the death from web posts. Some say Twitter is too quick to report deaths, and the same is true for Facebook. While social media can be good for finding sources, leads or tidbits of information, it can be problematic to gather correct details without backup from reliable sources. Parrish and her managing editor knew this, but even that knowledge did not prevent reporting mistakes.

The two editors did not communicate well about how to find more information about the death of the student. Parrish knew Carroll and had just seen her on campus less than a month before. She was in shock when she heard the news and told her managing editor to find out more information, but they didn't discuss exactly how to do that.

The managing editor posted on social media as "The Johnsonian," hoping to crowdsource information about the student's death. Parrish did not know about the social media posts until she received phone calls from other staff members asking why she was posting on Facebook seeking information about the death.

It was true that the death of Carroll was a mystery. Because it was so late in the evening, calling authorities or the family for a cause of death was not practical. But in his zeal to seek additional information, the managing editor had made the newspaper guilty of insensitivity. Worse, many of Carroll's friends found out about her death through The Johnsonian's Facebook page and Twitter feed, which resulted in backlash from the university community.

Following are The Johnsonian's Facebook and Twitter posts and comments from The Johnsonian's page. The original posts were later deleted from Facebook and Twitter.

Carroll was well known across the campus and had many friends. She was an excellent student and was involved with multiple organizations such as the National Collegiate Scholars.

FIGURE 12.1 Facebook post

SOURCE: The Johnsonian. Used with permission.

FIGURE 12.2 Twitter post

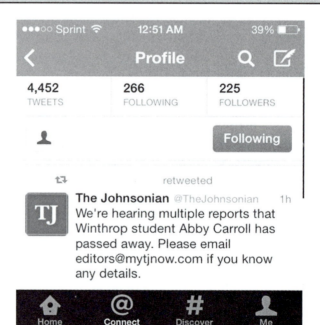

SOURCE: The Johnsonian. Used with permission.

FIGURE 12.3 Comments on the original Facebook post

Erin Parker
Shame on you Johnsonian staff. One would think out of respect for the family and the deceased you would wait until details are provided from them. No need to seek and sensationalize.
Yesterday at 11:45 PM · Unlike · 👍 7

Amber Marie Schilling
I know you guys only have the best intentions, but this isn't really a crowdsourcing moment.
9 hours ago · Like · 👍 1

Julia Greiner
This post should be removed for the privacy of the family during this time.
9 hours ago · Like · 👍 4

Will Waldrep
Bad form, Johnsonian, bad form.
7 hours ago · Like

Ty Strickland
Even as a TJ employee, I have to agree with the other commenters here; Facebook day after is neither the place nor the time.
19 minutes ago · Like

SOURCE: The Johnsonian. Used with permission.

In response to the social media posts, Parris received an email from a cousin confirming Abby Carroll's death.

"The family is understandably distraught at this time and I am hesitant to even make a statement about this without the permission of her parents, but as it is already all over Facebook I would rather you hear it from someone who knows the details of exactly what happened," the cousin wrote.

THE CHALLENGE: HOW TO REPORT A CAUSE OF DEATH

While crowdsourcing may be an effective method for gathering information in some cases, it quickly became apparent from the reaction on social media that this was not the appropriate way to gather information in this case. Parrish realized she needed to take action.

The Johnsonian had heard rumors and had off-the-record conversations with several people, including friends of Carroll, indicating that she had committed suicide. This was not confirmed through official sources at that point, though, so The Johnsonian did not immediately report that detail.

Still, believing the suicide information to be true made the case more delicate. Writing about a death of a student is difficult, but writing about a student who committed suicide can be even more difficult. Reporters have an obligation to find the truth and report it to the public. But journalists also have an obligation to respect those who are in mourning. Mourners may wish to speak or not, but whatever the situation, reporters must be mindful of people's feelings and wishes when dealing with the family of the deceased.

The editor-in-chief wasn't sure how to handle the situation—especially after the blow-up on social media—so she spoke to former adviser Larry Timbs and the newspaper adviser, Guy Reel,[1] about handling the social media issue.

Parrish asked if the newspaper should publicly apologize for the social media posts, but she was advised not to because of the damage already done on Facebook.

The Johnsonian had lost integrity in a matter of 24 hours, and Parrish had to perform damage control. She realized the initial posts should

---

1. Reel is the co-editor of this textbook.

have never been made; editors should have privately messaged the people who were posting on Facebook about Carroll's death.

The posts were deleted by the social media editor, and Parrish decided that she would need to explore possible disciplinary action against the managing editor.

■ ■ TOOLS FOR ACTION: Using Facebook and Other Social Networking Sites

The internet is a valuable tool for reporters. But like any tool, if used improperly, it can cause harm. Here are some guidelines for using information posted at sites such as Facebook:

Verify. Some information posted online is public, but that doesn't mean it's correct. Check the validity of names, photographs, graphics— anything you find online. This should be done by contacting the sources of the information and getting direct substantiation of their validity. Remember, anyone can post a photo online and claim to be the person pictured.

Attribute. Using information from a publicly available portion of Facebook or other social networking site may be OK legally—courts have not definitively ruled on a specific case in this area. But if you use something from Facebook, it is your ethical responsibility to tell the reader, viewer or listener where the information came from—after you verify its validity. That way, if something turns out to be wrong, the error will be attributed to the source. At all times, be careful: You may not use copyrighted information from websites without permission or attribution.

Consider timeliness. As the web ages, so does the information on its static pages. Facebook postings rapidly go out of date.

Research and report. Facebook, Twitter, Instagram and other social networking sites can be a good first step for background.

(Continued)

However, they should never be your *only* step. Always do your own original reporting. What people tell you directly will be much more relevant to your story than the random musings they've posted online for their own purposes.

THE RESPONSE: GETTING THE STORIES

Until the time of publication, the family did not want to speak to student media, so Parrish's primary sources were school officials. She met with the dean of students, who wanted be informed of the social media situation. The meeting was off the record, and the dean did not officially discuss the cause of death on the record.

Parrish then met with the vice president of student affairs to get quotes for the story. He also would not officially release the cause of death, but he did talk about how students can deal with grief and that was made part of the story. Because no source would disclose the cause of death, The Johnsonian could not report the cause.

"Because of the delicate situation, we didn't confirm it was a suicide," Parrish said later. "At the time of her death and a week or two later, no one was too keen to talk about it, and we didn't want to drag out her death for weeks on end." Parrish had never covered a death before, and calling official sources (such as the coroner in Carroll's hometown some 140 miles away) for a cause of death never came up in the students' discussions.

Because of how The Johnsonian responded to the death through the social media posts, some people were hesitant to talk to reporters. Still, Parrish was able to get enough information for a brief story about the death, and the newspaper also reported on the availability of counseling services for grief-stricken students. But it was nearly a year later before the newspaper indicated a cause of death when it covered the Abby Carroll Walk for Suicide Prevention.

Note: The story below ran in The Johnsonian, nearly a year after Abby Carroll's death.

Remembering Abby

By Michaela Bishop, Oct. 3, 2014

Friends and family gathered slowly by the circle of chairs as the sun began to set. Silent greetings and soft hellos were whispered, while Donna Carroll passed out blue ribbons and welcomed each guest individually. She grabbed her husband's hand, took a deep breath and spoke.

"She inspired us all and she still inspires us," Mrs. Carroll said.

The Abby Carroll Walk for Suicide Prevention took place on Sunday, Sept. 28, at Winthrop University. Sponsored by the Department of Residence Life and the Honors Program, the walk began in the DiGiorgio Campus Center Breezeway and ended in the Honors Center at The Courtyard at Winthrop.

"This was something Abby wanted me to do," said Mrs. Carroll, mother of former Winthrop student Abby Carroll. "By doing this walk we want to raise awareness."

During the walk, Donna Carroll held a sign with a picture of her daughter and the words "Her Love Lives On."

Abby Carroll, a junior biology major at Winthrop, took her life last October, shocking all who knew her.

Through the American Foundation for Suicide Prevention, Donna Carroll came up with the idea of doing the walk to help raise awareness about suicide prevention on campus. Carroll got in touch with Dr. Kathy A. Lyon, director of the honors program, at the beginning of the 2014 fall semester with the idea.

"Donna emailed, asking if it could be done this quickly . . . it was actually quite easy to do," Dr. Lyon said. Dr. Lyon said she hoped the walk would raise awareness campus-wide about suicide and how it can affect any student.

"[Abby was] one of those people who seemed to have it all together," said Dr. Lyon, who said Carroll's death took her by surprise. "It was such a shock."

All those who knew Abby remember what she meant not only to them but also to an entire community.

One of Carroll's friends and former roommates, Ali Jensen remembers her as someone who you could always count on and believes that being able to advocate for Abby makes a difference.

"Abby was a light, and being able to advocate for her will make a positive difference in other people's lives," Jensen said. "This kind of thing has a huge impact on people and they should reach out if they feel any kind of sadness."

Nora Webb, another former roommate and friend to Abby Carroll, said it felt good to have an event where others who knew Carroll could come together.

Webb said that she hoped students who participated in the walk or saw it would now know that support is always available.

Abby was the member of many organizations across campus and worked hard to do her part in bettering the Winthrop experience for others.

As an honors student, she helped with a lot of programing for the honors program. She also lived in the Courtyard apartments where she would get to know the residence life coordinator Emily Tobin, who said Abby was more than just a resident.

"She was a name that touched a lot of people, a very respectful person," Tobin said.

Tobin wants students to know that there are places on campus to get help whether that be Grief Support, talking with their RLCs or going to the counseling center.

"It's really important that students understand what resources are available to them on campus and knowing that they have people they can talk to," Tobin said.

"I hope that this would help shape [students'] minds towards civic involvement," said Mark Carroll, father of Abby, who stressed how simple the idea of a suicide prevention walk is.

"But what a difference it can make," he said.

SOURCE: "Remembering Abby" by Michaela Bishop, from The Johnsonian. Used with permission.

TOOL FOR THOUGHT:
Carol Gilligan's Ethics of Care

Chapter 1 of this book notes that the "ethics of care," based on feminist theory, takes into account self as well as other. This view makes *relationships* central to ethical decision-making.

Carol Gilligan's "In a Different Voice," published in 1982, examined how women used a "different voice" in describing their ethical choices—that voice being one concerned with relationships.

If you were to apply ethics of care to the case study in this chapter, how might that have influenced your choices? Would you have carefully considered the family of the student before tweeting about her death? How might that have influenced your subsequent actions?

Consider other relationships in this case:

The relationship between the student and her family and friends.

The relationship between the newspaper and the community it serves.

The relationship between the editor and her staff members, including the managing editor.

Are there other relationships that might be considered in this case?

Journalists sometimes are guilty of going "after the story" at all costs, sometimes not considering the consequences of their actions. They often focus on the "right to know," but may not consider as closely the right to privacy or the rights of victims. Thus, many have argued that such a gung-ho attitude results in damaging the credibility of news workers.

As you work through this case, consider ways that reporters could better use understandings of communities and relationships in their reporting, and how that might influence their stories and their treatment of sources and victims.

The Aftermath: Taking Professional Action

Given how the initial social media postings had hampered the newspaper's reporting on the student's death, the student journalists did the best they could to follow up. But Parrish now faced decisions about what actions to take professionally.

Parrish met with her adviser to discuss possible disciplinary actions to take concerning the managing editor. This was not the first mistake the managing editor had made, but the adviser did not believe that any of them amounted to a firing offense. Still, action did need to be taken.

Parrish decided to demote the managing editor to staff writer. She believed she needed to send a strong signal to the staff that the newspaper must act professionally and sensitively in all cases, and that was particularly important when it was represented in tweets or Facebook posts as "The Johnsonian." That brought her to the necessity of developing a more comprehensive social media policy.

After the managing editor was demoted, Parrish met with the section editors to inform them of her decision, and she stressed the importance of being respectful to those they reported on. She told the staff that this kind of social media error should never happen again, and if something needed to be crowdsourced, the reporter or editor should double-check with the editor-in-chief.

■ ■ ■ TOOL FOR ACTION: Using Social Media

In 2011 the American Society of Newspaper Editors issued its "Best practice for editors crafting social media policies." Ten key takeaways follow:

1. Traditional ethics rules still apply online.

2. Assume everything you write online will become public.

3. Use social media to engage with readers, but professionally.

4. Break news on your website, not on Twitter.

5. Beware of perceptions.

6. Independently authenticate anything found on a social networking site.

7. Always identify yourself as a journalist.

8. Social networks are tools not toys.

9. Be transparent and admit when you're wrong online.

10. Keep internal deliberations confidential.

Full guidelines may be viewed at http://asne.org/Files/pdf/10_Best_Practices_for_Social_Media.pdf.

Parrish changed the passwords for Twitter and Facebook, the only social media that the paper used, to ensure only the multimedia editor and the editor-in-chief could post on them. All other social media posts would have to be edited and approved by the editor-in-chief.

Parrish, who was editor of the newspaper for two years, also specifically addressed the use of social media in future newspaper training workshops. Each semester, she addressed the Carroll case and the consequences that ensued from the way it was handled; other editors who followed were made aware of the case and the need for staff training on social media.

Social media training had always been a topic of discussion in the newsroom but never to that extent until Carroll's death. Previously, Parrish discussed what to post and not post on Facebook—such as not posting negative comments about co-workers, crowdsourcing inappropriately and maintaining objectivity, professionalism and respect.

Thinking It Through

1. Should a news organization report the cause of death? Should it report suicide as a cause? If it is a college newspaper, is the publication obligated to treat the subject differently from, for example, a large metropolitan daily newspaper?

2. Would you have taken the same action that Parrish did with regard to the managing editor? Why or why not?

3. Should the newspaper have apologized on social media or was deleting the posts enough? Why or why not? What about in the follow-up editorial?

4. Newspapers often consult social media after tragedies or crimes. How should this information be treated? Should it be reported verbatim?

5. What would be good elements to include in a news publication's social media policy? Do you think restricting social media passwords to the editor and multimedia editor is a good idea?

Go Online for More

Ellyn Angelotti of the Poynter Institute posted an online column about journalists' use of social networking sites titled A New Tool in the Box: Social Networks at http://www.poynter.org/column.asp?id= 67&aid=139520.

Read her column and share key points with your classmates. In particular, what do you think of the question and her answer, "Once you've verified someone's identity, what privacy issues should be considered?"

What If?

How to treat reporting involving social media sites such as Facebook can be tricky ethically as well as legally. Instagram, LinkedIn or Twitter help people connect, share ideas, shop for opportunities, and promote causes or entertainment events. But social media can have another side: online libel and scurrilous gossip. Yik Yak is a smartphone app that allows users within a five-mile radius to anonymously post and create discussion threads. Some schools have taken action to ban the app because of potential for abuse—cyberbullying, personal gossip and sharing of hate speech, for example.

Chances are you know of a gossipy website or app where people may anonymously comment on professors or students at your university by name. What if such a site became wildly popular? Do you think the campus newspaper or other media outlets should write about it? Should they report on what's posted on the site even if the postings are libelous or vulgar or hurtful? How specific should they be?

Let's say you keep hearing people on campus talking about a site, and, of course, anyone can read what's there. What are your ethical considerations in reporting on it? Think about how you'd feel if crazy rumors about you were anonymously posted on this kind of site. Would you consider those comments fair game for a news report?

If you've looked at any of the gossip sites that have pages featuring your university, think about what you've found there. Is reading content on such a website any more responsible than posting a falsehood is? Is gossiping about anything posted on the site a socially responsible thing to do? Do you think the act of reading posts on these sites poses an ethical dilemma? Have you ever posted to such a site? Why or why not?

Now try thinking as if you were the president of your university. You've seen this type of site do real harm to people on campus. Do you think the university should try to block on-campus access to the site? Why or why not? Are there *any* sites that a university should block?

Some people have argued that even gossip sites are a legitimate form of citizen journalism. In a time when the media are trying so hard to involve the audience, do we simply have to take the good with the bad? If you were in charge of one of the campus media, what ways could you think of to involve more people in generating news, without resorting to gossip?

CHAPTER 13

The Case of Ethics in Immersion Journalism

The White Noise

David R. Davies

Cassie Rodenberg

F or Cassie Rodenberg, the opportunity to blog for Scientific American magazine just a few years out of college was going to be a life-changing opportunity to explain science to the masses. But the job turned out to be much more than that: It led her to immerse herself in covering the lives of drug addicts and the homeless in one of America's poorest communities and, in the process, demonstrating the ethical challenges of immersion journalism.

The Situation: "Why Are You Writing About This?"

Rodenberg's path to journalism was indirect. A science communication major in college, she later took graduate coursework in journalism. She worked as a television producer and then was hired to do a science blog for Scientific American magazine's website. It was a dream job, to be sure, and it offered her a chance to explain science through writing articles focused on people.

"So much of Scientific American was blatantly science, I feel like it forgot a bit of the human aspect, which I think scientists missed some of the time," Rodenberg said. Knowing that much of the science on addiction had been covered by other writers, she decided to write about the people affected by it, specifically the inhabitants of the Hunts Point section of the Bronx in New York City, one of the poorest congressional districts in the country, with the highest crime rate in New York. She intended to juxtapose scientific studies of addiction with narratives of people living with it.

Rodenberg's blog was titled The White Noise, taking its title from Rodenberg's view that "addiction and mental illness is the white noise behind many lives." Her project was undertaken along with photographer Chris Arnade over four years. She posted about four articles a month during that time period.

"It is not within me to make my coverage traditional, to allow the precedence of widespread, global statistics, something I have fastidiously avoided throughout my work," Rosenberg wrote as The White Noise came to a close in 2014. "I believe science relies too heavily on numbers at the price of the individual. Statistics are too easy. In this, science has forgotten so much, has forgotten nearly everything."

Her editors were encouraging about her approach, but many Scientific American readers weren't—at least at first. While her work would ultimately gain a large and appreciative audience, at first readers were skeptical about the people stories—they just weren't the articles they'd come to expect from Scientific American. "This isn't science. Why are you writing about this?" Rodenberg's readers asked her. She responded that she was not only giving readers science in the stories she wrote but also giving them human interest stories, too.

The Challenge: Balancing Ethics and Protecting Sources

Working with addicts posed its own set of problems and ethical dilemmas. Rodenberg's goal was first and foremost not to harm the people she was covering by writing their life stories. Before embarking on any interview, her practice was to inform her interviewees of the nature of her work and to ask their permission to quote them. She routinely showed drafts of her blog posts to her sources before they went public. While these practices were outside the bounds of what many editors in journalism would permit, it seemed to her to be a necessity. Many of her subjects were vulnerable because they were involved in child custody or other legal disputes that could be swayed by her published accounts of their lives.

"My first commitment was always ethically to do justice to the stories that the people I met while being protective at the same time of their privacy," Rodenberg said. Since many of her subjects were taking part in illegal activity—prostitution, taking or selling drugs—she chose not to use her subjects' real names, instead using their "street names," the names by which they were known in their neighborhood. While occasionally sources would quibble with her over some aspects of her drafts, getting her sources' approval posed few issues, she said.

Rodenberg's goal as a reporter was to describe a group of people whom society was largely ignoring, and many of her sources were eager to tell their stories in hopes that doing so would help others. In fact, many readers said just that in online comments in response to the blog, specifically that her writing had allowed them to understand their own relatives and loved ones who were suffering from addiction. "It was a very unique, cathartic experience for both my subjects and

FIGURE 13.1

SOURCE: Cathy Rodenberg. Used with permission.

my readers online, which I think further opened up the stories that I heard," she said.

"Working with a vulnerable population underscored everything that I did," Rodenberg said. This required an approach to information-gathering that varied considerably from the standard approaches—and the ethical guidelines supporting them—used in reporting everyday stories. For Rodenberg, that meant she would not have been able to gather her subjects' intimate stories unless she had changed their names, had given them approval over her blog posts and had exercised caution in selecting the content of her stories so as to protect her sources in their day-to-day lives.

Moreover, Rodenberg said she couldn't help but become friends with her sources given the amount of time she spent in Hunts Point. On three different occasions, she invited sources to stay overnight at her home as they were awaiting housing placements upon leaving drug rehabilitation. "At times," she said, "it was almost laughable how enmeshed I was [with sources' lives]." On another occasion, she invited a homeless person to her apartment for Thanksgiving dinner. "Was I doing this person a service or not by having them for dinner for one day when they're going to be homeless for the rest of the year? Was that selfish of me? Or was that something that you do for a friend? That was how I considered it."

Once a few of Rodenberg's sources began to trust her, these interviewees vouched for her to others, thus widening her circle of sources. She ultimately grew to be such a fixture in the neighborhood it was almost as if she were invisible. She recalled one instance when she was in a crack house among people for whom she was such a persistent presence that they ignored her.

Rodenberg's interactions with girls involved in child prostitution posed another ethical dilemma. Although minors were often willing to talk to her, Rodenberg was unwilling to interview girls who were underage because she could put the younger women in danger. The rare times she wrote about these women, she used pseudonyms and photographs that did not reveal their faces.

Rodenberg was frequently a witness to criminal activity. She did not, as some ethics codes require, report that activity—prostitution, drug dealing—to the police. She knew first of all that the police knew about this already and would not be learning anything new or be spurred to take action should she go to them. She also knew that going to the police would ruin her relationships with her subjects and end her efforts to tell their stories to a wider audience.

THE RESPONSE: GIVING VOICE TO THOSE SELDOM HEARD

While "don't befriend your sources" is standard advice in America's newsrooms, for the stories Rodenberg was pursuing, friendship was necessary to understand the people and the community she was writing about. In fact, her methods were symptomatic of a strain of immersion journalism that dates back more than a century.

Going back to Nellie Bly and even further, journalists have been gathering information for in-depth stories by living among their sources. (Bly famously faked insanity in an asylum in the 1880s to expose poor treatment of patients.) Writer Robin Hemley, in "Field Guide for Immersion Writing," classifies immersion writing into three categories—travel writing, memoir and immersion journalism. While immersion journalism is not so common in the internet-driven journalism of today, it nonetheless has a long tradition. And it should be noted that Rodenberg was practicing a particular kind of immersion journalism, one in which journalists clearly identify themselves as journalists to those they are covering. She was not living as a homeless person as some writers have done or faking insanity as Bly did so many years before her. Hers was a more straightforward kind of journalism.

Moreover, codes of ethics in American journalism would seem to support Rodenberg's choices, both in the subject matter she chose and for dealing with sources as she did to cover her subject. The Society of Professional Journalists Code of Ethics, for example, urges reporters in all media to follow four principles: seek truth and report it; minimize harm; act independently; and be accountable and transparent. Rosenberg did all of these things. Specifically, while she did grant her sources anonymity, she followed the code's admonition to reserve the practice "for sources who may face danger, retribution or other harm, and have information that cannot be obtained elsewhere." Moreover, her entire series seemed to reflect a section of the code that encourages journalists to "[b]oldly tell the story of diversity and magnitude of the human experience. Seek sources whose voice we seldom hear."

To get the stories she wanted and to do justice to telling the details of her subjects' lives, Rodenberg said, she had to form relationships with her sources, to earn their trust, and to even become their friends in certain circumstances. These are the compromises of immersion journalism, and without these compromises, Rodenberg believes, stories of society's marginalized communities simply cannot be told. At the same time, Rodenberg said she understands that editors' standard warnings not to get too close to sources make sense for most routine stories.

"I'm sure I could have gotten some of these things had I maintained distance," Rodenberg argues, "but not nearly to the depth and level that I was able to this way."

TOOL FOR THOUGHT:
Carol Gilligan's Ethics of Care

Psychologist Carol Gilligan has argued that ethical decision-making is often guided not by rigid rules but by an "ethics of care," that is, by a concern for others and for the community that trumps a concern for self. This ethical approach has been expanded by other academics and also applied to numerous fields, including journalism. Assuming, as Gilligan does, that care for others often guides our decision-making, consider how this approach might inform your own reporting and writing.

1. Carefully assess the impact of your journalistic work upon your sources. How will what you write affect those you write about? Rodenberg was first and foremost committed to "do no harm" to her interviewees as they represented a vulnerable population who could face arrest, legal repercussions, or worse if their identities were made public. As private individuals (not public figures or public officials who had sought the limelight), they seem to deserve special consideration. What communities that you

(Continued)

(Continued)

cover or might cover deserve similar care?

2. Consult with your editors in sensitive stories about vulnerable populations. Gilligan's "ethics of care" centers on individuals making personal choices, but the collaborative nature of journalistic work requires writers and reporters to consult closely with their editors in decision-making in sensitive stories. Be prepared to make your best case to your editor for the ethical choices you propose in dealing with your sources. As Rodenberg did, you will need to balance your commitment to truthfully telling your story with your concerns for your sources.

3. Be transparent with your readers. Your audience has every right to understand what compromises, if any, you made in covering your story. If you changed names to protect sources, say so and explain why. If your own interactions with sources could be interpreted as having some impact as to how you told the story, explain those interactions.

Journalists must be somewhat flexible in their ethical approaches to stories depending upon the unique aspects of each. The multiyear nature of Rodenberg's coverage of Hunts Point, and the freedom Scientific American gave her in her blog, make her situation unique but instructive. The routine stories you cover may not challenge you as Rodenberg's did, but her in-depth journalism illustrates a nuanced approach to important stories that should serve as a model for beginning reporters.

The Aftermath: "Just Talk to People"

Rodenberg ended the project after four years as it became clear to her that she had explored the issues she had set out to illuminate. In addition, her initial hopes that she could shed some light on the solutions to the poverty and drug use she described had faded. "I learned after four years there's very, very little hope," she said, and she left the project to pursue other interests. Still, she sees herself as doing more work in the future to explore the issues of poverty.

She also views her time writing for Scientific American as a particularly uninhibited time for science writing. "That was sort of a beautiful bubble in time where I was free to do really whatever I pleased," Rodenberg said. "I don't know if I would have that would I have started today."

The project not only offered her freedom but gave her a chance to interact with journalism students who seemed interested in replicating her kind of reporting. When students ask her how to go about reporting on people in poverty or otherwise on society's fringes, she offers this advice: "Just talk to people. Go to the neighborhood and be honest about your intentions; hang out there and be genuine. It's as easy as that."

And, she said, it's important for students to remember that ethical lines may sometimes have to be reconsidered in the interests in covering something bigger.

Thinking It Through

1. Rodenberg says she became friends with her sources because of the long-form nature of the story and of the amount of time she spent covering Hunts Point. When is it justified to become friends with your sources? In deciding this, does it matter whether the source is a public figure? Are there certain kinds of stories for which friendship with a source is permissible and other kinds for which it is not? Understand the need to be open with your editors and your readers about the nature of your relationships with your sources.

2. For her blog, Rodenberg routinely changed the names of her sources to protect the vulnerable. Most journalistic codes of ethics, including that of the Society of Professional Journalists, caution journalists against granting anonymity except in rare cases in which information could not be obtained otherwise. What are other situations in which you think the use of anonymous sources is justified? Would you agree with some journalistic critics who say that anonymous sources are cited far too often?

3. Hunts Point became Rodenberg's home for much of the time she was writing her blog. Her kind of immersion journalism gave her the advantage of a deep understanding of the plight of the community and its inhabitants. Did her closeness to the story have disadvantages as well?

What If?

The White Noise blog offered readers a close-up view of a stunningly poor community and of the havoc that drugs, crime and addiction can bring to its residents. The coverage of poverty has declined markedly in recent years, a fact that raises questions about media institutions' commitment to covering the entirety of society.

According to the Census Bureau, 45 million Americans, or 14.5 percent of the population, lived below the federal poverty line in 2013. Obviously, political approaches to addressing poverty vary widely, and Americans disagree about the extent to which government should intervene. Still, what is journalists' responsibility to cover poverty and the Americans who suffer from it? Given the extent of the problem, can journalists justifiably ignore a problem faced by so many people? National surveys report that one in 10 Americans use illicit drugs. What are journalists' obligations to cover such a significant health story? Given the illegalities involved, what are the challenges of covering these stories and how might you overcome them?

Since World War II, the continuing professionalization of journalism has meant that the vast majority of reporters beginning work in America's newsrooms are college graduates. If you're middle class and you're reading this textbook, you mirror most journalism students today. A challenge to beginning journalists is to think beyond the boundaries of their own experiences to cover a diverse world that becomes more complicated by the day. How does your background— economic, ethnic, and otherwise—limit your understanding of what constitutes a story and what does not? How do you plan to expand your understanding of and appreciation for whom and what deserves coverage?

A good place to start is by reading widely. Read the best newspapers and news outlets, and watch a varied range of news. To serve your development as a journalist, read not simply for content but also to understand the multiple approaches to covering a story.

Go Online for More

Cassie Rodenberg's stories remain a part of the Scientific American website, and her posts provide rich and varied models for covering poverty and addiction:
http://blogs.scientificamerican.com/white-noise/

The Grady College of Journalism and Mass Communication and the University of Georgia have published a tool kit for journalists who are covering poverty:
http://www.coveringpoverty.org/

The Society of Professional Journalists offers journalists tips on diverse ways to approach a poverty story:
http://www.spj.org/divws4.asp

Nieman Reports laments the lack of coverage of poor people:
http://niemanreports.org/articles/it-cant-happen-here-2/

The Association of Health Care Journalists offers reporters a wide-ranging set of advice on how to cover health issues:
http://healthjournalism.org/

CHAPTER 14

When Privacy Outweighs the Public's Right to Know

The Case of the Rape Victim

Nathaniel Frederick II

Aimee Pavia Meader

The practice of naming rape victims varies depending on a news organization's ethics policy. Although identifying information can be obtained in the public record and is permissible to publish, news organizations must make ethical decisions, balancing their legal right to publish with potential harm that could face the rape victim if identifying information is published. Some names have been changed in this chapter to protect the privacy of the individuals involved.

THE SITUATION: "THIS ISN'T THE AVERAGE MURDER"

Jonathan McFadden, 25, was a 2012 graduate of Winthrop University in Rock Hill, South Carolina. His first professional job was crime reporter at The Herald, a newspaper in Rock Hill. In August 2012, he broke a story about Tony Brown, a 22-year-old who was accused of killing 39-year-old Michael Jamar Taylor in the street after Taylor allegedly raped Brown's 16-year-old half-sister. McFadden knew it was against The Herald's policy to name the rape victim, but by naming the murder victim, would he inadvertently identify the rape victim? Furthermore, revealing the exact location of the crime, specifically the street name and the relationship between the shooter and the murder victim, could potentially identify the rape victim. McFadden had never encountered this dilemma before and he needed assistance. Several meetings ensued between McFadden and the editor-in-chief of The Herald about how to report the story while protecting the privacy of the rape victim.

McFadden talked to Sheriff Richard Smith about the circumstances of the crime. He reported that sheriff's investigators had spent much of the day after the murder following leads and searching for suspects but had not developed anything specific. "This isn't the average murder," the sheriff told McFadden.

THE CHALLENGE: CONCEALING ISN'T ENOUGH

McFadden began by canvassing the neighborhood to determine what people knew of the crime. He interviewed one neighbor who mentioned that Michael Jamar Taylor was the father and he sexually assaulted the girl. McFadden later interviewed the sheriff, who confirmed on the record that Taylor was the father of the victim and suspected of the sexual assault. As McFadden gathered more information, it became apparent that he would have to make decisions that would affect the way the story was reported for the sake of protecting the victim's identity. "We had the information," McFadden said. "We could've run with it but were very cautious about how we were going to report this story because we don't identify sexual assault victims."

The subsequent murder of Taylor, allegedly by Tony Brown, posed another problem for McFadden. It was also revealed through interviews and later confirmed in police reports that Tony Brown was the half-brother of the sexual assault victim and apparently murdered Taylor in retaliation for the rape. Brown was released on $40,000 bond.

Protecting privacy went beyond concealing the name of the street where the crimes occurred. The challenge was that by revealing the familial relationships, McFadden could inadvertently identify the sexual assault victim. The relationships the sexual assault victim shared with her alleged attacker and the alleged murderer of her attacker were all confirmed through official police records and a subsequent bond hearing for Tony Brown. Yet ethical decisions by McFadden and the editors at The Herald shaped the way the story was told to protect the identity of the victim.

THE RESPONSE: LEAVING OUT DETAILS

After a series of meetings, the editing team decided not to name the rape victim. The crime of rape carries a stigma, and by revealing the name of the girl, the journalists were afraid they would traumatize the 16-year-old victim. "Obviously, our goal was to get as much information out there to inform the public," McFadden said. "But we also wanted to protect this young woman. She was in high school." The fact that the girl was underage played a major role in the decision. Although it's the general policy of the paper not to name rape victims, her status as a minor helped guide their decision.

The second decision was to omit the name of the road where the 16-year-old girl was raped. Because the community was small, knowledge of the road would connect the girl to the crime and expose her identity. The team also decided to downplay the relationship between the girl, the alleged rapist and the accused killer. The paper decided that any reference to the girl's half-brother would be "a relative" and any reference to her father would be "someone she knew." Making these decisions was difficult. "Of course there's a lot of concern about misleading the public," McFadden said. "That's a huge thing. We don't stand for that. We stand for transparency. These were tough conversations."

A major mission of the press is to inform the public. However, those at The Herald came to the conclusion that they could not reveal key facts and still protect the victim. "There's a lot of things that as journalists we can do and a lot of things we can print and write legally, but that doesn't mean you should do it just because you can," McFadden said. Though there were concerns that he would be scooped by the competition, McFadden stood by his ideals. "We have ethics to maintain, and you have to stand by those. The policy in and of itself is relatively simple. The execution of that policy is often times complicated."

With this in mind, those at The Herald decided that protecting the girl's identity was a core mission. Although the information was part of court documentation and the paper had the legal option to print the girl's name, McFadden and his team chose to preserve her anonymity to the best of their ability. In this case, minimizing harm outweighed the public's right to know every detail.

TOOL FOR THOUGHT: W. D. Ross

Scottish philosopher W. D. Ross argued that the rightness of one's actions does not depend upon the consequences of those actions and that morally good actions generally follow morally good motives. He wrote that one must weigh several duties to determine the right course of action. He came up with seven prima facie duties:

Fidelity: A duty to keep one's promises

Reparation: A duty to make up for an injury to another

Gratitude: A duty to be grateful for the kindness of another and do something kind in return

Nonmaleficence: A duty to cause no further harm

Justice: A duty to distribute benefits and injury fairly

Beneficence: A duty to do something good for others

Self-improvement: A duty to improve one's self

When determining whether or not to reveal the name of

(Continued)

(Continued)

the victim you must consider at least two duties: fidelity and nonmaleficence. You have a duty to tell the truth (fidelity) because you have an unspoken agreement with your audience that you will provide the whole truth. This is what helps you establish credibility. However, you also have a duty to protect the victim (nonmaleficence) and revealing her name could cause her further harm. It's your job to determine which duty has more weight.

In his book "The Good and the Right," Ross said:

"It appears to me that the duty of nonmaleficence is recognized as a distinct one, and as prima facie more binding. We should not in general consider it justifiable to kill one person in order to keep another alive, or to steal from one in order to give aims to another." (p. 22)

Do you agree that non-maleficence outweighs other duties? Is it more important to protect the victim from further harm than to keep your promise to tell the truth? Which duty do you think holds more weight?

You must also consider beneficence. Revealing the whole truth could be a matter of safety. If the public is aware that there is an accused rapist living in their neighborhood, they might choose to lock their doors at night or watch where their children play. Is this duty of beneficence more important than avoiding causing the victim further harm?

THE AFTERMATH: HANDLING FUTURE COVERAGE

It's three years later, and the victim is now 19 years old. Even though the victim is a legal adult, McFadden said that it was unlikely that her name would be revealed in follow-up stories. However, he added that The Herald might reverse its decision to withhold the relationships among the victim, Taylor and Brown. Not only is the victim an adult, but this information is readily available to the public through court records. Although rival news outlets may choose to run with the name, relationship and street name in future coverage, journalists at The Herald say they have a duty to protect the girl from further harm.

McFadden said it was a hard case, but that he's happy it happened so early in his career. He advises aspiring journalists to never lose their humanity. "Always think about it this way: What if you were in the situation? What if it was someone you loved?"

Thinking It Through

1. Would you have named the rape victim in this case? Would you have revealed the relationship between the accused perpetrator, the victim of the murder, and the rape victim? How about in follow-up stories?

2. If a rival newspaper names the victim, is it OK for your paper to name the victim?

3. If the victim's family comes to you and makes a personal request to maintain the family's privacy, does that change the way you should cover the case?

4. In this case deputies confirmed the rape, but what if they hadn't? If you find out from neighbors that Taylor raped the girl, but that was unconfirmed by the sheriff's department, should you go ahead and report their comments? How much does hearsay impact your coverage?

5. When covering the court case, is it fair to publish the name of the victim—especially if she takes the stand? Does the practice change when covering a civil case as opposed to a criminal case?

Go Online for More

To read an article about the case, visit this site:
http://www.heraldonline.com/news/local/news-columns-blogs/andrew-dys/article12284645.html

To learn about how the media traumatizes rape victims:
http://tribune.com.pk/story/338953/journalistic-ethics-how-the-media-traumatises-rape-victims/

To get tips on rape stories from the Poynter Institute:
http://www.poynter.org/2002/rape-and-american-journalism/4480/

CHAPTER 15

Free Speech, Official Pressure

The Case of the Visiting Foreign Student

Daniel Reimold

I t began with a campus newspaper article that shared an international student's critical views of his home country. It ended with the young man's remorse at what he had said, U.S. government officials' concerns that the article might jeopardize his safety and a weeklong debate in the paper's newsroom. The main question for the newspaper staff, in the words of its editor-in-chief, was this: "What do we do when a source—who may not have understood the American media process and who might be in physical danger or danger of being repressed by his government—wants something removed or changed after publication?"[1]

All the names in this story are real. The student whose identity the paper was debating whether to protect is safe back in his homeland.

---

1. Holly Miller, "No Longer Written in Stone: Online Distribution of News Content Presents New Ethical Challenges," *The Minnesota Daily*, Aug. 11, 2009, http://www.mndaily.com/2009/08/11/no-longer-written-stone.

Amid the controversy, he publicly stated he had no fear that his comments would endanger himself or his family. Simply to be safe, however, this chapter does not use the student's last name.

THE SITUATION: "AMERICAN CULTURE, WITH A MINNESOTAN TWIST"

After spring semester classes end each May, The Minnesota Daily goes into summer mode. The award-winning campus newspaper at the University of Minnesota prints one edition a week rather than four, operating with a much smaller staff of students who are either adapting to new editorial positions or working on the paper for the first time.

In summer 2009, Katherine Lymn fell into the latter category. As a new reporting intern with The Daily, Lymn was eager for story assignments to feed her burgeoning journalism passion and to prove she could pull her weight on staff. She searched for something—anything—she could transform into a publishable piece.

Early in her tenure, while scrolling through the university's online events calendar, she spotted an interesting item: A group of North African college students was visiting UM through an exchange program sponsored by the U.S. Department of State. The 20 students—natives of Algeria, Egypt, Libya, Morocco and Tunisia—were spending a month on the school's campus learning about U.S. "politics, policies and people," in part to provide them with a fuller vision of modern America beyond stereotyped or biased media depictions they might have seen at home. As Lymn later wrote, the program, called the Study of the U.S. Institute for Student Leaders, engaged students "in a series of classes and field trips that educated them on the U.S. government as well as providing a sample of American culture, with a Minnesotan twist."[2]

Lymn pitched the program as a possible story to her editors. By chance, they had just received a press release about it and gave Lymn an immediate green light. She contacted the program's university directors,

---

2. Katherine Lymn, "Tunisian Visitor Shares Philosophies, Views of the U.S.: Ashref, a Student from Tunisia, Visited the U with a Group of North African Students," *The Minnesota Daily*, July 28, 2009, http://www.mndaily.com/2009/07/28/tunisian-visitor-shares-philosophies-views-us.

receiving permission to speak to participants and attend some events. When the North African students arrived on campus, she interviewed a number of them.

Her first draft focused on the group's activities as a whole. The editors were encouraging but asked her to rethink her angle. Instead of an overall summary, they suggested she spotlight one member of the group in a profile, someone with an intriguing background and a voice that could bring the program to life. Lymn thought this was a good idea, and one person immediately popped into her head: Ashref.

The 23-year-old Tunisian student studying English and American literature and civilization had impressed her at their first meeting. Smart, passionate and fluent in English, he spoke candidly about his upbringing and about Tunisia as he saw it. During her early chats with program participants, Ashref had been one of the few willing to provide his full name for attribution. She contacted him right away to set up a more in-depth face-to-face interview.

The Challenge: "Bold Statements, Straightforward Views"

The pair met soon afterward in a campus coffee shop. Lymn knew that Ashref and the other participants had received basic information about U.S. media policies as part of their program, but she wasn't sure about its focus or breadth. So she erred on the side of caution, telling Ashref as they sat down that the conversation was on the record and that she planned to use it for a story she hoped The Daily would publish. "The whole time we met, I had my recorder out," she said. "I had my notes out. I was writing down almost everything he said from the moment we sat down. It wasn't an environment where we were just walking around, chatting."

As he spoke critically about different facets of modern Tunisia and mentioned his father's past involvement in opposition politics, Lymn asked one more time whether Ashref was OK having his story shared with Daily readers. He consented, smiling. He later posed for a picture taken by a staff photographer.

On July 29, 2009, Lymn's article ran on the bottom of The Daily front page, under the headline "Tunisian Visitor Shares Philosophies, Views of the U.S." Ashref's first and last names appeared in the sub-headline and body of the piece, along with the names of his father and sister. Lymn's story introduced Ashref as an impassioned young man from a family of academics with big dreams for himself and the place he called home. As she wrote in the lead, "Ashref wants to be a leader of his country. And with his bold statements, straightforward views and ambitious visions, this Tunisian's statement is not unrealistic."[3]

In the story, Ashref denounced his country's education system, notably the poor conditions in university classrooms, which he said often lacked air-conditioning and enough seats for all students. He said he was proud of his father, whom Lymn described as a former "revolutionary leader" with a history of "standing up to the Tunisian government." He criticized Tunisia's ruling party at the time, noting, "We need only to feel somebody fighting for the people." Ashref also repeatedly declared that his country was missing the type of optimism he saw expressed by President Barack Obama. "He has what is lacking in Tunisia," Ashref said, "which is hope."

A photo of a seated Ashref accompanied the text. In the shot, he sports blue jeans, a sweater, red Keds sneakers, a canvas satchel, some chin scruff, a hint of sideburns and a bright smile stretching from ear to ear.

The smile perfectly captured his mood during Lymn's reporting and immediately after the story's publication. As Ashref wrote later,

> I felt pride and happiness to see my ideas shared with the students and people of Minnesota, a place that I love. I was proud because I felt that I am telling the truth, that I am helping my people express themselves and making their voices reach the United States. I was proud because I was expressing the ideas that a lot of my compatriots are afraid to say.[4]

---

3. Ibid.

4. Ashref, "My Reply to Minnesota Nice," *The Minnesota Daily*, Sept. 7, 2009, http://www.mndaily.com/2009/09/07/my-reply-minnesota-nice?page=2

Lymn also felt good about the story and her interactions with Ashref. "He was very happy to talk about almost everything," she said. "Everything was fine for a while until the calls came."

The Response: Story's Up, But Government Wants It Down

The first call that Daily editor-in-chief Holly Miller received came from one of the UM program directors for the student leaders institute, on the day the article appeared in print and online. As Miller recalled,

> He said, "I got this call from the State Department. We really need Ashref's name removed from the story [online]. He said some things about the education system there and his father's political activism that could really get him in trouble."

The same director also phoned Lymn, the reporter, to express similar concerns.

Next, a State Department representative called Miller, urging more heatedly that either the full story be taken down from the web or Ashref's name be immediately removed. According to Miller, the conversation's civility quickly deteriorated, ending with the representative calling her "unpatriotic and unwilling to help my country."

Miller acknowledges now that her initial instinct was to ignore the requests. Especially when dealing with the State Department employee she found hostile, she did not want to give even the slightest impression that student media should or can be bullied. But soon after hanging up, she realized she at least needed to do some research to ensure that she understood all the potential implications of the decision.

First, Miller contacted the newspaper's lawyer. He advised her that from a legal perspective, the newspaper was within its rights to maintain or remove the content as it wished. Next, she oversaw a staff meeting and engaged in more informal newsroom chats and phone calls with other top Daily editors and Lymn to discuss the situation. In addition, Miller and other staffers reached out to journalism ethics experts on and off campus, including the Poynter Institute's values scholar, Bob Steele.

During these talks with experts and one another, the staff considered a number of factors. The first—and many felt, most important—was that the article was already in the public sphere. "Already 20,000 copies of this thing were out there," Miller said. "It had been tweeted. It was on Facebook. It was all over the internet."

To maintain the integrity of its reported news, the paper's general practice was not to alter or remove accurate information once it had been published. For years, UM students, alumni and even former Daily writers had been asking editors to remove their names from stories or fully delete articles appearing online that they wrote or in which they were featured. The typical reasons given for the requests, according to Miller, included "change of opinion, regret, or fear of it being found in a Google search by potential employers."[5]

For example, Miller said a former columnist once requested that all his pieces be erased from the newspaper's website because he had been on drugs while he was writing them. Miller refused.

TOOL FOR THOUGHT: SPJ Code of Ethics

The Society of Professional Journalists Code of Ethics (at www.spj.org/ethicscode .asp) is built on the belief that a journalist's role involves "seeking truth and providing a fair and comprehensive account of events and issues." Some of the code's key statements are useful in thinking about the dilemma that faced the Minnesota student journalists.

• **Seek Truth and Report It.** The tenet topping the SPJ ethics code stresses the value of a complete, accurate telling of all news fit for print and online consumption. It does, however, encourage journalists to "examine their own cultural values and avoid imposing those values on others." Do you feel The Daily imposed its

---

5.   Miller, "No Longer Written in Stone."

values on Ashref through its reporting, even if he did participate of his own accord?

- **Minimize Harm.** Specifically, SPJ advises journalists to "show compassion for those who may be affected adversely by news coverage. Use special sensitivity when dealing with children and inexperienced sources or subjects." What type of sensitivity is SPJ referring to? And how do you decide what constitutes true potential danger or an adverse effect for a source or subject you report

upon? Does it matter whether, like Ashref, the person does not feel he or she needs protection?

- **Be Accountable.** In one item under this heading, the SPJ code says, "Journalists should . . . [c]larify and explain news coverage and invite dialogue with the public over journalistic conduct." Do you think Miller went far enough with her explanation to readers? How do you properly invite readers into the editorial process without sacrificing your journalistic integrity?

Andrew Mannix, The Daily's managing editor in the summer of 2009, recalled a separate situation in which a UM student repeatedly called the newsroom and even cornered Miller one evening in a bar, begging her to remove his name from a Daily article in which he had willingly identified himself as a gambling addict. He was concerned the gambling stigma was hurting his job prospects. "Our response was, basically, 'Tough sh-t,'" Mannix said. "Of course, we said it nicer than that. But to me, there are very few reasons to go back and actually edit an article after the fact."

Yet staffers had purposely not instituted a written or blanket policy, partially in deference to the still new, murky ethics of online journalism. The newspaper's lawyer had advised them to handle such matters instead on a case-by-case basis.

In this case, however, the reasoning behind a possible online information change went well beyond mere source remorse or writer embarrassment. The personal safety and future of a student, and possibly his family, might have been at stake. "It wasn't like someone saying, 'Oh, I wish I hadn't done this beer pong [drinking game] article five years ago,'" said Miller. "You know, we didn't want to ruin [Ashref's] education or his opportunity to become a leader in his country. And we certainly didn't want him to be imprisoned, beaten up or killed."

When wrestling with the safety issue, part of the problem for the paper was that no one on staff or among those The Daily contacted knew much about Tunisia—specifically the level of tolerance Tunisian government officials exhibited toward those who spoke out against them. Thus, it was hard for the editors to determine the credibility of the State Department's claims that Ashref and his family would be in peril.

"None of us really knew enough about the history or government of Tunisia to really be able to say if it was a legitimate threat," Mannix said. "Like, is he going to go back to Tunisia and they're going to be waiting for him when he gets off the plane? It was unclear." The staff conducted some research, finding that the international Press Freedom Index released annually by the journalism advocacy organization Reporters Without Borders confirmed that Tunisia was a country known for holding free expression and free press in low esteem.[6]

Staffers also considered concerns brought to their attention by SUSI and the university that Ashref's criticisms might lead the government of Tunisia or those of other North African countries to distance themselves from the student leadership program. Ashref, in particular, was worried about this implication, one he acknowledged he hadn't considered when speaking so candidly with Lymn. As he told a State Department representative at the time, "If you think that my article represents a threat to the program in my country and that the government may cancel it because of me, you'd better remove my name." He wrote later, "I did not want to be selfish. I did not want to be the force preventing other Tunisian students from coming to the United States and having the same experience I had."[7]

A separate but no less significant question is this: Had Lymn truly done all she could to ensure that Ashref, someone new to the country, was

---

6. Reporters Without Borders, "Press Freedom Index 2009," http://en.rsf
.org/press-freedom-index-2009,1001.html

7. Ashref, "My Reply to Minnesota Nice."

completely aware of how the American news media operated? Did he fully understand that what he was saying would appear in public, exactly as he said it, with his name attached? As far as how he interacted with her during the interview, "I was confident he totally understood what I was doing," Lymn said. "He just didn't understand what some of the implications could be after the fact."

In particular, James Anderson, editor of The Daily campus section at the time, said Ashref most likely did not fully consider the internet factor. "I think he probably just thought what he was doing was going to be seen by people strictly in the U.S.," Anderson said. "He was just maybe unaware of our media culture and the way things get posted online and spread like wildfire. I think if it was someone who sort of understood the way newspapers and the Web 2.0 era worked, it would have been a different issue."

Other staffers were less swayed by the "foreign naivete" argument, especially considering the State Department's oversight of the student leadership program and the media training that participants had received. "It also just sets a bad precedent," Mannix said. "It's kind of like someone coming here and driving 100 miles per hour and getting pulled over and then saying they didn't understand the speed limit."

Even those staffers who felt some revisions were necessary were unsure how far they should go. Some argued that removing Ashref's name would only slightly delay—not actually stop—Tunisian officials from discovering that a native had badmouthed them while abroad. After all, a directed Google search would still yield the name of the country, the program, Ashref's comments and even his smiling face in full color, enabling even the lowliest government employee to connect the dots quite quickly.

But removing the whole article, descriptions of his family history or his most critical quotes represented a different and troubling prospect: tinkering with the published truth.

THE AFTERMATH: "NO LONGER WRITTEN IN STONE"

In the end, concerns about Ashref's safety proved too large to ignore. The editors removed all mentions of his last name from the online version of the story. To ensure transparency in the process, they added an editor's note below Lymn's byline for clarification. It read,

> The last name of the main subject of this story, Ashref, and his family members has been removed from this story since its original publication. The source became concerned of the negative implications that may come from speaking critically of the Tunisian government and its programs upon his return to his home country.

Overcoming their initial anger at being asked to change their content, staff members agreed that while State Department officials were possibly being overprotective and could certainly have been more polite, the department was a trusted and knowledgeable source whose concerns could not be ignored.

Basic human instinct also entered into the equation. Simply put, no one wanted to see Ashref hurt for taking a stand and speaking the truth, especially if he did not quite understand the circumstances or consequences involved while he was doing it. "The big thing we were having a hard time with was this idea that he would be in jail or killed from this piece," Mannix said. "If this person were to be executed, that would be hard to deal with and [make it] hard to sleep at night."

It was important to editors that the story essentially stayed the same. "For him [Ashref], it's changed in that you can't find what he said unless you really Google in-depth," Anderson said. "From a content perspective, I don't think we changed anything at all."

Even so, Miller favored total transparency, buttressing the editor's note with a separate column explaining the newspaper's decision. In the column, headlined "No Longer Written in Stone," she discussed what Poynter's Steele called the "new form and new intensity" of ethical dilemmas for journalists. "In the days of print only, it was unlikely for a source to come back and ask for all remaining versions of the paper to be burned or removed from libraries," Miller wrote. "There used to be a sense of permanency with print versions. . . . The internet changed that."[8]

---

8. Miller, "No Longer Written in Stone."

The newspaper did not stop with an explanation to its readers. It also changed its staff policies, adding a requirement that all reporters fully explain to their sources the publication possibilities of a story and how a source's words might be used. Lymn described the new policy this way:

> Be clear—be annoyingly clear—with the people you talk to about what's going to happen to the information they give you. Don't try to hide it just because you're nervous they won't talk to you because it will come back to bite you. Repeat things. Say, "This is going in the paper. This is going on our website." At times, it might make it harder to get information out of your sources, but it will make you feel better at the end of the day that you were clear. And you won't have the State Department calling you.

FIGURE 15.1 **This screenshot of the online article shows the changes and the editor's note that was added after its original posting.**

CAMPUS

Tunisian visitor shares philosophies, views of the U.S.

Ashref, a student from Tunisia, visited the U with a group of North African students.

By Katherine Lymn

Editor's note: The last name of the main subject of this story, Ashref, and his family members has been removed from this story since its original publication. The source became concerned of the negative implications that may come from speaking critically of the Tunisian government and its programs upon his return to his home country.

Ashref wants to be a leader of his country.

And with his bold statements, straightforward views and ambitious visions, this Tunisian's statement is not unrealistic.

A 23-year-old student of English and American literature and civilization, Ashref was chosen to partake in the U.S. Department of State's Study of the U.S. Institute (SUSI) for Student Leaders.

date 2009 / 07 / 28
sectionNews > Campus

Printer-friendly version
PDF version

SOURCE: The Minnesota Daily. Used with permission.

Figure 15.2 A column by the newspaper's editor-in-chief explained why the staff had decided to remove a visiting student's last name from a story.

SOURCE: The Minnesota Daily. Used with permission.

Thinking It Through

1. According to Poynter's Bob Steele, The Daily's situation was unique, and any solution rendered was ultimately going to be imperfect.[9] Do you agree with the newspaper's decision? What options do you think the paper had for dealing with the "unpublish" request, and which would you have chosen?

2. Lymn said the biggest lesson she learned from interviewing Ashref was to be "annoyingly clear" with sources about her intentions for a story. The problem with such an approach, Miller noted, is that you don't want to scare away people before they start talking. So the question remains, what should you say to the people you interview? As a reporter, would you feel an obligation to be more thorough in your explanations with young adults, foreigners or those inexperienced with news media, or do you think it's not up to you to make those judgments?

---

9. Ibid.

3. College news media have access to journalism professors, local professional journalists, campus officials and publications boards, all eager to help when tough situations occur. Whom should you consult on or near your own campus during more complex ethical dilemmas? How should you use their advice?

4. Miller wrote a column explaining the newspaper's decision about the Ashref story. Would you make the same choice? How much explanation of these sorts of matters do you think readers want or deserve? More generally, how should you cover news when the story involves your own news outlet?

What If?

The removal or alteration of accurate information from an online news story should be rare and handled with the utmost care. In this case, The Daily decided to drop the last name of an international student from the online version of a story in order to protect him from possible harm back home. What other cases might be worthy of a change of some sort to content already published and placed online?

For example, are there ever circumstances in which you should protect a suspected or convicted criminal? What if a student arrested for drug possession pleads with you to drop his name from your story, swearing that a local drug dealer will hurt or kill him if he finds out the student was caught with his stuff?

What if a 17-year-old freshman convicted of a minor underage drinking charge asks you to erase his name from your story because he deserves greater compassion as a legal minor?

What if a student convicted in connection with a hit-and-run asks you two years later to add an editor's note atop the story in your online archive, explaining that two of the more serious charges against her were later downgraded? One of the reasons she gives is her fear that potential employers who Google her name will be dissuaded from hiring her when they see the original story, which was accurate when published.

Go Online for More

See the article "5 Ways News Organizations Respond to 'Unpublishing' Requests" from the Poynter Institute:

http://www.poynter.org/latest-news/top-stories/104414/5-ways-news-organizations-respond-to-unpublishing-requests/

The group Reporters Without Borders compiles an annual Press Freedom Index measuring the degree of freedom for news organizations in various countries:

http://en.rsf.org/

CHAPTER 16

Sins of Omission

The Case of the Not-So-Free Pet Party

Giselle A. Auger

In their first professional jobs, new graduates are eager to take on responsibilities, enthusiastically applying knowledge gained in school to real-world situations. Yet sometimes unethical managers can take advantage of youth and inexperience, assigning new staff members to projects that appear to be legitimate but are partially, or not at all, acceptable.

A recent college graduate was asked by her supervising manager to create a publicity campaign for free events, only to discover later that the people attending would actually be charged. The situation forced the new employee to weigh competing loyalties: to her employer, to the company's present and potential customers and—ultimately—to truth and professionalism. The young communications manager still feels some loyalty to the company where she interned and worked; therefore, she asked that the names in this chapter be changed.

The Situation: Come to Our First Barking Barbecue!

Lauren Henderson, 24, was delighted when a local dog day camp hired her as communications manager. She had interned at the camp while a student at the University of Florida and was excited that the owner liked her work enough to offer her a position where she could get real professional experience. "When I was an intern, I helped with a lot of their activities, like dog birthday parties, but as communications manager I got to develop and plan new promotions from A to Z," Henderson said.

Happy Tails Dog Day Camp and Spa provided companionship and activities for dogs during the day while their owners were at work. Grooming services, such as nail trimming and baths, were also available. Between 15 and 25 dogs took part in the day camp services offered Monday through Friday. Including Henderson, the business had five employees plus the owner, Flo Sawyer, who Henderson said was rarely on site.

Liz Dillon, the general manager who was licensed for training and grooming, ran the camp and managed overall operations. The associate manager, Cynthia Brand, handled scheduling, worked with the dog owners during drop-off and pickup times, and was Henderson's direct supervisor. "I knew Liz from when I interned, but Cynthia was hired later," Henderson said. "She seemed really nice, and we all got along really well until the barbecue event."

Henderson's first project as communications manager was to help develop new brochures, stationery and business cards for Happy Tails. Once that was done, Brand talked to her about developing a new event to thank current clients and attract new ones. Together they came up with the idea of a "Barking Barbecue" with food for pets and their owners as well as games, grooming and training tips. The event would be free and open to the public, Brand said.

"I thought it was a great idea," Henderson said. "It is so important to take care of the customers you already have, and this sounded fun. It's a little crazy, but the owners of the pets love the pet-centered activities we do, like the birthday parties. They really get into it and bring special cakes and dog ice cream and party favors. The barbecue would be a good way to thank them and also show potential new clients what a fun place this is for their dog."

Henderson developed an event plan and created a schedule of activities for the day, which Brand critiqued and approved. Henderson designed advertisements for the local newspaper and postcards to hand out to customers and distribute to local veterinary offices and animal rescue groups. She arranged for volunteers from the animal rescue groups to have informational tables at the event; solicited special offers from local pet retailers; and created gift bags for participants that included dog cookies and information on Happy Tails' services and fees and on pet health and safety, as well as the special offers and coupons.

"It was a lot of work but really exciting to be creating and implementing a plan from start to finish," Henderson said. The fun ended, however, when Henderson asked Brand to pay the deposits for the extra dog trainer who would be coming in for the day and for the table and chair rentals and the food order. "She said we didn't have enough money for the deposits and she'd negotiate a 30-day grace period from the vendors," Henderson said.

Henderson was surprised. She'd been working for more than a month planning the event, discussing it with Brand frequently, and had seen no indication that money was a problem. "It wasn't like business had changed or anything," Henderson said. "We still had about the same number of clients as we had when we started planning, so I was really confused. I didn't really want to question her because she was my boss, but I wondered whether maybe the owner had decided to do some expansion or something that I didn't know about."

Henderson decided to wait a few days while she figured out what was going on.

The Challenge: Follow Orders or Serve the Truth?

In the days that followed, Henderson looked for indications of impending expansion or other activities that might explain the lack of money to pay vendors. Finally, she casually asked Brand if there were any such plans. When Brand said there were not, Henderson expressed her concerns about the barbecue expenses and asked for more information. "I told her I was worried about how we were going to fund the barbecue if we couldn't pay the deposits."

In response, Brand acknowledged that the company had never had enough money available to run the barbecue as a completely free event. She said participants would be asked to make donations at the event and would be charged for extras like the training and grooming activities. She said she had asked Henderson to advertise it as a free event because it sounded good that way. In her view, the advertising was partially true because some activities would be free, and people didn't have to make a donation if they didn't want to.

Henderson was shocked by Brand's response and attitude. She now faced a bigger ethical dilemma than she'd first realized: All the promotional materials she'd been so proud of creating were, in fact, deceptive. Worse, they had already been disseminated. True, she'd believed the barbecue would be free when she wrote the ads and postcards, but that didn't change the fact that the people who'd seen the promotional material, or were about to, would not be getting the real story.

When Brand said the company would charge for some of the services, "I told her we couldn't do that because we had advertised it all over the place and we'd said it would be free. Cynthia said it was no big deal; people would understand."

In the next few days, Henderson broached the subject several times with Brand, suggesting that new publicity materials be created and distributed in order to clarify what "free" meant. Finally, Brand lost patience and told Henderson that she was the boss, and if any problems resulted from the publicity campaign, she would deal with them. "She told me to keep working on promoting the event and firming up the details," Henderson said.

Henderson felt angry and confused. "I knew it was wrong and I just couldn't keep advertising the event as free, but I didn't want to make Cynthia mad and I didn't want to lose my job," she said.

For a few days, Henderson deliberated and discussed the issue with friends. She considered various options: pulling the newspaper ads or changing them without Brand's approval; calling clients to clarify which activities at the barbecue event would be free; and, finally, bringing her concerns to upper management. She worried about her reputation and the reputation of the business. She wondered if she should quit.

"Then I figured if I felt bad enough to quit, I might as well talk to Liz," she said. So she brought the issue to the general manager. "I thought Liz should know what was going on," Henderson said. Even as she chose this course, she recognized one possible implication: If the boss already knew about the false advertising and didn't have a problem with it, then Henderson would have some tough thinking to do about whether she could continue to work for the company.

THE RESPONSE: REALITY MEETS PROMOTION

About a week after finding out that she'd inadvertently been doing false publicity for the barbecue, Henderson met with Liz Dillon, the general manager, to discuss her concerns. She had prepared carefully for the meeting, assembling all the relevant material and thinking through what she wanted to say and how her boss, Dillon, might respond. To help explain her position, she brought copies of the advertisements and postcards that had been distributed, details of the event schedule and the expected costs associated with the event. She included the anticipated number of attendees, both current customers and potential clients, which Henderson and Brand had estimated to be between 200 and 250.

As Henderson had suspected, Dillon did not know the details of the event and had not concerned herself with its financing. She was aware that the event was going to take place; she was scheduled to present many of the training and grooming sessions herself. However, one of the reasons she had hired an associate manager who was adept at finances was to relinquish that part of the operation and focus on her other duties. Although Dillon still reviewed ledger balances monthly and had asked Brand for forecasts for the coming two months, she had not seen anything alarming relating to the barbecue because no shortfalls or major expenses were indicated.

Henderson explained to her supervisor that she was worried about upsetting customers and hurting the camp's reputation if people were charged for an event that had been advertised as free. "I wasn't really sure if it was legal or not, but I knew that from a public relations standpoint, it would be a really bad thing," she said. "People would feel we had cheated them, and we could lose customers." She also pointed out the longer-term implications: "People might feel that if they brought their pets to us, then there would be hidden charges in their bills afterwards."

Dillon was sympathetic to Henderson's concerns and told her she would discuss the matter with both the owner and Brand. "She was nice, but it seemed like she thought maybe I didn't understand what was happening," Henderson said. Dillon explained to Henderson that she wanted to hear all sides of the story to find out what was really going on, plus she needed to review the accounts. "I thought that was the right thing to do, but I was still scared Cynthia would be mad at me, and I really hate confrontations," Henderson said. She returned to work, and she and Dillon did not discuss the subject again.

Dillon and Sawyer, the owner, reached a decision quickly. Within a few days of Henderson's meeting with Dillon, Sawyer had committed funds to cover the costs of the event, which would be run as advertised—free. Brand was asked to leave the company and was not replaced. "Liz never came right out and said why Cynthia left, but it seemed pretty obvious that it had something to do with the barbecue and Mrs. Sawyer having to come up with the money to cover it," Henderson said.

TOOL FOR THOUGHT:
Provisions of Conduct in the PRSA Ethics Code

In addition to its six core values—advocacy, honesty, expertise, independence, loyalty and fairness—the code of ethics of the Public Relations Society of America (at www.prsa.org/AboutPRSA/Ethics/CodeEnglish/) provides what it calls "provisions of conduct," designed to help practitioners determine the appropriate and ethical course of action in various situations. These provisions fall into six broad categories:

1. **Free flow of information.** Ask yourself whether the information you are providing is accurate and truthful so that those receiving the information can make informed decisions. Are you trying to hide information in small type? If so, do you think that facilitates the free flow of information?

2. **Competition.** You and your company should not engage in bad-mouthing or otherwise undermine a competitor. Rather than engage in underhanded behavior, think about competition this way: No one likes to lose an account or a client; however, losing to a competitor allows you to review your campaign. Did you listen to the client's needs? Were you too controversial or too conservative? Remember that it is in the public interest to have the strongest and best businesses from which to choose.

3. **Disclosure of information.** It is not OK to deceive people about who is paying for or sponsoring an event. We've all heard about fake bloggers who promote a company or product without disclosing that they were paid for their support. Such practice is unethical. As an ethical practitioner, you should try to correct misinformation or provide disclosure if you find information has been withheld.

4. **Safeguarding confidences.** If your client shares "Gramma's Secret Recipe" with you, it is not yours to share, either professionally or informally with friends, nor is confidential information about upcoming retirement of the chairman or anything else you hear on the job.

5. **Conflicts of interest.** Be open about any potential conflicts of interest, either your own or your company's. For example,

(Continued)

it is possible to have competing companies as clients, but the clients should be aware of that fact.

6. **Enhancing the profession.** As a professional practitioner, you should be aware of ongoing changes and growth of the profession. By practicing ethically, you serve to strengthen public trust in the profession.

THE AFTERMATH: COMMUNICATION IS A MANAGEMENT FUNCTION

The barking barbecue went well, pleasing existing clients and bringing the company some new ones. Henderson stayed in the job for another year and now works in sports event management. She remains proud of the way she handled her first big ethical dilemma, but looking back, she can see even more implications than she realized at the time.

Students of public relations are taught that PR is a management function. As such, practitioners should be part of decisions and planning that may affect both the company and its stakeholders, whether those stakeholders are customers or other members of the public. At the time of the incident, Henderson realized the implications for Happy Tails Dog Day Camp and Spa if the business deceived people through false publicity. Once she learned of her boss's intentions, she knew she had to do something. Only later did she realize that the situation could have been avoided if she had been part of the strategic planning for the camp as a whole and not involved in the planning just for one event.

"I planned the event and the budget for the expenses and it was OK'd by Cynthia, so I thought it was OK," Henderson said. "It would have been better if all of us—me, Cynthia and Liz—had talked about the barbecue event as part of the whole plan for the camp."

Having figured out how to handle her first big ethical dilemma hasn't made it easier for her to spot or deal with other ethics problems, Henderson said, but it did bring home to her the potential conflicts inherent in all public relations jobs. "On the one hand, we're supposed to work for the client, or our bosses, but on the other hand, we have to make sure that what we communicate is true," she said. "Sometimes that's harder than you think."

Thinking It Through

1. Think of yourself as a public relations consultant to the business in this chapter, Happy Tails Dog Day Camp and Spa. What alternate promotional activities could you recommend to your client that would meet the need to increase revenue while also serving current and potential customers? Explain how these activities would benefit both the client and the customer.

2. What if Henderson's boss had told her to place a disclaimer in small type on the advertising for the barbecue, explaining that free dog grooming would be provided only to those who made purchases of $100 or more and that some activities would involve a fee? Use the PRSA ethics code to think about whether this move would be valid and whether you'd be comfortable being held accountable for publicity material worded this way.

3. If you think your immediate boss is doing something unethical, in any type of job, is it always OK to report your concerns to the person who supervises your boss? Should you worry about whether doing so might endanger your immediate boss's job, or is that not your problem? If you were supervising people yourself, and one of them thought some of your actions were ethically questionable, what would you want that person to do? If that person came to you and you thought her concerns were not valid, what do you think should happen next?

What If?

The many ways of communicating online—websites, blogs, video news releases, social media—provide an unparalleled resource for public relations professionals to reach targeted and diverse audiences. The ever-changing nature of the internet also creates new challenges to professional ethics. Consider the infamous case of a blog called "Wal-Marting Across America."

Launched in September 2006,[1] the blog shared the adventures of a couple named Laura and Jim as they drove a recreational vehicle across America, parking in Wal-Mart lots along the way. The posts recounted the couple's wonderful experiences as RVers and included stories from happy store employees who helped them. Quickly, however, readers of the blog became suspicious, and soon the bloggers were exposed.[2]

Jim, it turns out, was Jim Thresher, a photographer for The Washington Post working on his own time, and Laura was Laura St. Claire, a freelance writer.[3] The trip had been organized by Edelman, a large international public relations firm that handled Wal-Mart's business; it had made the arrangements through a group called Working Families for Wal-Mart, which is funded by Wal-Mart. That group was paying Thresher and St. Claire to blog and providing money for the RV and gas.

What if you worked for Edelman in an entry-level job and you knew about plans for the blog? What would you have said about it, and to whom? What reasons could you have given to support your position? If you were the photographer's boss at The Washington Post, what would you have done in response to his participation in the blog? The Society of Professional Journalists ethics code may help you think about this question.

If you were an executive at Wal-Mart, would you have fired the Edelman firm over the blog episode? If you ran the Edelman firm, what would you have done once the deception was exposed? Ironically, the company at that point was looked to as a leading authority on how to use the internet for public relations.

Would it be fair for either Wal-Mart or Edelman to put all the blame on the other party? Do you think the newness of blogging in 2006

---

1. Pallavi Gogoi, "Wal-Mart's Jim and Laura: The Real Story," *Bloomberg Businessweek,* Oct. 9, 2006, http://www.businessweek.com/bwdaily/dnflash/content/oct2006/db20061009_579137.htm.

2. Ibid.

3. Ibid. See also http://walmartwatch.org/blog/archives/identity-of-wal-marting-across-america-rver-revealed.

makes what happened more understandable? If so, what would you suggest for establishing ethical standards in a continually evolving technological world?

In the aftermath of the Wal-Marting Across America expose, Richard Edelman produced the following statement[4]:

> I want to acknowledge our error in failing to be transparent about the identity of the two bloggers from the outset. This is 100 percent our responsibility and our error; not the client's. Let me reiterate our support for the [Word of Mouth Marketing Association's] guidelines on transparency, which we helped to write. Our commitment is to openness and engagement because trust is not negotiable and we are working to be sure that commitment is delivered in all our programs.

Edelman's apology refers to transparency, openness and trust. Remember these things when you begin to practice—truthfulness leads to trust. What do you think of his statement? If you worked for the Edelman firm, would it make you feel good about continuing? If you worked for Wal-Mart, would it feel like enough?

Go Online for More

Word of Mouth Marketing Association guidelines on transparency, referred to in the Edelman/Wal-Mart blog case:
http://womma.org/ethics/code/

The Arthur W. Page Society, a professional organization that works to strengthen the role of public relations as a management function, sponsors an annual competition for case studies written by college students. See the rules and winners here:
http://www.awpagesociety.com/insights/winning-case-studies/

The Institute for Public Relations provides practical research on measurement and the science of public relations:
http://www.instituteforpr.org

---

4. Richard Edelman, "A Commitment," Oct. 16, 2006, http://www.edelman
    .com/speak_up/blog/archives/2006/10/a_commitment.html.

For anyone interested in public relations, blogs are a good place to "eavesdrop" and learn about the hot topics in the profession. Several sites provide links to their own version of the best PR blogs:

Blogrank listing:
http://www.invesp.com/blog-rank/PR

Blogs for PR students:
http://www.bachelorsdegreeonline.com/blog/2011/50-best-blogs-for-the-public-relations-major/

PR Web's list of "25 essential PR blogs":
http://service.prweb.com/learning/article/public-relations-blogs-25-essential-pr-bloggers-you-should-be-reading/

CHAPTER 17

Please Don't Use the Video

The Case of the Fatal Accident

Ray Niekamp

J ournalists must often report on the ugly side of life—and death. People affected by tragedy often bear their pain bravely but are reluctant to share it publicly. When video of a fatal traffic accident was shown to jurors during a trial, reporters covering the case were faced with a decision: to air the video or not to, at a grieving family's request.

THE SITUATION: A SOLDIER, A GIRL, ALCOHOL AND A RED LIGHT

In El Paso, Texas, 19-year-old Valerie Talamantes sat waiting at a red light early on the morning of Dec. 29, 2007. Suddenly, an SUV traveling at an estimated 60 mph crashed into the back of her car and another one waiting beside it. Talamantes' car took the brunt of the crash. An ambulance rushed her to a hospital, where she died later that day.

The driver of the SUV was Staff Sgt. Edison Bayas, a soldier stationed at nearby Fort Bliss. He had returned from a tour of duty in Iraq just 10 days before the crash. Police charged him with intoxicated manslaughter. Bayas had a blood alcohol count of 0.27, more than three times the legal limit.

At Bayas' trial a year and a half later, his lawyer argued that Bayas suffered from post-traumatic stress disorder that had not been diagnosed by Army doctors. They said he was having a flashback when he hit Talamantes' car. Prosecutors, however, contended that Bayas had a history of alcohol abuse, including two previous arrests and four referrals to the Army's substance abuse program.

Reporter Ramon Herrera of KDBC-TV in El Paso covered the Bayas trial. He had graduated from Texas State University only six months before and was working part-time for the CBS affiliate. The news department's budget had been cut, and as the only dayside reporter, Herrera was sent to the courthouse.

A few days into the trial, the judge's clerk tipped off the media that the district attorney would present a red-light camera video in court that day. This video, taken by a camera positioned to catch drivers who run red lights, showed the SUV hitting Talamantes' car and pushing it through the intersection. The reporters were excited about the tip but faced some complications: Neither the police nor the district attorney would provide reporters with copies of the video. Not only that, but news cameras were not allowed in the courtroom. Reporters worried that they might not be able to show their viewers the trial's most compelling evidence.

Video coverage of the trial was operating on a "pool" system, meaning one camera took video that was then made available to all four El Paso TV stations. In this particular courthouse, it was common for news cameras to shoot through a window in the door of the courtroom. Herrera said most judges allowed that kind of shooting. When the crash video played on a large projection screen in the courtroom, the pool camera operator was able to aim through the window in the courtroom door and capture the footage. In addition, newspaper and website photographers took still pictures through the window.

The red-light video, in a fixed position above and behind the stoplight, clearly showed Talamantes' car stopped at the light alongside another car. Suddenly, a blurry vehicle came in from the left—behind the cars. It slammed into them and pushed Talamantes' car into the intersection. The video was in color but did not show great detail because the crash happened before daybreak. However, it did show the impact clearly enough that jurors gasped when the video played in court. Bayas was shaken and wiped his eyes.

THE CHALLENGE: "CAN YOU PLEASE NOT USE THE VIDEO?"

After the district attorney showed the video in court, the trial recessed for lunch. As people straggled back to the courthouse after the break, reporters clustered in a small group and chatted about the morning's developments. The victim's father walked up to the group. "I know you guys have a job to do," he said to the reporters, "but if you guys can, can you please not use the video?"

He explained that the graphic nature of the video would be likely to stir up strong emotions among Valerie Talamantes' family and friends. The discussion was polite and civil. Reporters told Talamantes that they couldn't make any promises because they wouldn't be the ones making the final decision—that was up to their news directors. The father said he understood then made a final plea: "Put yourself in my shoes, please."

The request made Herrera uncomfortable—not because he thought it was unreasonable but because he empathized with the father. When he'd watched the video as it played in the courtroom, "I had a lump in my throat," he said. "Personally, I couldn't imagine seeing my daughter's last moments on earth."

Herrera and his photographer headed back to the station. There, he told his news director and executive producer about Talamantes' request. They all looked at the video together.

TOOL FOR THOUGHT:
Telling Truth Versus Doing Harm

When doctors take the Hippocratic Oath, they begin by reciting, "First, do no harm." But of course doctors often do cause harm—for example, by subjecting patients to painful treatments in an attempt to cure them. So, too, can journalists cause harm. By its nature, reporting information can hurt people. The Society of Professional Journalists ethics code (at www.spj.org/ethicscode.asp) recognizes this reality. The first guiding principle in the code is Seek Truth and Report It. The second is Minimize Harm.

In the story in this chapter, the fact that the Talamantes family was a group of private individuals, not public figures, imposed an even more rigorous standard on journalists. In the words of the SPJ ethics code, "Recognize that private people have a greater right to control information about themselves than do public officials and others who seek power, influence or attention. Only an overriding public need can justify intrusion into anyone's privacy." Although the case of

Talamantes' death had thrust her family into the public eye, they weren't there willingly. And although the video was seen by everyone in the courtroom during an official proceeding, showing it to the rest of the world outside that room was a separate question, especially once the father had made the family's feelings known.

The "minimize harm" principle, like everything else in journalism, comes second to reporting the truth. The red-light camera video was central to the case against Bayas because it dramatically showed the speed of his vehicle and the force with which he hit Talamantes' car. The availability of the video helped television stations tell the story. For a television station, video is important. Not only does it show viewers what happened, but it also adds interest to the narrative that would be missing without it. In this case, the video of the crash was the key element in the trial, which was certainly a factor in KDBC-TV's decision to use it. However, as Herrera remembers the discussion, the most important consideration was that it showed what the case and the trial were all about. The video had news value because it helped viewers to understand the manslaughter case.

In attempting to minimize harm, determining the stakeholders in a story is a key consideration. The Talamantes family was a stakeholder, but so were viewers, who depended upon the station for a full and accurate account of the trial proceedings. The journalist must weigh those stakeholders and the harm that could be done to each in order to make an ethical decision about using the video in question. For example, how badly would the Talamanteses be harmed if the video were shown on TV? Some family members had already seen the video in the courtroom, so the shock might have worn off by the time the newscast aired. Even given that many people who knew or were related to the dead teenager were not in the courtroom that day, the number of family members and friends was still small compared with the number of viewers of a newscast. Would the audience members be able to appreciate the impact of the crash without seeing it as it happened?

When the news director made the seemingly callous comment that the family shouldn't watch the news (see below), he was verbalizing the idea of minimizing harm. If the people most likely to suffer emotional distress didn't watch, harm would be minimized. The reporter tried to further minimize harm with the narration in which he warned viewers about the video's content, so they could make the choice of whether to watch.

Plenty of people like to watch gory movies, but does that mean journalists should cater to those instincts? The SPJ ethics code calls for journalists to maintain good taste and "avoid pandering to lurid curiosity." In this case, the red light camera was shooting from above and behind the intersection, in a wide shot, not a close-up. While the video of the crash itself resembled what viewers often see in television shows that feature police chases, in this case no people were visible on screen. The video was not lurid or gory. It was the clearest way for the TV station to show its viewers what was at stake in the trial.

THE RESPONSE: RUN THE WHOLE THING

Herrera says both the news director and the executive producer found the video to be "kind of shocking." When he realized that no body or gore was visible, the news director said he wanted to use the entire video on the air. Herrera presented the father's concern about family members seeing the video, and the emotional trauma it might provoke. The news director, however, said his response to those people would be simple: "Then don't watch the news." Herrera did not disagree with the news director. "I guess you have a point," he responded.

The video ran in its entirety on that night's newscast. In his lead-in, Herrera explained that the district attorney had introduced the video into evidence, and he issued a warning to viewers that they were about to see a graphic video. Because it did not have sound, Herrera narrated over the video: "You can see Bayas quickly cut into the view of the traffic cam, colliding with Talamantes." As it turned out, that was not the only time the station aired the crash video. It was used from then on whenever the station covered new developments in the story, to remind the audience of the issues involved in the trial. "I thought the video was essential in telling Valerie's story," Herrera said.

Herrera and his bosses considered the video to be legitimately newsworthy, even though Herrera felt "somewhat bad" about using it. At the courthouse, other reporters had indicated that their stations would probably be using the video. They told Herrera that their news directors would not sit on it, and he had doubted that his would either.

"We all knew everyone else was going to use it, and our competitiveness was a factor," Herrera said. "I wasn't going to fall behind the other stations by being the only one who didn't use it." As University of Maryland professor Carl Sessions Stepp points out, "Clobbering the heck out of competition is a long-glorified value that has motivated and terrorized reporters for decades."[1] If all the stations aired the crash video, the playing field would be level; if one station didn't, that station would get clobbered. Knowing he wasn't alone in using the video, Herrera said, made him feel better about the decision.

---

1. Carl S. Stepp, "Whatever Happened to Competition?" *American Journalism Review*, 23, No. 5 (2001, June): 22.

The Aftermath: No Second Thoughts

As the trial continued, Herrera talked with reporters from the other stations in town. All said their news managers had used the same reasoning: Show the entire video because it was the best material to come out of the trial. In addition, the reporters all said their news directors had a similar response to Mr. Talamantes' request not to use the video: The family does not have to watch the news.

No one in the reporting corps had second thoughts about the decision, Herrera said. Because none of them had promised the father their stations would not use it, they considered themselves free of any ethical conflict.

The community apparently wasn't concerned about the red-light camera video either. Although station executives had expected some reaction, Herrera said no telephone calls or emails came from viewers after the video aired. Not only that, but the members of Talamantes' family did not complain about use of the video. They appeared ready to let bygones be bygones. "The next day in court, the father still said hello to all of us," Herrera said.

Bayas was convicted of intoxicated manslaughter in the death of Valerie Talamantes; he was sentenced to 15 years in prison and ordered to pay a fine of $10,000. He appealed but lost his case.

Dealing with the question of the red light video was a learning experience for Herrera, the young reporter, and he was happy with the way it turned out. "I like to think I handled the situation the way I had to," he said. "The only thing I would do differently is get the video to the station ASAP, during the lunch break, so we could be the first to post it online."

Thinking It Through

1. As a journalist, you have many loyalties—to your sources, your employer, the community, your colleagues, the news, the truth. What loyalties came into conflict in this case? What considerations can you think of that might help you weigh the value of various loyalties in a particular news situation?

Do you believe that competition is a legitimate journalistic value, to be considered along with other high-minded goals, or is it simply a fact of life?

2. The mantra of most photojournalists is, "Shoot now; choose later." In other words, grab all the visuals you can while you're at a news scene, on the theory that you can't decide later to use a shot that you never took. Now that nearly all reporters for all types of news organizations shoot photos and video, does this idea seem helpful to you? Can you imagine situations in which you feel that you should not be shooting photos or video at all? If you shoot visuals even though you're pretty sure you won't be posting or publishing or airing them, can you think of any potential problems you might be creating for yourself or your organization?

3. A person without empathy can never be a great journalist. A journalist with too much empathy may be paralyzed. If you had a personal code of journalistic ethics, what would it say about your responsibility to put yourself in others' shoes? Given that thought, would you have done anything differently when faced with the grieving father who didn't want the video aired? If you were fairly sure that your bosses were going to air the video no matter what you said, would telling the father that the decision wasn't up to you be an ethical response? Do you have any responsibility to explain to him how the decision looks from a journalist's perspective?

4. Most news organizations routinely air graphic footage from a far distant place—from the Japanese earthquake and tsunami, for example, or the war in Afghanistan. What would you say if someone asked you why it's fine to show a dead child from a faraway country but not a dead child from down the street?

5. Once your bosses have made a decision to run a particular photo or air particular footage, is that the end of your ethical responsibility as a reporter? Do you think it's OK to run something because others are doing it, or to keep running it because a decision to do so was made weeks ago? Do you believe that each re-airing of a clip, such as the red-light video or the video of the World Trade Center towers collapsing, should be its own, new ethical decision?

What If?

News reporters get a look at scenes from life that nonjournalists rarely encounter. Stories involving death and mayhem are common. Reporters have to decide whether unpleasant images are necessary to tell a story and if so, how to balance the need to report the truth with the need to minimize harm. Many broadcast, print and online news organizations have stopped routine coverage of traffic accidents because they affect few people. At times, though, accidents are newsworthy because of the circumstances.

Let's say that two semi-trailer trucks collide head-on on a busy two-lane highway in your coverage area. Both drivers die in the crash, and rush-hour traffic is backed up for many miles for multiple hours. You are sent to cover the accident. Whether you're reporting primarily for broadcast, print or online, you're now expected to submit video as part of your duties.

By the time you arrive, one of the bodies has been moved to a nearby ambulance, but the other has yet to be pulled out of the wreckage. The mangled truck cabs and trailers are strewn along more than a hundred yards of the highway, with their cargo scattered on the asphalt and in roadside ditches. With those scenes and the backed-up traffic, you have plenty to shoot; the possibilities seem endless.

The county coroner, who has been summoned to the crash site, lets you know that the ambulance crew will soon remove the second driver's body from his crushed truck cab. He urges you to approach the overturned cab from the front and motions you to get down on your knees to see what's inside. The upside-down face of the dead driver stares out at you. "That would make a good shot, wouldn't it?" the coroner asks.

Within a few minutes, "Jaws of Life" equipment has pried open the cab enough that rescuers can get the body out and onto a gurney. They wheel the gurney past you as you stand with your video camera or cell phone in hand. The body is uncovered, and the face is smeared with blood. You point and shoot as the gurney goes by. Then you position yourself near the ambulance and get shots of the crew putting the gurney inside.

How much video is necessary to tell the story? Do you accept the coroner's invitation to shoot the face of the dead man while it's still in the cab? Do you shoot video of the body as it is moved to the ambulance? As it is put inside? Are there ethical considerations in simply shooting the video, as opposed to airing it? As long as you stay out of the way and don't impede emergency workers' efforts, is anything you do OK, so long as you know you'll think carefully later about what to air?

Now, picture yourself as a viewer watching the newscast or checking the website at home. Would your understanding of the story by improved by seeing the dead man's face? What objections might you raise?

Let's alter the situation. You're sent to cover a fatal accident in a residential area at a corner that has seen more than its share of fatalities. When you arrive, you find that a 5-year-old boy has been struck and killed by a car. The boy's body, covered with a sheet, lies in the street as police complete their investigation. You take out your camera and are shooting the accident scene when the boy's distraught father walks up to you, puts a hand over your camera lens and says, "No pictures." What do you say? What do you do? How do you balance the requirement to report the truth with the need to minimize harm?

The tension between two "right" courses of action creates ethical dilemmas that you must reason your way through then explain your reasoning to others.

Go Online for More

Tips for covering tragedies can be found at the Poynter Institute:
http://www.poynter.org/how-tos/newsgathering-storytelling/diversity-at-work/29537/tips-for-covering-tragedy/

The Dart Center has a comprehensive guide on journalism and trauma:
http://dartcenter.org/content/tragedies-journalists-6

For a discussion of journalism and loyalties, see this essay from The Digital Journalist:
http://digitaljournalist.org/issue0612/the-changing-problem-of-a-journalist-s-loyalty.html

As many as 200 people jumped to their deaths from the World Trade Center on 9/11. Most U.S. television stations avoided airing any of that footage because of its traumatic impact. See the 2006 documentary about this issue, "The Falling Man," here: http://topdocumentaryfilms.com/911-falling-man/

CHAPTER 18

Source Remorse

The Case of the Requests to "Unpublish"

Michael O'Donnell

T he palest ink is better than the best memory, an old Chinese proverb says. Certainly, a printed story lives far longer than the people mentioned in it. But should the same be true for a story on a web page, available for anyone in the world to see? Should electrons on a web server be "permanent"?

What's written about us on the lowliest of websites can follow us everywhere. When a young professional Googles herself and the top result is an embarrassing story in the college newspaper from years earlier, "source remorse" sets in. A request to take the story off the web may soon follow.

Student journalists and their advisers at the University of St. Thomas received their first request to "unpublish" in fall 2008. Though that plea seemed like an easy call at the time, subsequent unpublishing requests showed the complexities that journalists must negotiate in these situations. Because the point of this case is one woman's effort to separate herself from a newspaper story, the name of the woman making the request has been changed for this chapter.

THE SITUATION: "I'M AFRAID MY EMPLOYER WILL GOOGLE MY NAME AND SEE MY STORY"

The email from a graduate arrived two years after a story about school drinking policies had run in The Aquin, the student-operated newspaper at the University of St. Thomas in St. Paul, Minnesota. The story had appeared on the front page of the print edition and in a PDF version posted on the paper's website. Alexa Kelly, who was a senior at the time, had spoken frankly in the story about her objections to the university's new enforcement measures for dealing with people found intoxicated on campus.

FIGURE 18.1 A story about alcohol policies in The Aquin caused embarrassment to a student.

SOURCE: University of St. Thomas, Communication and Journalism Department. Used with permission.

In her email to the paper's adviser, Kelly wrote that she now worked for a suburban school district. When she entered her name in a Google search, The Aquin story always came up first in all its embarrassing detail. "If my employer sees this, it could do serious harm to me professionally," she wrote, adding that she knew the paper could do something to hide the story from search engines.

The story clearly was embarrassing to a young professional two years removed from college:

(Note: The story below ran in the print edition of The Aquin, the student newspaper at the University of St. Thomas. It also appeared online in a PDF version, shown in the figure. We present only that part of the story involving the source.)

Sobering Up to Reality

As a restricted campus, underage drinkers are not the only students affected

By Ann Nasseff, staff writer

St. Thomas students turning 21 soon will not be as free from on-campus alcohol consumption policies as they might think. Contrary to popular belief among students and even some faculty, the university is not a wet campus. It is a restricted campus, meaning that Public Safety can reprimand even individuals of the legal drinking age.

Under the conditions of a restricted campus, alcohol consumption by students of the legal drinking age is allowed, but only at certain times, in certain places and in a quantity deemed appropriate and safe by Public Safety. Regardless of a student's age, if he or she demonstrates severe intoxication or is shown to be above the legal driving limit of 0.08 percent blood alcohol content while on campus, a course of action by university officials is warranted.

Remember that Residence Life contract you signed as an incoming freshman? Although many students questioned remembered signing it, few could explain what it entailed. That contract is one of few places where the on-campus drinking policy for of-age students is explained.

William Carter III, manager of special projects administration for Public Safety, emphasized that it is not the responsibility of Public Safety to raise awareness of the policy among students and guests of the university. That accountability, he said, lies on the shoulders of Residence Life and the university's dean's office.

A few students who know of the policy do so only because they had experienced it in action firsthand. Last month, a Public Safety officer confronted senior [Alexa Kelly] after she returned to her residence hall from a night at the bars. The officer asked to see her license and, after calling for the assistance of two other officers, proceeded to give her a Breathalyzer test, she said.

"They told me that I was 'quite drunk' and I would have to go with them so they could call a parent," [Kelly] said. "I didn't want my parents to get a phone call at 2 a.m. saying they had to drive to campus to pick up their 21-year-old because she had been drinking. They then asked if any of my roommates were 21 and sober. One of them is, so they had her take a Breathalyzer test, as well. When she blew 0.00, they released me to her."

[Kelly] is one of a handful of students who have reported being stopped on campus and talked to by Public Safety officers. The action taken by a Public Safety officer under the guidelines of the policy depends on both the blood alcohol content of the individual as well as their cooperation and attitude, said Carter, who also is in charge of St. Thomas' Strategic Planning for Alcohol Prevention and Abuse program.

"In many cases the individual has more control over the outcome of the situation than they may initially think," he said.

A website created by the National Institute on Alcohol Abuse and Alcoholism includes numerous surveys taken of college students in recent years. According to a 2002 survey, approximately 5 percent

(Continued)

(Continued)

of four-year college students are "involved with the police or campus security as a result of their drinking" and close to 1,800 college students between the ages of 18 and 24 die each year from unintended alcohol-related injuries.

Ultimately, the officer uses the results of a Breathalyzer, along with his or her discretion and the student's behavior to determine the proper course of action. After being told of the university's policy on students 21 and over drinking on campus, many students find the policy too constricting.

"I think the entire situation is ridiculous," [Kelly] said. "Even if someone is 21, the policy is that they cannot be above the legal driving limit or a parent will have to be called. I guess I just don't see why it matters since I wasn't driving anywhere or doing anything wrong. I was being loud in the hallway when I was talking to my friends, but that's my personality."

SOURCE: University of St. Thomas, Communication and Journalism Department. Used with permission.

THE CHALLENGE: SMALL PAPER, BIG AUDIENCE

The Aquin distributed 2,600 copies a week to a university of more than 11,000 students on two Twin Cities campuses. The drinking story would have been seen by relatively few people had it remained print-only. But putting the PDF online made it available to anyone in the world with a web browser. Despite printing a minuscule number of copies, The Aquin was among the thousands of small newspapers that together make up a huge readership online, a "long tail" that reaches around the world.

The term "long tail" refers to statistical distributions in which the bulk of observations make up the steep part of the chart, with increasingly smaller numbers spread out in a "long tail." Chris Anderson of

Wired magazine is credited with first using the term to apply to online content, specifically music. He noted that while hit songs on major labels add up to millions of sales, millions of lesser-known songs sell a few copies each. Together, those small sellers could bring a retailer as much profit as the one big seller.

The chart shows how this business principle applies to the readership of 700 daily newspapers in the United States. A relative few make up a large part of total circulation, but many more newspapers make up the "long tail" of the chart, with combined readership rivaling that of the larger papers. And this chart does not include monthly, weekly or bi-weekly papers, nor does it include college and high school newspapers.

Larry Timbs, Douglas J. Fisher and Will Atkinson, writing in Grassroots Editor, note that smaller newspapers, and to some extent larger newspapers, once published in a state of "practical obscurity." While their archives might have been open to the public, finding an

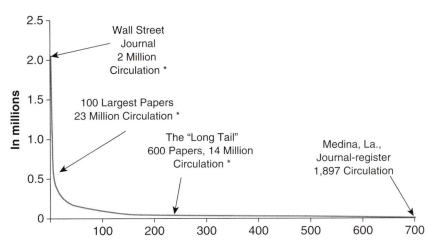

**FIGURE 18.2   U.S. Newspapers Average Daily Circulation*
for the six-month period ending 9/30/2010**

*Not including Sunday or combined Saturday editions

SOURCE: Audit Bureau of Circulations.

article "required going to the newspaper offices and likely working through a newsroom librarian or clerk."[1]

When the same archive moves online, that practical obscurity is lost. Stories posted by small dailies, weeklies, blogs, online newsletters and college newspapers, all of which make up that "long tail," are nearly as likely to turn up in a search as something from the New York Times—as Kelly, the student who had spoken out in The Aquin's drinking story, found out.

THE RESPONSE: TRYING TO DODGE THE SEARCH ENGINES

At the request of The Aquin's editors, the faculty adviser responded to Kelly's first email request by trying to return the drinking story to its practical obscurity. This meant taking steps on The Aquin's website to hide the story from search engines. Google offers online advice on how to do this but is firm in stating that it cannot alter or hide the content on any site. Susan Moskwa, a Google trends analyst, wrote in Google's Webmaster Central forum,

> If something you dislike has already been published, the next step is to try to remove it from the site where it's appearing. . . . Google doesn't own the internet; our search results simply reflect what's already out there on the web.[2]

Google provides instructions on how to block certain pages from its search engine, and others, by writing a "robots.txt" file. When a search engine robot "crawls" the web, it first checks any site for a robots.txt

---

1. Lawrence Timbs, with Doug Fisher and Will Atkinson, "How America's Community Newspapers Handle (Or Don't Handle) Their 'Digital Attics': An Investigation Into Ethical, Legal and Privacy Issues Emerging From Publications' Web Archives." Presented at the Newspapers and Community-Building Symposium XIII, National Newspaper Association Annual Convention, Norfolk, Va., Sept. 27, 2007. Appeared in *Grassroots Editor*, 48, No. 4 (Winter 2007): 11–18.

2. Susan Moskwa, "Managing Your Reputation Through Search Results," *Google Webmaster Central Blog*, googleweb mastercentral.blogspot.com/2009/10/managing-your-reputation-through-search.html.

file that sets some pages off limits. All "respectable robots" will honor the directions in this file, according to Google's Webmaster Central, with the caveat "a robots.txt is not enforceable, and some spammers and other troublemakers may ignore it."[3]

The Aquin adviser installed a robots.txt file on the newspaper's website, but it didn't block the PDF file. His next move was to add password protection to the PDF file, but that, too, did nothing to prevent a summary of the story from popping up in Google when he searched for Kelly's name, although the file itself was now impossible to open. He also requested that Google remove the PDF from its index of Uniform Resource Locators. Still, the story kept popping up in searches.

All these efforts took time, and despite the adviser's attempts to keep her up-to-date, Kelly assumed that the newspaper was stalling. Her emails grew more insistent, and she began to hint at legal action.

In the end, the adviser removed the PDF from The Aquin online archive. He reasoned that the same information would still be available in The Aquin's paper files and on its production server for anyone asking for it. In his view, the possible harm caused by leaving the story online outweighed the value of keeping it on the website. He discussed the move with The Aquin's student editor, Shane Kitzman; neither of them anticipated that this problem would pop up again.

Two developments made the decision easier: First, the university was planning to discontinue The Aquin and launch a new web-only multimedia student news organization, TommieMedia.com. Second, the university library had completed a project to digitize all editions of The Aquin, going back 76 years to the first one. This archive, located behind a university firewall, was hidden from search engines. So the PDF was removed from the newspaper's own archive, and Kelly's youthful indiscretions became Google-proof.

In September 2009, the University of St. Thomas stopped publishing The Aquin and launched TommieMedia.com. The switch to web-only publishing introduced students to the hectic world of the 24/7 news

---

3. Google Search Console Help, "Block or Remove Pages Using a Robots. Txt File," http://support.google.com/webmasters/bin/answer.py?hl=en& answer=156449&topic=1724262&ctx=topic.

cycle, a shock to those who had worked under the leisurely once-a-week pace of The Aquin. They also found themselves exposed to a much larger readership—the whole world.

TOOL FOR THOUGHT:
Clifford G. Christians on Privacy and Morality

When journalists discuss issues such as the unpublishing of potentially damaging information, they cite professional standards such as the SPJ Code of Ethics. This code and others outline behavior that is first of all concerned with protecting the credibility of news organizations and of the profession as a whole.

Codes are admirable, of course, but they concern what we do as professionals, not as human beings. Clifford G. Christians, a scholar in philosophical and social ethics at the University of Illinois, writes that relying on professional codes ignores the wider scope of "general morality," in which privacy "is not merely a legal right but a human condition or status in which humans, by virtue of their humanness, control the time, place, and circumstances of communications about themselves."[1]

This definition of privacy takes on greater importance as communication technology is transformed, making privacy "increasingly fragile and unenforceable." Thus, Christians urges journalists to consider privacy issues not within the boundaries of professional standards but in the wider realm of general morality. With this wider focus, journalists must develop new ways of thinking as they deal with sources and issues of privacy. Christian's advice follows:

Challenge the conventional wisdom. Editors and publishers often put the reputation of the news organization first and justify their decisions by citing the public's right to know or the need to maintain reader trust. "Journalism's self-interested definition of newsworthiness, rather than the common good, becomes the standard," Christians writes. A journalist can become frozen in this mindset if he or she does not consciously try to think like the audience and sources—like Christians' "reasonable public."

Ask these questions: If you're citing a professional standard to justify an action, is that standard valid in this case? Is it universally valid? Will your news organization really lose anything important by violating the standard?

Treat people as people, not titles or roles. Journalists too often view the subjects of their stories by their roles: public official, victim, criminal, source. The SPJ code asks us to minimize harm but also implies that journalists should adopt some skepticism, advising them to "test the accuracy of all sources" and to "question sources' motives before promising anonymity." Christians advises that "sensitive journalists who struggle with these issues in terms of real people put more demands on themselves" because they refuse to see things only from the news organization's point of view.

Ask these questions: Are we treating a source differently from how we would want to be treated? If I replaced the source's name in the story with my own, how would I feel? How would my mother and father feel as they read it? Are we being totally open with sources about how we will use their information?

Consider the consequences, short term and long term, of maintaining information on the internet. The internet requires us to imagine consequences of our behavior that might occur long after we're gone. When someone is suffering because information published years ago pops up in web searches, we should consider that person's situation now, not as a source who should have known better back then. We think of student journalism as sort of a practice journalism, yet student-produced stories, like any other stories, have the potential to cause lasting harm.

(Continued)

Ask these questions: What could be the long-term consequences of the story you're reporting? Should you discuss these consequences with the source before publishing? Considering those consequences, should you offer anonymity?

"The ethics of privacy is fundamentally a citizens' ethics," Christians writes, "understood and implemented by professionals as human beings first of all, not practitioners."

1. Clifford G. Christians, "The Ethics of Privacy," in *Journalism Ethics: A Philosophical Approach*, ed. Christopher Myers (Oxford, UK: Oxford University Press, 2010), 203-213.

THE AFTERMATH: MORE REQUESTS, NEW STANDARDS

After TommieMedia.com launched, its editors received two other requests to unpublish stories. Realizing the importance of planning for future requests, three TommieMedia.com advisers and four of the site's student leaders met to discuss unpublishing.

As a multimedia news outlet, TommieMedia.com had a much more complex structure than The Aquin, with its one adviser and few editors. TommieMedia.com has five faculty advisers with limited roles in helping with writing, video, studio production and technical issues, and a senior adviser with overall authority. It has one "director," the equivalent of an editor-in-chief, and three second-tier editors who oversee day-to-day operations. A structure with so many editors and advisers made it imperative to set a policy on unpublishing; otherwise, any staff person might decide to grant or refuse a request without informing the others.

In their discussion, the TommieMedia.com group used The Aquin story about drinking as an example because it represented the ethical dilemma of source remorse in all its untidiness, complicated by the special situation of student journalists. Unlike the adviser or editors at the time of Kelly's unpublish request, the 2009 TommieMedia.com student leaders had little sympathy for Kelly and her desire to have the embarrassing material removed. They were aware that the SPJ Code of Ethics (www.spj.org/ethicscode.asp) urged journalists to "minimize harm," but they reasoned that Kelly had spoken to the paper voluntarily.

Though her becoming a source set up what production editor Michael Ewen called an "unfortunate circumstance," Ewen didn't consider that a strong argument. "I don't think it's fair to go back and take her name out of the article because it's a problem for her," Ewen said. "Maybe she can address it in interviews, but I don't think it's up to us to change that."

TommieMedia.com director Katie Broadwell agreed that it's not a journalist's problem if people start regretting things they said years before. "Where do you draw the line?" she asked. But Broadwell did acknowledge that if she had read the drinking story with her name in place of Kelly's, she wouldn't have been happy.

"I'd regret talking to the person, the news organization," she said, "but at the same time I'd say, 'Well, I probably shouldn't have done that, but I'm not going to hold them responsible for me messing up.' Because it is ultimately their decision to talk or not."

They also understood that information on the internet is different. Production editor Miles Trump said that "to look up the first story ever done on TommieMedia would take five seconds, versus the first story from The Aquin. That would take . . . I don't know how you'd find that."

■ ■ TOOL FOR ACTION: Questions to Guide "Unpublishing" Decisions

Kathy English, public editor of the Toronto Star, surveyed editors at 110 newspapers in the United States and Canada in 2009, asking whether they believed their organizations should ever unpublish online articles (meaning web-only content and content published in print and online). Surprisingly, slightly more than 78 percent said yes. The editors cited inaccuracy or unfairness

(Continued)

(Continued)

as the most valid reason to unpublish (67 percent). However, none said they would unpublish because a source "rethinks what they want wider audience to know about them."[1]

English titled her report for the Associated Press Media Editors "The Long Tail of News," meaning that even a minor story is instantly available to anyone using a search engine, even if the story wasn't what the searcher was seeking. Because half the newspapers she surveyed had no policy to deal with requests to unpublish, she offered a set of questions that news organizations can ask when considering such a request. The questions can be summarized into a set of action points:

1. Establish a basic philosophy on the question of removing content from your website and create guidelines that reflect this philosophy, understanding that some "will want information to disappear because they don't like what was written about them or have changed their mind about being interviewed."

2. Make it part of your guidelines to listen and consider the potential harm to a person by continuing to publish, and weigh that against the journalistic values of transparency and trust with readers.

3. Decide what measures you can take to maintain the accuracy of published content and how you might update online content in a truthful and transparent way.

4. Consider how you will handle requests to remove comments and other reader-generated content.

5. Consider cases when you might veer from the guidelines and decide to unpublish content.

6. Explain the policy to all readers and to those individuals who

seek to have content unpublished.

7. Determine who can decide to unpublish web content and set up a decision procedure, understanding that each decision should never rest on the shoulders of one person.

8. Most important, examine carefully how you handle sources as an organization and what you publish online when you know that anyone in the world can see it.[2]

9. Read the full report here: www.apme.com/?page=Unpublishing.

---

1. Kathy English, "The Long Tail of News: To Publish or Not to Publish" (APME Online Journalism Credibility Project, 2009): http://www.apme.com/resource/resmgr/online_journalism_credibility/questions_for_your_newsroom.pdf.

2. Ibid.

As the discussion continued, TommieMedia.com leaders talked of two other requests to unpublish a story. Both of the later requests were more clear-cut than The Aquin drinking story; taken together, the three cases led the group to a number of conclusions.

Unpublish for the right reasons. Journalists considering requests to unpublish must have firm standards while remaining flexible. If that seems contradictory, it's because ethical standards are only guidelines. "I don't take our code of ethics as rules, like when you play Monopoly, no one can ever pass 'Go' without collecting $200," said Kris Bunton, TommieMedia .com's senior adviser. "The question to me is what's the guideline in these kinds of cases? What's the sort of default position? Then you figure out, OK, when do we stick to that because we think this case merits sticking to it? The general guideline would be that we publish and it stays online."

Though the group agreed with that general goal, TommieMedia.com had unpublished stories twice in its first year. Bunton said one of those stories was an easy call because it contained apparent plagiarism. A student writing for TommieMedia.com had used material without attribution from another website, and the piece was removed as soon as someone brought the plagiarism to the staff's attention.

"Web, old-fashioned newspaper, whatever—we don't steal other people's words," Bunton said. "Maybe that was a snap decision, but I just don't think you let that live on."

The other story seemed innocent enough: It concerned a charity event, and its only source was a St. Thomas graduate working for a public relations firm. After the story was posted, the source's employer contacted the reporter and said that the story was completely inaccurate, although the employer's real motivation seemed more complex, with issues of proprietary information involved.

Shane Kitzman, TommieMedia.com's incoming director at the time, said he was "shaken" when he got the request. "I thought, 'A whole story being wrong? Who's at fault here?'" The source's arguments for unpublishing the story "were simple and they were emotional," Kitzman said. "She said, 'I was completely wrong and shouldn't have done this story with TommieMedia, and now I need it to be deleted or else I will be terminated at my job.'"

Though they thought that the source's unprofessionalism was her own problem, Kitzman said he and Bunton "agreed that, under the circumstances, we were naïve enough to publish a one-source story in the first place." The story was deleted from the website.

Do the right thing before you publish. In their discussion of unpublishing, TommieMedia.com student leaders and advisers considered how the realities of the digital world might alter approaching and interviewing sources. When she talked to a reporter for the drinking story, Kelly might not have anticipated that this one story in a college newspaper would come to define her for anyone Googling her name. In her emails, Kelly sounded like someone who felt ambushed—not by the original story but by its persistent life online.

TommieMedia.com published a series of similar stories on campus drinking in October 2010. By that time, students, faculty and staff members were thoroughly familiar with TommieMedia.com as a news site available to the whole world.

Although the series quoted few students, reporters still felt the need at times to discuss where the interview would appear. Theresa Malloy, TommieMedia.com assignment editor, said she thought to warn one administrator, an assistant dean who admitted to being a "hard-core partier" in his student days.

"I said, 'You know this is going to be online,'" Malloy said. "'I'm going to represent you fairly; do you mind that I share your story?' And he said, 'No, I'd like students to know this story. I'm not sure what my boss will think, but I think it's an important message that needs to get out there, and I trust that you will represent me fairly.'"

He and his boss liked the finished story.

The Canadian Association of Journalists Ethics Advisory Committee, led by Kathy English, believes that journalists should help sources understand the implications of digital publishing. In its recommended best practices, the committee stated,

> Many who seek to have articles unpublished express surprise that the article was published online and remains available online, accessible through Google and other search engines. Print and broadcast journalists should inform sources of the implications of multi-platform publishing.[4]

Many journalists take a harder line, maintaining that most people who talk to reporters in the internet age know what they're doing and understand what publishing means. "They know it's online, they know it's going to be in an article, they know they're going to be quoted," Broadwell said. "If they can't connect the dots to that, I don't think we need to say, you know, if you're applying for a job in two years, this could show up in a search engine."

Embrace the differences of the web. The editors whom English surveyed recounted many situations where the web itself could provide remedies to common problems. For example, when a website publishes a story reporting that someone has been acquitted, links to that story should be added to any earlier stories that reported the charges against the person. That way, people who find one story through a search engine will see the acquittal as well as the original charges.

---

4. Kathy English, Tim Currie, and Rod Link, *The Ethics of Unpublishing: A Panel Report,* Canadian Association of Journalists, Ethics Advisory Committee (Oct. 27, 2010): http://www.j-source.ca/english_new/detail.php?id=5845.

FIGURE 18.3 Screenshot of TommieMedia story on discipline issues related to alcohol.

SOURCE: Theresa Malloy, TommieMedia, University of St. Thomas, Communication and Journalism Department. Used with permission.

Brad Dennison told English that GateHouse media had started a "sunset" policy pilot project in its New England Group. Most police blotter reports would be removed from the online archive six months after first publication, although the articles might not disappear from the web entirely because of search engine caches.

"How long does something minor like a shoplifting charge have to follow someone on the web?" he asked English. "My moral barometer tells me that's not fair. There's no rule that says this stuff has to live forever."[5]

---

5. English, "The Long Tail of News," 18.

Computer technology makes this sort of practice much simpler and automatic. In the digital world, journalists should shake themselves out of the linear habit and begin to think of a story as dynamic, continuing information that can be updated or linked in ways that ensure a reader gets the complete picture.

Recognize that students are different. Students make up the most important audience and an important pool of sources for TommieMedia.com. Student journalists are urged by their teachers and advisers to act professionally, but does that mean treating other students the way professional journalists treat their sources? Do college students, who are still trying out possible lives and futures, deserve a special kind of privacy? Members of the TommieMedia.com leadership group differed in their views on this question.

"We try to be professionals, so it shouldn't be different," Katie Broadwell said. "Yes, we're students, they're students. But if our true goal is to try to practice journalism in a professional environment, it's not student to student, it's professional and student."

In theory, that should be true, but Miles Trump said it wasn't always true in practice. "We look at it like we're professionals talking to people out there, but in reality, we're students talking to students," said Trump, who was TommieMedia.com sports editor in fall 2010. "Sports people I talk to, some of them are people I know [as friends]. So in reality, the relationship is different."

The new realities of digital publishing call for new sensibilities from student journalists. Someday, "student" will be what you once were. If once you were a student in a dorm who got stopped by Public Safety for drinking, and now you're a respected church member who serves with charitable organizations, are you allowed to leave your former student self behind? What if a student news site won't let your former self go away?

Thinking It Through

1. Given that one of the four main tenets of the SPJ ethics code is to minimize harm, would you have removed the story about drinking at Kelly's request? Or do you agree with the editors in

the APME survey that "source remorse" should never be a reason to unpublish a story? Do you think student media should have different standards from professional media?

2. Have you had experience with requests to unpublish stories, either as the person seeking to unpublish or from the perspective of the news organization? Do your student media organizations have a policy on how to handle such requests? How is that policy made known to student journalists and to the audience?

3. Kathy English, who wrote The Long Tail of News report on unpublishing, suggests this "script" for staffers to follow in responding to someone who's asking for a story to be removed from the web:

Thank you for writing (calling). We are guided by a newsroom policy that says it is inappropriate to remove published content from our website. If an article is inaccurate, we will correct it and tell readers it has been altered. If relevant new information emerges, we will update the article or do a follow-up story.

As with our newsprint version, our online published content is a matter of public record and is part of our contract with our readers. To simply remove published content from the archive diminishes transparency and trust with our readers and in effect, erases history. This is not a practice engaged in by credible news organizations or in line with ethical journalism.

What do you think? If you worked in a newsroom, would you feel comfortable saying those words or posting them on your site? If not, how might you revise them?

4. Most newspaper websites are shaped by the print product, with its editions and sections, and with the "first the story, then the follow-up" approach. What ways can you make sure readers get the whole story as it develops over time? How might stories be deployed on the website or archived in a way that allows long-past indiscretions to fade away? Should they fade away? What

do you think of one newspaper group's policy of having police log archives disappear from the web after a certain number of months?

What If?

You're a student reporter who covers crime for your university's student news website. In your routine check of the campus police blotter, you see this item: "Officers answered a disturbance call at Wingnut Hall. Joe Smith, a student, was cited for being intoxicated on campus property." Do you post this item to the site? If the site does routinely publish police log items, what's the reason? What purpose does the police log serve? What rules does a media organization need in order to ensure that the police log is handled fairly?

Several tabloids and websites, including websites of law enforcement agencies, publish mugshots of those who have been arrested and charged with, but not necessarily convicted of, crimes. Would you publish those on your news site? Why or why not?

The web offers several advantages over print that allow us to be more specific in identifying people. If several Joe Smiths attend your school, how might you use the power of the web to clearly identify the particular Joe Smith in your article? Do ethics require you to do this, or can you just write "Joe Smith" and let people draw their own conclusions?

In Kathy English's study, one common complaint was that news organizations publish or broadcast stories about arrests but then never do follow-up stories to explain what happened to the charges. If you were in charge of proposing policies for a student news organization, what policy would you recommend regarding use of the names of suspects? Or about following up on charges that were reported?

What might Clifford Christians say about identifying Joe Smith in a published police log item, mistakenly or otherwise, in your news stories? Christians urges us to consider our actions not as professional journalists, but as members of a wider community applying the tenets of general morality. Rethink your news organization's policies in light of his recommendations.

Go Online for More

Kathy English and a group of fellow Canadian journalists have developed a set of best practices for handling requests to unpublish—and for preventing them in the first place. Here is her report:
http://www.j-source.ca/english_new/detail.php?id=5845

Doug Fisher provides a summary of studies and articles related to unpublishing in his blog "Common Sense Journalism":
http://commonsensej.blogspot.com/2010/01/unpublishing-growing-
    challenge-for.html

Many newspapers are wrestling with these same questions, including The Washington Post:
http://www.washingtonpost.com/wp-dyn/content/article/2010/08/06/
    AR2010080604341.html

The Poynter Institute for Media Studies offers a webinar on the subject that is available for a fee:
http://www.newsu.org/unpublishing-online-content-credibility

CHAPTER 19

Friend of the Victim

The Case of the Murdered Student

Lois A. Boynton

Adam Rhew

B efore dawn on a March morning, a body was found lying in the street in a university town. The young woman, it turned out, was the university's student body president, and she had been shot. Media descended upon the town to cover this apparently random act of violence. Also covering the tragedy were student journalists, including at least one who knew the victim.

It's difficult to cover any murder, with constant deadlines, devastated friends and family, and ever-changing information from sources that may or may not be reliable. In this case, the novice reporter faced the additional challenge of balancing his dual roles as professional journalist and caring friend.

THE SITUATION: STUDENT BODY PRESIDENT FOUND MURDERED

It was early spring 2008 in Chapel Hill, and students at the University of North Carolina were facing midterms and longing for spring break. Right before the vacation began, news broke that a young woman had been brutally murdered a half-mile from campus. Initial reports said authorities had not yet identified the young woman.

Then, the day after the murder, police identified her as 22-year-old Eve Carson, a senior and the university's student body president. The town and campus communities were in shock.

For Adam Rhew, a senior broadcast journalism major who also worked part-time as a reporter for community radio station WCHL, the murder carried not just news impact but personal impact. He knew Carson from his work covering student government for the journalism school's television station; he had come to consider her a friend. Like others in the community, Rhew realized that Carson's death was an important story that needed careful attention. But given his friendship with the victim, should he cover the story as a reporter?

Rhew quickly decided the answer was yes. "I thought I could bring an interesting context to the story as a fellow student and one of Eve's friends, despite realizing that a conflict of interest could arise," he said. "Eve and I were friends because of our working relationship, not in spite of it." As a reporter for "Carolina Week," a student-produced television news program through the School of Journalism and Mass Communication, Rhew covered stories about student government, which included considerable contact with its leadership.

"It's something akin to a governor becoming friendly with the press corps assigned to cover him," he explained. "If the governor were killed, the state press corps would cover his death, even if they had become friendly. That's the way I looked at this situation."

Rhew decided he would proceed with covering the grisly murder. "I came at it from the perspective of a reporter covering the death of a public figure," he said.

The Challenge: Handling Emotion, Getting It Right

Once he decided to tackle the story, Rhew realized he would have to balance the emotions of losing a friend with his responsibility to remain objective. "There was a lot of raw, visceral emotion that I had to process, but at the same time, I had to process details, sound bites and deadlines," he said. "My job was to make sure the emotional trauma did not affect my work." While some people might think objectivity means not having emotions, Rhew knew that type of robotic response is neither possible nor desirable. "I think a good reporter can recognize what he's emotional about—and also can recognize when that emotion is affecting his work."

Emotion turned out to be just the start of the challenges the coverage posed. Murder was not regular fare for reporters in Chapel Hill, and soon they were immersed in the constant judgment calls that come with any big, developing story. WCHL, the radio station where Rhew worked, was the first media outlet to identify the victim as Carson, thanks to information received from a law enforcement source. "We would have been screwed had the information been wrong," he said. "Thankfully, our reporter was confident in the source relationship he had."

Rhew himself chose to report several details about the case based solely on law enforcement sources whose names he could not release. Because he had cultivated relationships with these sources through his work at WCHL and "Carolina Week," he felt confident the information they were giving him was accurate. Making a decision to use an unnamed source isn't something Rhew or his supervisors took lightly. News organizations' policies require verifying information from any source, particularly those who do not want to be identified. Exceptions to this rule are rare.

In this instance, the impact of the information and the established relationship between reporter and source led to the decision to report it. "I thought it was important to get the facts out there, and I was confident in the information," Rhew said. "But if my sources were wrong, I would be responsible. It was a risk I was willing to take because I trusted my sources implicitly."

As the investigation into the murder progressed, news unfolded quickly; information that reliable sources considered true one day sometimes proved wrong the next. For example, initial reports from police indicated that Carson had been carjacked, but officials later discovered that she had been taken from her home. Reporters all wanted to get information to the public as quickly as possible; unfortunately, not all of them were careful about verifying what they heard.

"There was a lot of speculation surrounding the case," Rhew said. "I had to constantly correct people who were making astounding assumptions about the case based on things they had heard from different people. As a reporter, it was my job to separate fact from gossip, assumption and innuendo—not only on the air but in my personal conversations, too."

Rhew also faced the challenge of his first hands-on experience with the 24-hour news cycle. As a student journalist and a reporter for a small radio station, he often had only minutes to check facts, confirm sources and write a story. The coverage became "an organic beast," he said. "Facts were changing; sources were skittish; and more often than not, I had to go live on the air without a written script. It was daunting."

The Response: "I Stood My Ground"

In addition to gathering reports about the murder from police and university authorities, Rhew also was among the thousands to attend a campus candlelight vigil in memory of Carson, held the day her identity was discovered. Students, faculty and individuals from throughout the area descended upon The Pit, a heart-of-the-campus student gathering place. The highly emotional event was also attended by an onslaught of local and national media. Helicopters flew overhead as cameras and recording devices captured the tributes and tears of the evening.

Rhew tried to balance people's need to grieve with his need to capture the scene for the audience listening live on the radio. He spoke softly into his microphone, crouched low to the ground and stood several feet away from the assembled crowd, attempting to paint a verbal picture of the vigil. The event was emotional and, at times, Rhew struggled to maintain his composure on the air. He believes he was simultaneously respectful of the mourners and effective for his listeners.

But not everyone appreciated the media coverage; some people lashed out at reporters, including Rhew.

While he was on the air during the candlelight vigil, "I had a woman tell me to 'get off the [expletive] phone and leave these students alone,'" Rhew said. "She tried to have the cops kick me off campus. But I stood my ground. The law clearly was on my side. But, more importantly, I still think I had a moral duty to be there, even though I know the media were not a popular presence at the vigil."

By "moral duty," Rhew meant that beyond his right to be physically present in a public setting, he saw covering the vigil as an important public service for the thousands of people who couldn't be there and thus were watching or listening from home. He believed that providing access to the vigil to the wider community far outweighed the occasional negative reaction to his presence at the event. And, by knowing his rights, he was able to provide that service. "Had I not stood my ground—or known my rights as a journalist—the situation could have had a completely different ending." Specifically, Rhew might have been persuaded to leave the event and not cover the story.

As the case became national news and journalists from around the country arrived in Chapel Hill, Rhew faced a new question: Should he be interviewed by other reporters? And, if so, interviewed as what—a journalist covering the case or a friend of Carson's? Or both? Journalists were seeking students, faculty and friends of the victim to speak about their feelings and reactions. Rhew was approached by Fox News, CNN and CBS, among others. Agreeing to do a few interviews, he soon learned it's not easy trying to be both a source and a journalist.

TOOL FOR THOUGHT:
The Philosophies of W. D. Ross and Sissela Bok

In thinking about the issues Rhew faced in covering the murder of someone he knew, two philosophical constructs come to mind: the competing duties defined by Scottish

(Continued)

(Continued)

philosopher William D. Ross, and the need to balance empathy and social trust as described by ethicist Sissela Bok.

Rhew faced competing duties and competing values: He was a friend of the victim, a source for other reporters and an on-air journalist. He needed to keep the community informed of a terrible crime while also respecting the feelings and sensitivities of those around him. His situation reflected elements of the philosophy presented by Ross,[1] who believed that many ethical challenges result from competing duties, two or more viable options that cannot be acted upon at the same time. What Ross called the "duty proper" in one situation may not carry the same weight in another situation.

For example, when Rhew covered the candlelight vigil, he had a duty to maintain his professionalism as a journalist and report the facts of the event (fidelity) while dealing with the sensitive nature of the case and the high levels of emotion at the event (not injuring others). In this situation, he reasoned that the benefit of serving the public interest outweighed some media intrusion; thus, his duty proper became sharing the information about the vigil.

In weighing his duties, Rhew was making the kind of decision that Bok[2] examines in her ethical decision-making model. Although he did not do it consciously, he followed a pattern in which he balanced his empathy for the grieving community with the social trust found in journalistic integrity. That is, reporters must maintain the obligation to "seek truth and report it," as stated in the Society of Professional Journalists Code of Ethics,[3] but also must understand how situations affect individuals involved in their stories.

Bok's approach involves three steps: (1) consult your conscience; (2) seek expert advice and identify alternatives; and (3) conduct a public discussion, as is feasible. Perhaps you could see Bok's approach at work when Rhew consulted his conscience as he tried to determine whether to cover the story at all. He realized there were potential conflicts between his roles as reporter and friend, a dilemma that many of his peers did not have to address. He "checked in" with himself about the rightness of covering the tragedy. He had responsibilities to his employer to cover the story accurately and as objectively as possible, but he also had obligations associated with his friendship with the victim.

His next step, according to Bok, would be to consult experts, people he trusted to provide him with sound advice. In this instance, Rhew consulted his supervisors at WCHL, a professor in the School of Journalism and Mass Communication, and his father, an experienced television reporter. They provided valuable insight as well as an emotional sounding board. Another "expert" is the standards of practice, or ethics code, for journalism. As a broadcast journalist, Rhew consulted the Radio Television Digital News Association Code of Ethics, which states that reporters should "continuously seek the truth"; "treat all subjects of news coverage with respect and dignity"; and be "accountable for their actions to the public, the profession, and themselves."[4]

You could also see how Rhew considered various options. One was not to present himself as either a reporter or a friend, but as both— someone who could offer a unique perspective in a highly emotional case. Though this seemed to make sense in theory, he later found it was difficult in practice.

Bok's third step is to conduct a public discussion, if feasible. Even in the social media age, it's not usually feasible—and many journalists would say it's not desirable—for a reporter to ask the audience's views on whether or not to cover a story. But Rhew did contemplate the views of others as he moved forward, which Bok advises in such instances. He considered whether others might perceive him as having a conflict of

(Continued)

(Continued)

interest, even if he didn't think so himself. He considered the importance the community placed on learning about Carson as a person, not as a murder victim.

Armed with data from his own conscience, his superiors and the community, Rhew made informed decisions about whether and how to cover this complex and highly emotional story.

1. William D. Ross, *The Right and the Good* (Indianapolis, IN: Hackett, 1988).

2. Sissela Bok, *Lying: Moral Choice in Public and Private Life* (New York, NY: Random House, 1978).

3. "Society of Professional Journalists Code of Ethics (1996)," http://www.spj.org/ethicscode.asp.

4. "Radio Television Digital News Association Code of Ethics and Professional Conduct" (2000), http://www.rtdna.org/pages/media_items/code-of-ethics-and-professional-conduct48.php.

THE AFTERMATH: REFLECTING ON DUAL ROLES

Rhew was a student journalist and novice freelancer when he confronted multiple hard choices and competing loyalties in covering Carson's murder. This case remains the most ethically compelling situation he has faced in his young career. He's proud of how he behaved and the work he did, and there are also a few things he'd do differently if put in the same situation today.

First, Rhew believes he made the right decision to cover the story of his friend's murder, despite the conflicts that subsequently arose. He took the time to weigh competing duties as friend and journalist, and he understood the importance of keeping his emotions under control. However, he did come to realize that the 24/7 pressure of the news business makes it extremely difficult to separate work from emotions. Looking back, he can see how the intense pace during the first days after the murder took its toll.

"A little decompression time probably would have done me some good in those first 72 hours," he said. "Instead, I was on the clock—and on the air—for a significant chunk of time." Today, he would try to find some breathing room—even if just for a moment—to be alone with his thoughts. Reporters must recognize that they, too, are human and require time to process emotional trauma.

Second, Rhew recognized the importance of using his journalistic training to guide him in decision making. For example, it was crucial that he understood both his rights and his duties as a journalist when facing criticism of his coverage of the candlelight vigil. He also understood the importance of checking facts and verifying what sources told him. Although he did report some information without revealing his source, he sees the practice as a rare exception to be made only when he's sure of the source and no other means of obtaining the information is possible.

Third, he recognizes that working in journalism is a lifetime learning process. Decisions made in the moment, even if carefully considered, might not apply to future situations or hold up perfectly in retrospect. For example, in hindsight, Rhew thinks he probably should have declined all interviews with national media outlets. He tried to be selective about which reporters he spoke to, and he turned down a network TV show when the producers pushed for him to make statements about security at the university. "I got frustrated," he said. "I told them my opinion didn't matter; I deal in facts. The producer kindly told me they weren't interested in talking to me on their show after that."

Although he is glad he didn't risk losing his journalistic credibility by spouting opinions on TV, he now wishes he had not served as a source for other reporters at all. "My one regret about the whole situation is that I decided to do interviews with the national media as a reporter who also was a friend of Eve's," Rhew said. "My rationale was that interviewing me meant they'd leave some of her closer friends alone." Now he believes a better idea would have been to speak to the national press only as a journalist—"in other words as 'WCHL Reporter Adam Rhew, covering the tragedy,' rather than 'Adam Rhew, a student who knew Eve Carson.'"

Still, dealing with reporters as a source did help Rhew appreciate how stressful that position can be. In his career as a broadcast journalist, he continues to face ethical dilemmas of varying intensities, and building on his experiences during college helps ensure that he does his job as ethically as possible.

One week after Eve Carson's body was found, a video of someone using her ATM card led to the arrest of a 21-year-old Durham resident. He and a 17-year-old accomplice were sentenced to life in prison. The University of North Carolina now awards the Eve Carson Scholarship to a junior who has "exhibited passion and transformative growth." Establishing a student-run merit scholarship had been one of the changes Carson advocated while running for student body president.

Thinking It Through

1. Television news and talk shows frequently interview reporters as experts on various topics, including foreign policy, health care issues and even crime. What do you think about this practice? Would you feel comfortable appearing on a show talking about a story you wrote on a beat you continue to cover? Would it be OK to state opinions on the show that had not been reflected in your reporting?

2. Is it appropriate for a reporter to have his or her own blog? If so, what guidelines or limitations would you institute if you ran a news organization? Can a reporter write different sorts of things on a personal blog than on a blog hosted on his or her employer's site? Does it matter whether the two blogs are linked? Is it OK for a reporter to do a "guest post" on someone else's blog and reveal opinions about stories and people on the reporter's beat?

3. Do you think news consumers understand the nature of breaking news and the way information from reliable sources can change? In the online, deadline-a-minute news environment, where anyone with a smartphone can tweet any kind of unverified information from a news scene, what is the role of the trained journalist? Do audiences make a distinction between citizen tweets and

information presented by a journalist? As a media professional, how can you help the audience understand the nature of news and judge the reliability of information?

4. Do you believe that objectivity in reporting is attainable? Is it desirable? What aspects of objectivity are most relevant? Can a reporter be neutral? Independent? Unemotional? What does a balanced story entail? If you do not believe objectivity is attainable, what do you consider a valid alternative goal?

What If?

In all breaking news situations—crimes, emergencies and disasters— information changes fast and hard facts are difficult to identify. The new prevalence of citizen journalists and the wide variety of words and visuals available online can make the challenges even tougher. If "everyone" is reporting something but official sources refuse to confirm it, what do you do?

If you were a reporter covering Eve Carson's murder and you heard from a student that Carson knew one of the men charged with attacking her, would you report that information? What if the source was a campus police officer? Let's take it a bit further—what if 10 different people from different parts of town were reporting this information on Twitter? What if you ask the police about this information and they tell you it's not true? What if you get this information from someone you trust, but the authorities will not confirm it? What if that individual doesn't want to be identified? Before you promise someone confidentiality, what steps might you want to take?

When reasoning through your decision, consider the advice of the RTDNA Code of Ethics, which states,

> Identify sources whenever possible. Confidential sources should be used only when it is clearly in the public interest to gather or convey important information or when a person providing information might be harmed. Journalists should keep all commitments to protect a confidential source.[1]

---

1. Ibid.

Consider another situation: A vital component of television reporting is the visual impact. One document that was available as a public record was Carson's autopsy report, which included a graphic illustration of her wounds. If you were a broadcast reporter, would you have wanted your station to show this document on TV? Should the autopsy report be posted on the website of any news organization? How about the illustration? Suppose that someone who lives near the intersection where the body was found approaches you with a photo he took with a telephoto lens of the crime scene, which shows the foot of the victim while the rest of her body is covered with a cloth. Would you air or publish that photo? Would your answer be different if the photo had been taken by a professional photojournalist? Who are the stakeholders in this decision, the people you'll want to consider as you debate what to do?

The National Press Photographers Association offers this advice about sensitive photos: "Treat all subjects with respect and dignity. Give special consideration to vulnerable subjects and compassion to victims of crime or tragedy. Intrude on private moments of grief only when the public has an overriding and justifiable need to see."[2] In addition, RTDNA provides Guidelines for Breaking News Events[3] that may help you decide what information is important and how to proceed.

Go Online for More

To read more about the case, see the following:

"Vigils for Slain UNC Student Body President Draw Thousands," posted on WRAL-TV on March 6, 2008: http://www.wral.com/news/local/story/2534527/

---

2. National Press Photographers Association Code of Ethics (n.d.), http://www.nppa.org/professional_development/business_practices/ethics.html.

3. "Guidelines for Breaking News Events" (n.d.), Radio Television Digital News Association, http://www.rtdna.org/pages/media_items/guidelines-for-breaking-news-events400.php?id=400.

UNC-Chapel Hill site to honor Eve Carson:
http://universityrelations.unc.edu/alert/carson/

Carolina Week Special Report: "Remembering Eve":
http://www.carolinaweek.org/carolina_week_special_reports/carolina_
    week_special_remembering_eve.html

Photos of those remembering Eve:
http://www.wral.com/news/local/image_gallery/2536400/

Criminal Justice Journalists, "Covering Crime and Justice:
A Guide for Journalists":
http://www.justicejournalism.org/crimeguide/

CHAPTER 20

When Ethical Compasses Collide

The Case of Following One's Conscience

Kathy K. Previs

Have you ever been put into a situation where you disagreed with your boss on a fundamental issue? On the one hand, you want to stay true to your conscience; on the other hand, you want to be a team player and not ruffle any feathers in the workplace. Indeed, one of the most difficult ethical problems a public relations practitioner can face is having to make a decision between serving the public while remaining loyal to the organization that signs his or her paycheck. This case study provides an example of such a conflict and provides several possible solutions based on the Public Relations Society of America (PRSA) Statement of Professional Values and well as other public relations industry codes of ethics.

THE SITUATION: FACILITATING COMMUNICATION WITH THE PUBLIC

John (we're using his first name only) worked for a public relations consulting firm (we'll call it "Energy Public Relations" or

EPR) that specialized in the development and facilitation of community advisory panels (CAPs). These panels operate like focus groups in which citizens of a community agree to meet with city or county managers on matters that affect citizens' daily lives. Such CAPs are quite common in towns that have chemical, coal, oil, nuclear, petroleum or other energy industries that create concern due to environmental issues such as pollution and hazardous waste products. Regardless of the industry, the goal of a CAP is to build mutual respect and trust between organizations and community members. Thus, the makeup of these panels should involve key audiences and should reflect the diverse opinions held within the community.

EPR, a small, family-owned firm in a mountainous region of the eastern United States, employed approximately one dozen employees. It represented clients in a variety of energy-related fields, including electric power plants as well as chemical, coal and oil companies. John and his team put together groups of stakeholders in the community and facilitated meetings between the local companies and these stakeholders. In keeping with the purpose of CAPs, the goal was to develop an ongoing understanding of the energy industry through transparency with the object of building trust to minimize conflicts and be able to reach a compromise on any issue that might arise. Therefore, John said, one of the most important aspects of his and his group's work was to stay as neutral as possible. "For me, this was not difficult," he said. "I had been trained as a journalist, had taken ethics courses, and knew how to be as neutral as possible in most settings."

Despite each of these companies being in competition with one another, the goal of EPR was to serve the community. For John, representing each company was not a problem given his ability to remain neutral. For him and "Jane," his coworker, however, keeping neutral became difficult when they arrived at work one day and noticed that "Jackie," the owner of EPR, had placed a bumper sticker on the company car that he and Jane were expected to drive while meeting CAPs in the community. The bumper sticker promoted a nonprofit organization that advocated the coal industry. For the purposes of this paper, we will call it "Coal Advocacy Group" (CAG).

The Challenge: Maintaining Neutrality

John and Jane, who was also trained as a journalist, expressed their discomfort to Jackie, who did not live in any of the communities that John and Jane served. Jackie lived in a coastal resort/vacation town in the Southern region of the United States. Sometimes, public relations practitioners work for people who are not familiar with, or who do not fully understand, all of the nuances associated with bumper stickers and other advertisements or symbols that endorse certain organizations. Such promotional material can be polarizing in a geographic area, and in many instances, owners of PR agencies are not privy to the tensions within the communities. So, how did this create an ethical dilemma for John and Jane?

The challenge, of course, was deciding whose moral compass to use to determine what was right and wrong. Jackie's moral compass pointed in the direction of a client that was paying her to represent her company. On the other hand, she was asking John and Jane to drive a vehicle that touted an organization that may be in opposition to the clients John and Jane served. Driving a car with a CAG bumper sticker would give the appearance of John and Jane being biased toward the coal industry, and possibly against the interests of the many CAPs they devised and facilitated and to whom they promised to remain neutral. However, the pair also wanted to remain loyal to their employer who signed their paychecks.

As communications professionals, when we find ourselves in such dilemmas, codes of ethics can often guide our behaviors and decision-making processes. Public relations cases can require even more guidance because of the bad reputation of practitioners dating back to the early days of the profession. During the Industrial Revolution, when public relations experienced its biggest growth as a profession, big businesses disregarded the interests of workers and consumers, and the media "muckrakers" exposed the corrupt practices of these businesses. In response, businesses began to hire communications experts (some of whom were former journalists) to counter the negative stories. This marked the beginning of press agentry (also called publicity): any form of public relations that involved sending material from the press agent to the media with little opportunity for interaction and feedback. However, it often involved conduct that would nowadays be considered deceptive, and thus unethical. Still today, many people believe (falsely) that public relations practitioners are paid to disguise the truth, or to act as "spin doctors," to turn a tale that makes an organization look good in the public arena. For these reasons, it is imperative that public relations practitioners consult codes of ethics, so they can adhere to the integrity of the profession and remain loyal to the publics they vow to serve.

TOOL FOR THOUGHT: The PRSA Member Statement of Professional Values

The Public Relations Society of America, founded in 1948, established its own code of ethics in 1954 to improve the industry's image by pledging to "conduct ourselves professionally, with truth, accuracy, fairness, and responsibility to the public."[1] Using this case study as an example, let us examine the PRSA's ethics code, specifically the PRSA Member Statement of Professional Values in the Code of Ethics. In so doing, we find there are several values that John and Jane could apply to this case.

1. **Advocacy:** "We serve the public interest by acting as responsible advocates for those we represent. We provide a voice in the marketplace of ideas, facts, and viewpoints to aid informed public debate." Here, John and Jane were faced with the challenge of what to advocate: their boss' client with the bumper sticker (CAG), or the public that John and Jane promised to serve (CAPs).

2. **Honesty:** "We adhere to the highest standards of accuracy and truth in advancing the interests of those we represent

(Continued)

(Continued)

and in communicating with the public." Because of their primary responsibility to the CAPs, John and Jane felt compelled to advance the interests of those they represented.

3. **Expertise:** "We acquire and responsibly use specialized knowledge and experience. We advance the profession through continued professional development, research, and education. We build mutual understanding, credibility, and relationships among a wide array of institutions and audiences." Like No. 2 above, as creators and facilitators of the CAPs, John and Jane's job was to build relationships among the diverse energy groups, not favor one over the other.

4. **Independence:** "We provide objective counsel to those we represent. We are accountable for our actions." John and Jane represented a variety of energy companies and CAPs; not one. To have been seen driving a vehicle with a bumper sticker promoting one industry over another would have meant they were not being objective.

5. **Loyalty:** "We are faithful to those we represent, while honoring our obligation to serve the public interest." Here, John and Jane served the public by remaining neutral. In addition, the public in this situation is the communities (CAPs) they serve.

6. **Fairness:** "We deal fairly with clients, employers, competitors, peers, vendors, the media, and the general public. We respect all opinions and support the right of free expression." While the bumper sticker on Jackie's car would

have been a symbol of her free expression, it was not for John or Jane. John and Jane believed that they were fairly dealing with the energy companies and the general public by remaining neutral.

1. Public Relations Society of America (PRSA), "PRSA Code of Ethics," https://www.prsa.org/AboutPRSA/Ethics/CodeEnglish/index.html#.ViaRDn6rSt8

THE RESPONSE: CONSULTING CODES OF ETHICS

John and Jane asked for a meeting with Jackie to discuss the matter, which was granted. At the meeting, Jane explained that she did not feel she could properly act as a neutral party who could listen to the public's point of view if she drove to community meetings in a car with a bumper sticker that supported an entity with whom the stakeholders may be in conflict. John supported Jane. John recalls what he said in the meeting. "I said that I felt the bumper sticker worked against the assurances we had given the stakeholders that, while paid by the companies, we pledged to maintain as neutral an attitude as possible as facilitators. How could we appear neutral when visibly supporting one side?"

In the 2015 PRSA Code of Ethics, under the "PRSA Code Provisions," core principles are listed that guide ethical dilemmas. Specific to the case at hand, consider the "Conflicts of Interest":

> Core principles avoiding real, potential or perceived conflicts of interest build the trust of clients, employers and the publics.
>
> **Intent:** To earn trust and mutual respect with clients or employers.
>
> To build trust with the public by avoiding or ending situations that put one's personal or professional interests in conflict with society's interests.
>
> **Guidelines:** A member shall:
>
> Act in the best interests of the client or employer, even subordinating the member's personal interests.

> Avoid actions and circumstances that may appear to compromise good business judgment or create a conflict between personal and professional interests.
>
> Disclose promptly any existing or potential conflict of interest to affected clients or organizations.
>
> Encourage clients and customers to determine if a conflict exists after notifying all affected parties.

John and Jane sought to earn trust with clients, to build trust with the public by avoiding conflict, to act in the best interest of client and employer, and to promptly notify Jackie that they believed a conflict existed between the affected organizations.

In his quest to remain neutral, John also recalled other codes of ethics he had seen. "At the time I was a member of the International Association of Public Participation (IAP2), whose code of ethics 'guides the actions of those who advocate including all affected parties in the public decision-making process.' The code goes on to define stakeholders as 'any individual, group of individuals, organizations, or political entity with a stake in the outcome of a decision.' Moreover, the code defines the public as 'those stakeholders who are not part of the decision-making entity or entities.'" IAP2's code of ethics stresses, "We will undertake and encourage actions that build trust and credibility for the process among all participants. . . .We will carefully consider and accurately portray the public's role in the decision-making process. . . . We will advocate for the public participation process and will not advocate for interest, party, or project outcome."[1] Thus, for John, the ethical decision was clear.

After listening to John and Jane for a brief time, Jackie cut the conversation short and in no uncertain terms outlined her case stating, "As long as they're the client and paying the bills, we'll side with CAG." But from the standpoint of John and Jane, Jackie was not as involved in the community as they were on a daily basis and did not have a solid understanding or appreciation of their dilemma. John explained, "As someone who lived remotely from the conflicts in the energy community and instead among wealthy business owners, her compass tended to point

---

1. International Association of Public Participation (IAP2), "IAP2 Code of Ethics," http://www.iap2.org/?page=8.

toward the opinions and interests of those sustaining her company." Jackie had heard John and Jane's pleas to remove the bumper sticker and remain neutral but to no avail.

John and Jane recognized the fact that Jackie, as owner of EPR, could do what she pleased with the company vehicle. They also realized the discussion had ended shortly after it began, and Jackie was not willing to compromise on the issue. "Jane and I both said we believed the company was portraying itself in a poor light by visibly supporting one side, and we feared it might eventually have consequences with the groups for which we worked," John explained.

■ ■ TOOL FOR ACTION:
Considering Your Options

Given that Jackie was unwilling to compromise, what options did John and Jane have in solving their ethical dilemma? When you are asked to do something by your employer that you do not believe is ethical, what course of action do you have? Using the case study at hand, let us discuss the different ways John and Jane could have handled the problem.

1. **Educate your organization.** John and Jane could have taken copies of the codes of ethics from PRSA and IAP2 to Jackie and explained why they believed driving the company car with a polarizing bumper sticker

was in direct conflict with the codes of ethics. In this situation, they would need to be prepared to accept that Jackie could respond by saying she was upholding her code of ethics in remaining true to the client who was paying her to represent CAG.

2. **Refuse to do the task.** John and Jane could have refused to be involved in all of the energy industries that opposed the *one* advertised with the bumper sticker— the coal industry—and pledged *only* to represent the coal industry. However,

(Continued)

(Continued)

this was in opposition with their conscience because it would mean not representing the CAPs they worked hard to create and serve. Thus, this would not have been an option in this particular case. On the other hand, John and Jane might have refused to drive any company vehicle on which a bumper sticker promoting any of the industries was affixed. In other words, they could keep their jobs the way they were and refuse to drive the company car.

3. **Ask to be given another task**. In this scenario, John and Jane could have asked to be removed from the energy industry CAPs altogether. However, if this were the lion's share of the firm's payroll, John and Jane might not have had another task on which they could have worked, forcing them to choose between one of the other three options.

4. **Take the assignment**. A final option for John and Jane would be to take the assignment and accept the consequences attached to doing so, such as offending one energy company over another. Keep in mind that accepting the assignment does not necessarily mean "say nothing." One might take the assignment after voicing opposition to the supervisor. If the supervisor still refuses, then the employee would still need to decide which actions to take.

THE AFTERMATH: COMPROMISES MAY BE MADE

Can you guess which of the four decisions John and Jane made? It was actually a combination of Nos. 2 and 4 above. Refusing to drive the company car with the CAG bumper sticker, John and Jane kept the assignment and continued to work for Jackie. "I did not drive it to meetings I facilitated for my clients in the other energy industries,"

John said. "I drove my personal car or a rental car instead." As it sometimes happens in the communication industry where there are gray areas in matters of ethics, compromises can be made where the employee can reach an agreement with the employer. John and Jane were able to find a solution that did not contradict their value system.

Aristotle believed ethical behavior is a result of achieving a balance between two extremes of beliefs or behaviors. However, this does not mean that a compromise can or must be made in every case. Regardless of the ethical dilemma, public relations practitioners must always be truthful. If a compromise between serving the public's interests and serving the client who employs you can be made that is based on truth, the practitioner is serving her or his profession. According to the PRSA Code of Ethics, serving the profession by being truthful should always be the clear choice above serving the employer or self in situations that involve not being truthful.

Thinking It Through

Would you have handled the situation differently than John and Jane? Based on the PRSA and IAP2 Codes of Ethics, why or why not?

1. Pretend you are an ombudsman, a neutral party hired to negotiate an agreement between Jackie and her employees. How could you defend the actions Jackie took, or could you? Why or why not?

2. Can you think of a situation where you would be willing to compromise your personal beliefs to satisfy the requests of a client or the public? Be specific. Does your scenario conflict with the codes of ethics discussed above? If so, how?

3. Would you have handled the case differently if John or Jane had personally opposed the CAG bumper sticker for political reasons, or do you think their involvement with the CAPs should have been the only force behind John and Jane's opposition to the bumper sticker?

What If?

1. What if Jackie had asked John or Jane to place a bumper sticker on their own personal vehicle and they refused? Would their ethical dilemma have been different? (Hint: Revisit the PRSA core principles above.)

2. What if we were to apply this case to the Bok Model for Ethical Decision Making? Do you think the outcome would have been different? How specifically would you say John and Jane should consult their conscience, consider alternatives, and take the point of view of all parties involved, including Jackie's?

3. In terms of "educating the organization," what if John and Jane were to have done some research, found a similar ethics case, and brought it to Jackie's attention in hopes she would change her mind? Can you find such a case based on a quick internet search that deals with a public relations practitioner who opposes her or his supervisor on an ethical matter?

Go Online for More

Many resources are available online at the Public Relations Society of America (PRSA) website, https://www.prsa.org/index.html. In the search box, type "ethics" and you will have access to articles pertaining to ethics research, commentary on ethics, professional opinions and a variety of ethics cases from which students and practitioners alike can learn valuable lessons.

For a brief account of why public relations practitioners have a poor reputation when it comes to ethics, read "Public Relations & Ethics: Why the Bad Reputation?" http://www.ereleases.com/prfuel/public-relations-ethics-bad-reputation/

The following study examines how leadership and internal communication plays a role in making ethical decisions and in building an ethical organizational culture. "Exploring the Role of the Dominant Coalition in Creating an Ethical Culture for Internal Stakeholders" by Shannon A.

Bowen. Public Relations Journal, Vol. 9, No. 1 (Spring 2015). http://www.prsa.org/intelligence/prjournal/documents/2015v09n01bowen.pdf

For more on ethical principles for PR practitioners, read "Out of the Red-Light District: Five Principles for Ethically Proactive Public Relations" by Sherry Baker and David Martinson. The authors suggest a TARES Test. TARES is an acronym for five action-guiding principles: Truthfulness, Authenticity, Respect, Equity, and Social Responsibility. Public Relations Quarterly, Fall 2002, Vol. 47, Issue 3, p. 15. http://connection.ebscohost.com/c/articles/7514920/out-red-light-district-five-principles-ethically-proactive-public-relations

Consider the 2006 movie "Thank You for Smoking," based on the 1994 satirical novel by Christopher Buckley. If you haven't seen it, do so, as some very interesting ethical questions arise for the film's leading character, Nick Naylor, a lobbyist for a cigarette manufacturer who is constantly torn between remaining true to his profession and being a good role model to his 12-year-old son. He is loyal to his company, but his conscience tells him cigarette smoking can and does harm millions. For more information about the movie: http://www.imdb.com/title/tt0427944/ or the book: http://www.amazon.com/Thank-You-Smoking-A-Novel/dp/0812976525.

CHAPTER 21

You Sent Me What?!

The Case of Sexual Harassment at an Internship

Kelly Scott Raisley

Internships in the "real world" make college lectures and assignments come to life. Third-year public relations students Breanne Jackson and Sydney Hulse were eager to put their new PR skills to use at their internships with a sports team during spring semester 2015. The two students from Colorado were excited to gain experience and network to kick-start their careers. Both were taken by surprise when their experiences taught them more about workplace harassment than crafting press releases and planning promotional activities.

THE SITUATION: QUESTIONABLE REQUESTS FROM A SUPERVISOR

Jackson and Hulse were both offered internship positions with an indoor football team. The corporate offices were in a neighboring city to the university they attended, so both women could easily manage the weekly time commitment. Jackson approached her faculty adviser, inquiring about earning college credit for the internship. She received approval, and in January 2015, she began her new position alongside Hulse, who did not seek college credit.

During the first weeks of their semester-long internships, Jackson and Hulse brought in framed family photos and newly purchased office supplies to personalize their office spaces. It didn't take long, however, until they began to question the instruction and guidance they were receiving from their on-site internship supervisor.

The questions began when Jackson, who was enrolled in a media ethics course, was asked to sensationalize press releases. "We were continually asked to make the team look better," she said. She knew press releases were to report facts and inform the public, not paint the team favorably when there was nothing overly positive to report. But that was just the beginning of the questionable requests from the supervisor. As time went on, his comments turned sexual in nature and sexual comments began to come from others in the organization as well.

Hulse, who has advanced photography skills, was asked to model the new fan jersey for photos to be used in a social media campaign. She agreed even though the assignment did not really utilize her skills as a photographer. Hulse said she was chosen from the pool of interns because she was "the only intern the kid's shirt would fit." However, it wasn't the minimizing of her skill set that started to make her skin crawl; it was the sexual comments and innuendoes made by co-workers and players that accompanied her modeling. "I just brushed it off," she said—and Jackson was doing the same.

Jackson had several encounters with coworkers and players who made sexual comments, advances and innuendoes. For example, at the beginning of the internship, Jackson was told by her supervisor to stop wearing jeans because they were too distracting for the men.

"Everyone else wore jeans," Jackson said. "I always wore nice, professional jeans—nothing tight or anything like that." This request by her supervisor was, of course, a red flag, but she, too, brushed it off. Being singled out and given a special dress code no one else was given became a concern; being told what to wear because others in the organization cannot control themselves is an arbitrary policy and discrimination. However, the two women ignored their moral judgments and values, trusting the supervisors—who allegedly had more "experience" in the profession—to not misguide them.

Jackson explained she actually had minimal contact with the players; the only contact she had with them was in the corporate office where she worked. "Most players never said much," she said. "Some would tease a little about dates, but I didn't think anything of it." Then it happened.

Jackson received a Snapchat from one of the players exposing himself. The player, who she only knew from a few brief exchanges at the office, was sending her an image of his penis.

The Challenge: What to Do?

Who do you turn to when one's internship supervisor cannot see the dilemma and does not take action? That is the question Jackson said she asked. She spoke with her faculty adviser, who was also the journalism program's internship coordinator, and disclosed her entire experience. The adviser's immediate response was to protect her and Hulse. Although Hulse was not receiving college credit for the internship position, the faculty member was dutybound to help both women. Jackson explained to the adviser how she attempted to discuss the harassment with her supervisor, but he would not take her complaints seriously. At one point he told her: "Good luck reporting that to HR; we don't have an HR."

Abuse of power and silencing the victim—factors that all too often contribute to unreported sexual harassment—were evident in these students' dilemma. Jackson knew what she and Hulse were experiencing was wrong, so she approached a trusted authority at her university, her adviser, for support. However, it was not just her adviser who gave support; it was also friends and family, other faculty in the program and administrators in the university's Dean of Students office.

TOOL FOR THOUGHT:
The Doctrine of the Mean and the Categorical Imperative

The female interns in this situation had gut feelings something was not right about the goings-on in their office. Still, they believed that the so-called professionals with whom they worked must know more than they did about appropriate behavior in the workplace, so they tolerated the harassment even though they didn't feel right about what was happening.

Finally, though, their experiences escalated to the point of being hostile and their supervisor did nothing. Although it would have helped if they had a primer on sexual harassment in the workplace before their internships started, they were in an ethics course and were learning about how to stand up for themselves—and they were also learning about theories that might help them work through such dilemmas.

Two theories they had already learned might have helped in their situation. First, Aristotle's Doctrine of Mean with its two extremes, or vices, could help with deliberation. On one extreme the women could have done nothing. On the other end, they could quit. Was there a middle ground to explore in their dilemma? Yes, and that was discussing the matter with their supervisor; however, nothing happened. So their decision had to move toward the extreme of quitting after making their concerns known.

Kant's Categorical Imperative, or universal law, could also help. The CI says that if you can will a behavior, or principle, to be followed by everyone, then it is a maxim, or law, to keep. One could look at this two ways: Would you want everyone to be allowed to create hostile environments in a workplace? Of course not. Would you want everyone to shy away from confronting their supervisors when they felt uncomfortable? No. Nothing about the women's situation creates a maxim to keep.

The Response:
Leaving the Internship

As Jackson explained the sexual harassment she encountered from male employees and players to her adviser, she kept repeating, "I can't believe this still happens." According to a study conducted by the Association for Women for Action and Research, 54 percent (of 500 respondents) had experienced some form of workplace sexual harassment, and not all were women; 21 percent were men.[1] While Jackson was surprised that women still get harassed at work, her response to the mistreatment parallels the Socratic method.

The Socratic method relies on critical thinking to resolve questions of ethical behavior, and such thinking is stimulated when questions are asked and discussion is engaged. Jackson and Hulse made attempts to report the harassment, yet direct supervisors ignored their pleas. Dissatisfied with the inaction of the supervisor, they asked additional questions to people outside of the organization.

In April, Jackson offered to show the picture of the player's penis (of which she had taken a screen shot for evidence) to the adviser; she explained that after this inappropriate communication she now felt uneasy walking to her car after working promotional events at home games. It became clear to the adviser that this intern was not only in an uncomfortable situation but was also in an unsafe work environment. Jackson also explained that she had approached her internship supervisor to explain how the actions and comments were inappropriate, and he justified them by saying, "Well, you are beautiful—sorry, but what do you expect?"

With just under three weeks until Jackson's internship experience concluded, her adviser along with another faculty member instructed her to discontinue the internship and explained that based on Title IX,[2] her experience needed to be reported to the Dean of Students office. Although Hulse was not receiving academic credit for her work, she was still a student at the university and she had protection. She also was

---

1. http://www.aware.org.sg/

2. http://www.justice.gov/crt/overview-title-ix-education-amendments-1972-20-usc-1681-et-seq

advised not to return. Hulse told Jackson's adviser that the modeling wasn't the real problem; it was remarks that followed. "I'll 'like' that photo," was an example of one of the comments, which were unprovoked and brewed feelings of discomfort for Hulse. She believed the problem stemmed from the office culture.

A culture of sexism had made it seemingly OK to turn a blind-eye to harassment. However, these women were courageous enough to report it, and when their internship supervisor did nothing, they found a trusted university authority to help. Once in contact with the Dean of Students' Office, Hulse and Jackson were told to have no contact with anyone from the internship site, and the adviser was only to contact the direct supervisor to inform him the interns would not be returning and the situation had been reported to the Dean of Students. At this point, the internships were over for Jackson and Hulse, but the lessons learned will stay with them for a long time.

■ ■ TOOL FOR ACTION: Dealing with Sexual Harassment or Sexism at Work

Both men and women can face sexual harassment by a co-worker, supervisor, customer or client. Although Jackson's situation was isolated to one day, you should know that a persistent uncomfortable situation on the job may be considered against the law.

According to the U.S. Equal Employment Opportunity Commission, it's unlawful to harass a person in the workplace because of that person's sex. The EEOC defines harassment as follows:

[It] can include "sexual harassment" or unwelcome sexual advances, requests for sexual favors, and other verbal or physical harassment of a sexual nature. Although the law doesn't prohibit simple teasing, offhand comments, or isolated incidents that are not very

(Continued)

(Continued)

serious, harassment is illegal when it is so frequent or severe that it creates a hostile or offensive work environment or when it results in an adverse employment decision (such as the victim being fired or demoted).[1]

Both the victim and the harasser can be either a woman or a man, and the victim and harasser can be the same sex. Harassment does not have to be of a sexual nature, however, and can include offensive remarks about a person's sex. For example, it is illegal to harass a woman by making offensive comments about women in general.

If you believe you are in a situation that fits one of the above examples, you should take these actions:

- Tell your employer immediately; if you wait too long, you may lose your ability to defend your rights. Keep notes on the alleged harassment, including times and dates.

- If your company has a sexual harassment procedure, follow it and expect your employer to follow it, too.

- Get legal counsel if your employer doesn't take corrective action or takes action you believe won't really protect you.

- Contact the nearest EEOC office if you think you are a victim, have additional questions, or want to file a charge.[2]

It's ethically unacceptable for someone to use his or her authority to demand favors or create a hostile work environment. It's important to note that a business may be held liable if a client, customer or other nonemployee sexually harasses an employee and the business supervisors were notified but did not take immediate corrective action.

---

1. Definition taken from http://www.eeoc.gov/laws/types/sexual_harassment.cfm.

2. Information compiled from http://www.workplaceethicsadvice.com and http://www.eeoc.gov.

The Aftermath: Looking Forward to Their Careers

As they left behind the family photos and that newly purchased stapler in their offices, the women left their internships wondering how this happened. Jackson explained she was hesitant to say anything about the sexual harassment at first because she worried that her actions had provoked the interactions or that she would ruin a player's career. However, when actions by others make a person feel uncomfortable and unsafe it needs to be reported, and the appropriate staff members need to deal with the situation.

Jackson and Hulse did nothing wrong. They were confident yet somewhat naive interns who were excited to work in sports as public relations practitioners. Instead, they worked in a male-dominated organization and, unfortunately, experienced sexual harassment, which both women said they thought was something of the past.

As unpleasant as this experience had been for Jackson and Hulse, both women still look forward to careers in public relations and advertising. As these women advance toward their career goals, they now have experience to identify, call out and take action when sexual harassment occurs. When another person's comments or actions alert one's inner "this doesn't feel right," one should remember the Jackson and Hulse story and speak up until heard and given support.

Thinking It Through

1. Imagine you were in this situation, but your supervisor did believe you and wanted to have a meeting with everyone involved. What would you do? If you agree to the meeting, how do you prepare?

2. Discontinuing the internship with three weeks remaining may appear to be unprofessional. What do you think? If so, what might be an alternative action? Consider using Aristotle's Doctrine of the Mean to help you deliberate.

3. Workplace culture can be difficult to change, but how might this organization reshape the culture to discourage sexual harassment? Could you create a code of conduct or create a list of workplace values to follow?

What If?

Knowing your rights is important when it comes to sexual harassment in the workplace. Federal and state laws protect citizens from such treatment. However, some—both men and women—may believe they provoked the negative and damaging attention. Like Jackson in the above dilemma, they also might not want the person doing the harassing to get in trouble.

What if you do not experience sexual harassment personally, but you witness it? How would you proceed?

Hoping to pursue a career in sports media relations as a recent college graduate, you are hired by a well-known regional sports team. The office culture seems relaxed and laidback with regular office discussion similar to what you discuss with your softball team. After less than a year in your position with media relations, you are asked by management to create, implement and coordinate an internship program.

As you develop the internship program, you understand that creating a safe learning environment is important to the success of those who are awarded a position. A concern you have is how women will fit into the current office culture. What steps do you take to ensure all genders feel comfortable in the office?

After weeks of developing the program, it is finally time to award the six summer internship positions. After deciding on the six senior college students, four women and two men, you are thankful you took time to consider the training materials related to sexual harassment and discrimination. About five weeks into the 15-week commitment, Darcy has a noticeable different attitude. She wants to work from home more often, but part of the internship experience is being on-site to familiarize students with the day-to-day operations of media relations.

The next time Darcy comes into the office you carefully observe her interactions and attitude. You notice topics of discussion change whenever she, Ashley, Megan or Heather are in the office. The talk among the men turns sexual and flirtatious when any of the four female interns are present. As the internship coordinator, how would you deal with this situation?

Which theory might help you work through this? Although this section focuses on the perspective of management, put yourself in the position of others involved in the situation. Consider John Rawls' theory of justice.

Go Online for More

U.S. Department of Education, Office of Civil Rights, provides a Know Your Rights page:
http://www2.ed.gov/about/offices/list/ocr/docs/title-ix-rights-201104
    .html

American Association of University Women provides case support for sexual harassment experienced in education or in the workplace:
http://www.aauw.org/

Feminist Majority Foundation's web page provides a variety of resources such as sexual harassment hotlines:
http://www.feminist.org/default.asp

CHAPTER 22

Advertiser Pressure

The Case of the School Lunches

Ray Niekamp

M edia outlets are businesses and must make money to pay their employees, pay their bills, buy equipment and make a profit. To do that, they sell advertising to local businesses. But often, advertisers decide, for whatever reason, they don't like a certain story planned for air on the station's newscast, and threaten to pull their ads if the story runs.

The pressures are greater in smaller media markets, because the pool of advertising money is smaller. To avoid angering an advertiser, media outlets often do give in and kill certain stories. This case is one example.

THE SITUATION: A COMPLAINT ABOUT SCHOOL LUNCHES

Susan Bennett (her name has been changed) anchors morning news on a small-market TV station in the Southwest. Once her anchoring duties are over, she becomes the "On Your Side" reporter, investigating consumer complaints and concerns and trying to create some response. One day, she received a letter from a man whose daughter attended a private elementary school. The man was concerned about the lunch menus at the school's cafeteria. He thought they were unhealthy, and he blamed the food for some health problems his daughter was having. The menu items included chicken fried steak, chili dogs and nachos.

Bennett spent several days working on the story. She first interviewed the father then a health expert at the local department of health. The health expert told her that school meals were sometimes the only meals children get, and that it's important to offer nutritional food. But her efforts to get comments from the school went nowhere, and she wound up settling for a written statement.

Several hours before the story was to air, the station's sales manager and general manager told the news director that the story would not run. The news director pulled Bennett aside and said the story was "being put on hold." The reason: A local advertiser with ties to the school had threatened to pull his advertising from the station unless the story was dropped.

THE CHALLENGE: ADVERTISER PRESSURE

Usually, if a station is faced with the prospect of losing advertising, it's because it had done a story about questionable practices at the advertiser's business. But this case provided a twist. The school did not advertise with the station, but one of its board members did. In fact, he was the president of a local auto dealer in the city. Auto dealers are the leading advertisers on local television, and this man's company was considered to be one of the station's biggest advertisers. He also was known for contributing large amounts of money to the private school, and his grandchildren, like his children before them, attended the school.

"He didn't want this story to run because he didn't want any bad press against the school with which he was affiliated," Bennett said.

The threat from such a prominent advertiser was enough. Station management immediately backed down and ordered the story pulled. Bennett asked her news director when the story would run, but the news director was vague. "She told me she was fighting for the story to air," Bennett said. "I was told the story was being put 'on hold' until things 'cooled down.'"

THE RESPONSE: "I WAS SHOCKED AND CONFUSED"

But even after the situation seemed to blow over, the station never ran the story. At the time, Bennett had been with the station for only a short while, after working at a station in a smaller market. She still doesn't think the story should have been killed. "I was shocked and confused, especially because it wasn't a controversial story," she said. "I had done numerous stories at my last station on healthy school lunches and there was never any sort of problem."

She also never found out exactly what kind of decision-making process took place regarding the story. If there were discussions about the appropriateness of the information, between the general manager, the sales manager, the sales person and the news director, she was never part of them. "However, my coworkers were quick to inform me it was not unusual at this station," she said. "Since then, other reporters have had their stories pulled because of advertiser conflicts."

TOOL FOR THOUGHT: Act Independently

It's an old story. For decades, industry leaders have been concerned about the possibility of undue pressure from advertisers on the news product. But independence is one of the cornerstone values of journalism. A virtual "Chinese wall" was expected to separate the sales department from the news department, so news could operate independent of sales pressures. That ideal still exists, but in reality, TV stations are very cognizant of the need to retain prominent advertisers, and that business imperative clashes with the journalistic imperative of independence from outside influences.

The Society of Professional Journalists ethics code tells journalists to "Deny favored treatment to advertisers, donors or any other special interests, and resist internal and external pressure to influence news coverage." The Radio Television Digital News Association, the professional association for broadcast journalists, says much the same thing: "Professional electronic journalists should gather and report news without fear or favor, and vigorously resist undue influence from any outside forces, including advertisers, sources, story subjects, powerful individuals and special-interest groups."

The RTDNA code goes further by suggesting ways for stations to deal with advertiser pressure. "Journalists, news managers and business-side managers must develop shared values, clear guidelines and practical protocols that serve the dual goals of journalistic independence and commercial success," the code says. The code exhorts stations to foster communication, respect and trust between managers and staff. "Business-side managers should be encouraged to understand that journalistic independence and credibility are among the station's most precious commodities," it adds. The RTDNA code addresses Bennett's situation head-on: "News operations should not show favoritism to advertisers," it reads. "It should be clear to all advertisers that they have no influence over news content."

The Aftermath: Self-Censorship

Bennett continues to work at the station, but her approach has changed. "It definitely changed the way I view the station," she said. She now engages in self-censorship before pitching an "On Your Side" report. The car dealer in question is still one of the station's biggest advertisers, and for that reason, she says she won't be doing any stories on car dealers. "I steer clear!" she said. "As a reporter, my mission is to deliver stories in the most balanced, accurate way possible. I still do that—but now I'm a little more cognizant of what the story is."

She also understands the financial pressures TV stations are under with viewers deserting "appointment viewing" of newscasts at the traditional 5 p.m., 6 p.m. and 10 p.m. times in favor of online news sources. That, coupled with the challenges of attracting viewers from a small number of households creates a difficult business environment for TV stations. And TV stations are businesses.

"Being in a relatively small market, we are always hurting for more advertisers," Bennett said. "In the end, advertising money took priority."

Thinking It Through

1. Bennett accepted the news director's decision to go along with station management and kill the story. What could she have done to change their minds and get the story on the air?

2. Suppose Bennett contacted the car dealer directly and made the case to run the story. Would that approach be appropriate? The question can be considered from both the news and the sales points of view.

3. If, some day in the future, Bennett is assigned to cover a story favorable to the car dealer, should she accept the assignment?

4. Bennett continues to work at the station but does not do "On Your Side" stories about car dealers in general. Is there another course of action she could take that would be more satisfying, from an ethical standpoint?

■ ■ ■ TOOL FOR ACTION: RTDNA Guidelines for Balancing Business Pressure and Journalistic Values

The RTDNA guidelines were issued in 2001 to directly face the danger external pressures pose to news credibility. A 1998 RTNDF (Radio Television News Directors' Foundation) survey showed that eight out of 10 viewers said they believed advertisers influence news content. A 2001 survey by the Project for Excellence in Journalism found that almost one out of five news directors said advertisers had tried to kill a story. Advertiser influence hit small market newsrooms even harder, where two-thirds of news directors felt pressure to give sponsors positive coverage. One researcher suggested that people who are well known in their towns might be able to exert their influence to get negative stories about them or close acquaintances from getting on air—exactly what happened in this case.

Al Tompkins of the Poynter Institute, who helped craft the RTDNA's guidelines for balancing journalistic values against business pressures, says television stations should deal with the issue of advertisers and news before problems arise. Among his ideas:

- Develop communication protocols between news, sales, and promotions while preserving journalistic independence.

- Promote interaction between news directors and sales managers so they may each understand the other's concerns.

- Establish protocols to prevent sales interests from clouding news coverage decisions.

- Encourage news directors to work with other station leaders to prevent reliance on short-term profit-seeking that could undermine the integrity of the news department.

- Sell news to advertisers based on its quality and credibility.

- Make sure advertisers understand that they have no role in determining editorial content.

- Ask: What would our viewers think if they knew about the business motives behind our newsroom decisions?

Bennett doesn't know to what extent her news director conferred with the general manager and sales manager about the lunch story. It's clear the station had not dealt with the kinds of issues that come up when money is on the line.

Now Try This

A quote generally attributed to British author George Orwell goes: "Journalism is printing what someone else does not want printed; everything else is public relations."

The car dealer was using his leverage as an advertiser to prevent what he viewed as potentially bad publicity for a school in which he had a stake. But being an advertiser only gives him the right to run his commercials on the TV station. It doesn't—or shouldn't—give him any editorial control over the station's news product. After all, that's an entirely different part of the TV business. However, many advertisers think paying money to the TV station to run their commercials does give them some say regarding news content. And that leverage can be a substantial tool.

Consider this: A woman and her daughter are driving along on a local highway, when, suddenly, their car speeds up on its own. The woman is able to hit the brakes and get the car back under control, then steer onto the shoulder of the road, and she and the girl get out safely. Local TV stations cover the incident and go beyond by asking whether the manufacturer of the car knew of the acceleration problem beforehand.

It turns out that the woman bought the car at a local dealer, who happens to advertise on your station. That provides a local angle to a potentially national story.

Is this a more newsworthy story than the car dealer and the school lunches? How would you treat it if you were a reporter in that city? What kinds of discussions would you have with your news director and your sales manager before you went out to cover the story?

Go Online for More

Although news and advertising are supposed to operate in two different spheres, in reality they're closely intertwined. TV stations need to sell advertising to operate, and that inevitably causes situations like the one facing Susan Bennett. The Poynter Institute's Al Tompkins presents a more detailed list of questions to consider when an advertiser tries to influence news coverage in a piece called "Balancing Business Pressure and Journalism Values" at http://www.poynter.org/uncategorized/1596/balancing-business-pressure-and-journalism-values/

Professor Lawrence Soley examines the kinds of pressures advertisers put on TV reporters in an older but still relevant piece on the Fairness and Accuracy in Reporting (FAIR) website: http://fair.org/extra-online-articles/the-power-of-the-press-has-a-price/

CHAPTER 23

Journalists' Judgments Versus Audience Clicks

The Case of Web Analytics' Influence

Gary Ritzenthaler

It is a balancing act as old as journalism: choosing between the stories the audience wants and the stories that journalists, from their training and experience, believe people need. For a long time, journalists made those choices based on instinct and perhaps a little market research. Today, web analytics can instantly show exactly which stories audience members are reading, commenting on and sharing on social media.

Once you have that information, what do you do with it? If your audience reliably clicks on stories about celebrity divorces but not on stories about the budget deficit, does that mean you should stop running budget stories? Such questions influence both story choice and story placement, as one young web producer found when she saw an international story that she thought deserved prominent play on her news organization's home page. Because this incident happened at a time when media organizations were just beginning to study the impact of web analytics, the producer does not want it to reflect badly on her former employer, and she asked that all names in this chapter be changed.

The Situation: When Is a Big Story Not a Top Story?

Web producers who work for newspaper companies keep their sites up-to-date technically and build frameworks for future content. They also manage the continuing flow of news on the site by assigning stories to specific sections and helping to determine which stories are important enough to be included on the home page.

Stacy Rodriguez was a web producer at The Florida Journal, a daily newspaper with an audience not just in its large metro area, but across the country and around the world. At the time, The Journal's newsroom was organized around a "command center" staffed with one photo editor, one copy editor and editors from different elements of the paper along with a web producer. The web producer had some control over what appeared on the home page and how the stories were arranged, but one of the editors from the command center always watched over the site and had the final say in news judgments. If that supervising editor wasn't there, the online producer would make his or her own judgments about the story, but those could be changed when the editor returned.

"At that time there was not a set of guidelines at The Journal for making decisions about prominence of specific stories; it was more subjective and free-form," Rodriguez recalled. She went on to say,

> In the mornings, when I usually worked, there was an editor next to the online producer. This editor was not an online editor by nature; none of them were. He was a good editor and reporter, though, on the print side.
>
> Because there was nothing to work on for that day's paper yet, in the morning, the editor's job was to manage the breaking news reporters out in the field, dispatch reporters to locations of breaking stories and edit the breaking news

stories to push to the web. If the reporter(s) needed to relay info quickly, that editor served as an anchor and would write the briefs for the web. This editor had general control in the morning over what articles were given the most prominence on the home page as well.

For example, she said, the supervising editor might say something like, "There's a fire on 10th Street? Make it the lead when we get the video in."

This case-by-case structure for deciding the play of stories online is still common in many newsrooms today though most news organizations produce far more web-only content than they did in 2008 when this case took place.

After uploading and placing stories on the site, web producers often checked other news sites to see how they were handling the day's stories. Doing this allowed them to compare the mix of stories elsewhere with The Journal's, and sometimes uncovered good stories that the web producer had missed.

At that time, the Journal's home page was designed with space for a large featured story at the top of the page, with two or three smaller featured stories to the right of the main story. Below these feature stories were headlines from the different sections. This design was similar to the sites of many regional or national news websites.

Rodriguez explained that the design of The Journal's home page reflected an understanding of how visitors arrived and moved around the site. "The lead feature and secondary features are a mix of what you want to see and what you need to see," she said. "That's the method for the majority of news sites." Web designers know it's important to get this mix onto the home page because of common patterns among audience members. "They often land on the front and then click into their topic areas, whether it is business, sports or news," Rodriguez said. Thus, the home page "is our only chance to present the majority of our readers with a significant story that they wouldn't necessarily search for or that wouldn't fall within their normal interests."

On a February morning in 2008, Rodriguez was managing stories for the site. The big story of the day was the unfolding Democratic and Republican primaries in 24 states, the Super Tuesday primaries for the

2008 presidential election cycle. In other news, severe weather was threatening the South and Midwest; it would spawn deadly tornadoes in Kentucky and Tennessee later that night. Locally, a celebrity had been sighted in the Waterfront District, a popular area of shops and clubs near the beach. This was not unique for the area, but because celebrity stories had long been big draws on The Journal's site, this item, too, had been added to the home page.

During her review of other sites, Rodriguez saw the headline "CIA Admits Waterboarding Inmates" on the BBC News website.

Rodriguez read through the story and thought it looked important. The international community had long been debating whether waterboarding, in which water is poured over the face of a prisoner being interrogated so that the prisoner feels as if he's drowning, constitutes torture, and the debate had intensified since a report the previous year saying that the CIA used the technique. In the story that Rodriguez saw on the BBC site that day, the head of the CIA had told Congress that waterboarding use was limited and hadn't happened in five years. Still, it was the first time the CIA had acknowledged that it did use waterboarding.

"This put the U.S. on the map as officially admitting they tortured human beings," she remembers thinking. In addition, because of Florida's location close to the Guantanamo Bay detention camp in Cuba, and many local residents' connections to Cuba, she thought the story had a regional angle as well.

Rodriguez turned to the supervising editor and told him about the breaking news, suggesting that the story merited a spot on the home page because the acknowledgment of waterboarding was so important. He responded, "Haven't we already admitted that?"

At that time, The Journal had an experienced reporter on the topic of U.S. activities at Guantanamo Bay, Kathy Ross. Rodriguez wanted to make sure her instincts about the story were correct, so she went to find Ross in her office. Ross confirmed that U.S. officials had not previously acknowledged the use of waterboarding. "I said, 'Is this significant?' and she [Ross] said, 'Yes, this is a very big deal,'" Rodriguez remembers. "This was coming from the Guantanamo Bay reporter, so I put a lot of weight into it."

To Rodriguez, this conversation confirmed the story's importance and suitability for feature placement on the home page. She went back to the editor and passed on what she had learned. Rodriguez suggested that they substitute the waterboarding story for the celebrity story because all the other spots on the home page were taken by important local news or stories on the political primaries. The editor disagreed, citing the good traffic numbers for the current mix of stories and in particular the celebrity sighting story, which was returning the second-highest traffic draw of all the stories on the site.

Rodriguez was surprised and frustrated by the editor's position. "The question I had was, what is the balance, and why were we doing that? I didn't feel like we should have been valuing the traffic over the integrity of the larger national story." To her, it seemed a question not just of news judgment but of ethics.

> If it was competing with a significant local story, then I think it becomes less of an ethical dilemma and more of a question of how we weight different aspects of newsworthiness. . . . In this case, I felt like we were sacrificing an important story for the sake of clicks.

THE CHALLENGE: WHO DECIDES WHAT'S NEWS?

For as long as editors have chosen stories and assembled news packages, they have faced some of the questions that Rodriguez faced that day in The Journal's newsroom. When does international news become important enough to take precedence over local news for a particular audience? When do the actions of a famous person become newsworthy, and how much more do those actions matter when the person turns up right there in town?

Other aspects of Rodriguez's dilemma were new, however, arriving only as newspapers, caught in intense competition for audience, began trying to make sense of the way their readers were using news online. Unlike their predecessors in print-only media, web producers and editors can see which stories are the most read and most discussed. The practice of collecting and analyzing data about a website's use is known as web analytics.

Knowing which stories are engaging the public can be a great benefit to a news organization. It allows producers to react quickly, focusing more resources and attention on trends that interest readers or issues they want to know more about. Over time, understanding web analytics can help a company make changes to its site, or to individual stories, that help those stories rank highly in the results when people use major search engines, a practice known as search engine optimization, or SEO. Usage data can also show what kinds of formats (podcast, slideshow, interactive graphic) work best for different kinds of stories.

When times get tough, knowing what readers want can help companies make decisions about what to cut and what to keep. In most cases, in addition to learning about site traffic for their own uses, newspapers also use information gained from web analytics to market to existing and potential advertisers.

Fans of web analytics say the information helps journalists make news decisions that are more scientific and more democratic than they previously could be. Why operate on instinct and experience alone, they ask, when now we actually *know* what people choose to read? The best news packages in the world are of little use if no one sees them; SEO and other tactics based on web analytics help journalists' hard work gain the audience it needs in order to make a difference.

Many journalists, however, fear that the new information provided by web analytics will tempt bosses and editors to use the data in ways that undermine traditional news values. They worry, as Rodriguez did, that producing online news might become a response to audience whims rather than an exercise of the hard-earned editorial judgments that are a big reason people turn to reputable news organizations. They're concerned that bosses will intensify old pressures to emphasize stories that attract advertisers, or will be tempted to lay off reporters whose stories don't have wide readership, even if those stories explore crucial issues.

How best to use web analytics was a relatively new question in 2008, when Rodriguez was advocating for the waterboarding story, and it is still an open question today. In a 2010 New York Times story, reporter Jeremy Peters explored whether web analytics was affecting traditional news judgments at some large U.S. newspapers. For example, he reported that at WSJ.com, the website of The Wall Street Journal, editors begin the day by looking at recent web data, then use it to position and update stories in ways similar to the day-to-day activities at The Florida Journal that Rodriguez described.

Peters quoted Alan Murray, executive editor at WSJ.com:

> We look at the data, and if things are getting a lot of hits, they'll get better play and longer play on the home page. . . . Conversely, articles getting low audiences will be moved down more quickly if there is no compelling news reason to keep them prominent.[2]

The Times article also describes news organizations using web analytics to determine resources, whether those resources are blogs to be expanded or people to be let go.

Although these could be viewed as worrying trends, Peters' story also shows how analytics can be a useful tool:

> Rather than corrupt news judgment by causing editors to pander to the most base reader interests, the availability of this technology so far seems to be leading to more surgical decisions about how to cover a topic so it becomes more appealing to an online audience.

Writing in American Journalism Review in the same month as Peters' article, Paul Farhi, a reporter for The Washington Post, described similar calculations in his newsroom. "There's no question that many of our

---

2. Jeremy W. Peters, "Some Newspapers, Tracking Readers Online, Shift Coverage," *New York Times*, September 5, 2010, http://www.nytimes.com/2010/09/06/business/media/06track.html.

daily editorial decisions [at The Post] are guided by what's 'working,' as defined by readers," he wrote. "Stories rise and fall on the home page throughout the day, based in part on what the traffic data indicate about a story's 'performance.'" Farhi suggests that the performance of stories has an effect on the editors, and that "universal desk editors are under constant pressure to maintain the paper's traffic goals; several told me that they believed their job evaluations depended, at least in part, on how often they meet these goals."[3]

Clearly, the questions about how web analytics should be used in news decisions weren't particular to Rodriguez or to her newsroom.

THE RESPONSE: "A MISSED OPPORTUNITY"

After the story broke, Rodriguez returned to the editor a couple of times during her shift to lobby for replacing the celebrity story with the waterboarding story on the home page. In the end, however, nothing happened. "The story pretty much fell flat," she said. The only mention of the waterboarding story on The Journal site that day came in an area reserved for an automatic feed of Associated Press stories; no link to that particular wire story ever appeared on the home page. Rodriguez says she contemplated discussing the problem with other editors or higher managers but decided not to, hoping it was just an isolated incident.

"As an online journalist, I understand how traffic conversion works, so I understand that we need to have high traffic numbers to show advertisers," she says. Still, she thinks of the decision to keep the celebrity story rather than the waterboarding story as "a missed opportunity." She believes large news organizations like The Journal have a responsibility to cover important national and international stories and to use news judgment to decide when those should be played above lighter stories that happen to be getting more clicks.

---

3. Paul Farhi, "Traffic Problems," *American Journalism Review*, September 2010, http://www.ajr.org/article.asp?id=4900.

"If it was a small paper, I wouldn't care about the article so much," she said. "There aren't that many international papers in the U.S., and my opinion is that such a role requires us to make sure that national issues are seen."

TOOL FOR THOUGHT:
W. D. Ross and Choosing Between Competing Duties

The Scottish philosopher W. D. Ross proposed that in each moral choice, you make a decision after thinking about a set of competing duties rather than trying to apply just one overall law or rule. In other words, Ross' theory is pluralistic, based on balancing and judging a variety of competing factors. He believed that theories of morality based on one absolute law or formula could create situations that violated common sense.

This distinction is important to the situation in this chapter. Rodriguez faced a situation in which she had at least two competing duties, both of them vital to her role as a journalist. On one side was the journalist's duty to inform the public of important stories; on the other was her duty to her employer to act in ways that would make money and keep the business going.

You can probably think of situations where each of these duties could be judged the most important. For instance, what if the celebrity was a local native who had become a big star and now was returning to his home? What if the story involved the U.S. president making a case for why the country had used waterboarding? Because each situation is different, it becomes harder to make the case that one principle or set of absolute rules can work for them all.

Applying a pluralistic moral theory like the one proposed by Ross means answering some important questions:

How do I learn what my duties are in a specific situation?

How do I decide which of these duties is, in these circumstances, the most important?

For the first question, Ross suggested some categories of duties (obligations to keep our promises, not to harm others, to improve ourselves, etc.) that we share as humans and members of society. You have duties when you take a job and assume the role of that profession in society. In journalism, for example, new journalists are often directed to the code of ethics created by the Society of Professional Journalists as an example of the duties shared by all journalists (http://www.spj.org/ethicscode.asp).

In addition to duties or obligations that come from assuming the role of a journalist, one also assumes the duties involved in being an employee, duties such as helping the company fulfill its mission and helping other employees do their jobs well. In any career field, conflicts can arise between our role as professional and our role as employee.

For media professionals, rapid change adds to the complexity of this balance. If the way journalists connect to the public changes, do journalistic duties also change? If economic times get tougher, how does that alter the relationship between duties as employees and duties as journalists? Although Ross acknowledges that determining our duties in each new situation can be challenging, he believes that, after sufficient training and enough time thinking about a situation, we should be able to decide which of our duties is most important.

THE AFTERMATH: MORE ANALYTICS, MORE OPTIONS AND QUESTIONS

Eventually, Rodriguez left her job to manage a website for a company outside of journalism. Although disagreement over the importance of the waterboarding story didn't cause her to leave, she says that in her time at The Journal she saw decisions in similar situations that "seemed to make sense from a business perspective but didn't when you took them apart."

"I'm out of the business now because I wanted a career that I knew was more stable," she says. "I still have a passion for the news industry, but my ideas about how we should manage such things are different than how they are run, even today."

Since 2008, use of web analytics has increased at news sites as analytics software becomes more powerful and more customized. In a 2011 survey of managing editors, executive editors and editors of community newspapers in the United States, done by the Reynolds Journalism Institute, 90 percent said they receive daily, weekly or monthly analytics reports, and 49 percent "reported that their newsrooms make decisions about what stories to cover based at least partially on the web analytics reports they receive." The survey also reports that circulation size was a factor in the responses, as "newspapers with a circulation of 25,000 or more (72 percent) make decisions about news coverage at least partially based on web analytics reports significantly more than those with a circulation of less than 25,000 (44 percent)."[4]

As the use of web analytics in news has increased, the power of the software has too. Analytics software now allows media companies to customize information on stories in a variety of ways, allowing reporters access to information on their own stories in real time that in 2008 was available only to management and only in less detailed forms.[5] Today's software can chart trends in visitors over time, show where they're coming from and enumerate links to your stories on Twitter or Facebook or other social media sites.

As journalists learn more about analytics, they'll be better able to produce compelling news packages that take SEO and audience behavior

---

4. Joy Mayer, "Highlights from the 2011 Journalists Engagement Survey," Reynolds Journalism Institute, July 7, 2011, http://rjionline.org/news/highlights-2011-journalists-engagement-survey.

5. For an example, see this discussion of recent Newsbeat software: http://www.niemanlab.org/2011/08/newsbeat-chartbeats-news-focused-analytics-tool-places-its-bets-on-the-entrepreneurial-side-of-news-orgs/.

into account. As companies learn more, they'll be better able to communicate with employees and help them balance new types of data with their traditional news skills and judgments.

This kind of communication makes a difference in the workplace. In 2010, Nikki Usher reviewed the practice of SEO in news organizations for Nieman Journalism Lab. "It seems that whether SEO makes your journalistic life miserable depends on how smart your news organization is about using SEO," she wrote, "and how your news organization does in making you feel invested in the process of combining SEO with quality content production." She went on to say,

> Organizations that understand the power of SEO and social news to drive traffic—rather than chase traffic—will keep their reporters in the loop and make them happy. Even if an organization has a good SEO strategy, it still needs to be communicated effectively to the newsroom, so journalists don't feel like they've been turned from trained professionals into slaves to Google Trends.[6]

Thinking It Through

1. When Stacy Rodriguez worked for The Journal, it had no specific guidelines about how stories should be selected for a featured spot on the home page. In the absence of those guidelines, do you think Rodriguez did a good job advocating for the waterboarding story? If not, what else might you have tried?

2. How has your campus news organization, or any other news organization where you have worked, handled the influence of analytics and the desire for web traffic? Have you ever experienced or witnessed any situations similar to the one faced by Rodriguez?

---

6. Nikki Usher, "What Impact Is SEO Having on Journalists? Reports from the Field," Nieman Journalism Lab, Sept. 23, 2010, http://www.niemanlab.org/2010/09/what-impact-is-seo-having-on-journalists-reports-from-the-field/

3. If you ran a newsroom, what guidelines would you establish to help employees learn how to balance web analytics with news judgment? Follow some of the links in this chapter to learn more about the kinds of info the new software can provide, so you can think about good (or not so good) uses of that information to improve your site's content and attract audience.

4. In his story for American Journalism Review, Paul Farhi asked about detailed web analytics, "What's this doing to journalism?" How do you answer? What have you seen already, and what do you think might happen? In your own experience looking for news online, is there anything a site could do to help you see the importance of a story you wouldn't immediately be inclined to click on? As a member of the news audience, do you like sites where the play of stories is determined entirely by audience interest, or do you prefer to visit news organizations whose judgment you trust?

5. As an actual or potential writer and producer of online news packages, how might an understanding of web analytics influence the way you report, write and think about multimedia? Start thinking about this question by following the link to "The Journalist's Guide to Web Analytics" at the end of this chapter.

What If?

In writing about journalists dealing with web analytics, Paul Farhi of The Washington Post describes some of the traffic-driving strategies news organizations use. He points out videos with headlines like "Fired for Being Too Sexy" and "Alligator Frenzy Caught on Tape." He then lists some examples of common site elements often used to drive traffic:

> There's no real playbook for this drill, but there are some gimmicks. The Post often throws up celebrity photo galleries, sometimes with dubious or tenuous news value (a recent gallery featuring the British royal family was pegged to mere speculation about a forthcoming royal engagement). Another gambit: frivolous "user polls" (a recent one asked if readers in

Montgomery County, Maryland, planned to flush their toilets in defiance of temporary water restrictions). Editors also monitor trending topics on Twitter and Google, and sometimes adjust their mix of stories to include something about a hot topic.[7]

Can you find specific examples of these kinds of headlines or elements on news websites that seem to be of "dubious or tenuous" news value, just there to get extra clicks toward the story's traffic numbers? How are these elements presented? Do they relate to a story on the same page? What's your opinion of these kinds of site elements? Do they change your ideas about a specific story? Do they change your opinion about the site itself?

If you reported, wrote and assembled a multimedia news package that you considered really important, but audience clicks were minimal, how would you feel if one of your company's web producers added some not-quite-accurate but sexy-sounding headlines and managed to get numerous other sites to link to them? Does that seem OK as long as what those visitors found when following the link was your good reporting? If you were trying to talk the producer out of what you considered misleading headlines, what ideas could you propose that seem more legitimate to boost traffic to your story?

Go Online for More

If you'd like to learn more about the skills and duties of a web producer, one easy way is to check the job descriptions for the position of web or online producer at job search sites like http://journalismjobs.com/.

For a detailed look at one company, read the PBS Web Policy Manual: http://projects.pbs.org/confluence/display/PX/Production+Requirements

"The Journalists' Guide to Analytics" at FishbowlNY: http://www.adweek.com/fishbowlny/the-journalists-guide-to-analytics/241831

---

7. Farhi, "Traffic Problems."

"What Web Analytics Can—and Can't—Tell You About Your Site's Traffic and Audience," from the Poynter Institute:

http://www.poynter.org/how-tos/digital-strategies/e-media-tidbits/
    104772/what-web-analytics-can-and-cant-tell-you-about-your-
    sites-traffic-and-audience/

CHAPTER 24

Are Public Officials Always on the Record?

The Case of the Councilor's Blog

Jan Leach

A young, tech-savvy beat reporter found controversial comments on a public official's blog. The comments related to issues on the reporter's beat about which the official had not spoken out at meetings or in interviews. Are all blog posts fair game for news stories? Can they be used verbatim? How public are the online comments of a public official?

Even today, when blogs are everywhere, these questions are complex and debatable. In 2008, when fewer people were blogging, reporters who understood blogs had to be newsroom educators to help find answers.

The Situation: A City Councilor Speaks Out

Meranda Watling was at her desk in the newsroom of the Lafayette Journal & Courier when she got a Google Alert relating to her beat. It was February 2008, and someone online was questioning a proposal to merge the West Lafayette city schools with the city itself. The school superintendent had brought up the idea as a possible cost-saving strategy at a recent public meeting, and no one had said much about it.

Watling, then 22, had been covering K–12 education for the Journal & Courier, a Gannett paper in west-central Indiana, for a little more than a year. It was her first job after college and, though she hadn't initially considered the schools beat her ideal first reporting job, she had come to realize how important the topic was to the community and to her news organization. Issues involving teachers, taxes, classroom activities, school accountability, student outcomes and many more helped Watling regularly produce eight or more education pieces a week, many of which wound up on the front page.

The education beat involved covering a lot of meetings at which all sorts of proposals came up. Some of these ideas would later become big stories while others would never be mentioned again; you could never be sure which were which. The idea of merging the West Lafayette Community Schools with the city had been one of several brought up during a meeting in which the new West Lafayette superintendent warned the community that school finances were dire and getting worse. West Lafayette was a high-achieving district that included Purdue University. A recent state report had suggested consolidating school districts that, like West Lafayette, had fewer than 2,000 students.

The idea started to sound interesting to Watling when she heard it again a month later at a joint meeting of the city council and school board. The superintendent proposed forming a committee to study such a merger, a provocative move that might mean increased student population and funding, expanded district boundaries, and encroaching on adjoining neighborhoods and schools in the name of cost savings. Because the city and the school district had different boundaries, merging the two could involve moving students from neighboring districts.

As bold as a city-school merger sounded, no one at the meeting raised any questions. Watling started digging, and the topic of school consolidation, already a big issue, started taking over her beat.

A few days after the meeting, a Google Alert led Watling to a blog belonging to Peter Bunder, a city council member. Bunder had posted five questions about the city-schools merger proposal, and his language made it clear that he opposed the idea. Bunder, then newly elected to the council, questioned the transparency of the process, especially the suddenness with which the merger had been proposed and the study committee created. "The clubbiness of all this is off-putting," he wrote. He sprinkled his blog entry with the words *wink* and *nudge*, apparently to indicate insider understanding not accessible to ordinary taxpayers. "It all feels way too clever," Bunder wrote.[1]

Watling knew who Bunder was, but she had never interviewed him because as a city councilor he was not a usual source on her education beat. Bunder's blog about the city-school consolidation committee raised important questions that Watling and the Journal & Courier were curious about: What was the motivation behind this idea? What positive or negative impact could a merger have? The paper was asking questions that Watling described as "due diligence," but until Bunder's blog post, no public officials had questioned the merger in public.

■ ■ TOOL FOR ACTION: Tips for Using Blog Posts in News Coverage

The internet is great for finding sources or monitoring reaction, but using material from a blog or other online source can be disastrous if you don't exercise due diligence as a journalist. Here are some tips to guide you:

(Continued)

---

1. Peter Bunder, "School Reorganization Study," West Lafayette District No. 2, Feb. 2008, http://wldistrict2.blogspot.com/2008/02/school-reorganization-study.html.

(Continued)

Authenticate: Accuracy requires that you independently verify authorship of any blog entry you plan to use. This means contacting the author directly. Public figures may have aides who write what appears on their blogs or Facebook walls, or in tweets under their names. Opponents of a public figure may create an authentic-looking blog or website for the individual that is in fact a hoax. Confirming the creator of what you see online is imperative.

Report: Do your research, just as you would with any story. Why is this blogger commenting on this issue, and why should your audience listen? Is the blogger in a position to know inside information or influence the outcome? What perspective can you add through good questions, beyond the quotes that anyone could see online? Take a hard look at the blog post. Does the content make sense? Is it similar to something else online, perhaps taken from another blog? Track similarities, and ask the blogger about them. Then make sure you stay on top of developments; blog posts can be outdated fast. You can engage your audience in online conversation, too. Use your own "beat blog," for example, to measure the public's response to the issue or to the blog post. You'll get good ideas for follow-up stories.

Be transparent: Acknowledge who you are online. Tell readers exactly where you found the information and where they can find it, too. Reveal any real or perceived conflicts of interest having to do with your coverage, your employer or your beat. Admit mistakes quickly, and explain how they happened. If you'll be posting a correction, follow your organization's policies on clearing the language before the audience sees it. Use technology to ensure that online corrections are prominently displayed. Be aware that anything you do or say online can spread far and fast.

Consider consequences: If something rings ethical alarm bells for you, take time, even on deadline, to think it through. Communicate internally with colleagues as well as externally with sources. Seek perspective from both the blogger you want to quote and other people with a stake in the story. Not everyone who posts online understands the instant, potentially negative response that can result. If you're using comments from a source on someone else's beat, be aware that you could "burn" that source for your colleague.

The Challenge: Are Blog Posts Newsworthy Quotes?

Bunder's blog offered important new perspective on a significant story, and Watling wanted to quote from it. "It was the first time I had seen someone in public office come out and question whether the haste of pursuing this [merger] was necessary," she said. She also wanted to find out whether other public officials thought this way—but first she needed to know for sure that Bunder was, in fact, the author of the blog post.

Watling took her concerns to J&C local editor Dave Bangert, who had been in the community for many years and would know the "back story." At this point in 2008, the paper did not maintain news blogs, and reporters weren't accustomed to using blogs as reporting tools. Watling, however, had been blogging for years. She had a personal blog about journalism that she'd started in college—it was not linked to the newspaper—and felt confident that she understood the public nature of the internet and blogs. To her surprise, though, her editor was hesitant to quote Bunder's blog in the paper, and her colleague, the city hall reporter, objected outright.

"The concern was whether it was Bunder writing and also whether it was fair to quote from [the blog], since many bloggers don't realize their writing is available to anyone," Watling said. "It doesn't have the same legitimacy, or real weight, as if he said it during a city council meeting."

Bangert was cautious; he believed that because Bunder had not written the blog for the media, it might not be fair to publish his posts in the newspaper. The city hall reporter said Bunder was outspoken, but that it would not be fair to quote from his blog because the blog was "private." Watling, in contrast, considered Bunder's blog completely public: It was written by a public official and posted online where anyone could find it, and it specifically addressed issues affecting his district.

"I told them that if he [Bunder] had put it in a flier or in an ad, we wouldn't hesitate to quote it," Watling said. "But the city hall reporter said, 'That's just Peter being Peter. It's not fair to quote him this way.'"

Discussion in the newsroom centered on privacy, accuracy and fairness. Quoting from blogs was fairly new at the time, and Watling realized that some journalists were less comfortable than she was with the idea and the technology. "As a blogger, I was aware that what I wrote on my site could be—and often was—quoted, dissected or debated elsewhere," she said.

Although Watling believed strongly that the blog posts of an elected official were "fair game," she appreciated her editor's efforts to consider her arguments and those of the city hall reporter who regularly covered the city council. "It was a high-profile story, and we had a public official questioning a major initiative," Watling said. "My only tool to share it then [in 2008] was a news article, and I had to make sure that was [an] OK source to cite."

Wanting to make sure her views were valid, Watling did more digging and found Bunder's first blog post, written just a few weeks after he was elected and about six weeks before the entry in question. Titled "Think of this as a Press Release," the post explained how Bunder planned to use the West Lafayette District 2 blog. He wrote, "I suppose I could litter your inbox. Litter your mailbox. But instead, perhaps a blog. You may want to know what I think or what I'm doing or what I think I'm doing as your District No. 2 councilman. Hopefully this blog will provide a way to do that."[2]

When her editor saw Bunder's "press release" post, he was satisfied that the paper could use the councilman's blog writing about the city-schools merger. His main requirement mirrored Watling's original concern: to confirm that Bunder had in fact written that post. While

---

2. Peter Bunder, "Think of This as a Press Release . . ." West Lafayette District No. 2, Dec. 2007, http://wldistrict2.blogspot.com/2007/12/think-of-this-as-press-release.html.

Watling called the school superintendent, the city hall reporter called Bunder, who said he had written the blog post and clarified his position on the merger proposal.

Watling wrote the story using what she considered a watered-down version of what Bunder had said online. She was satisfied, however, that she'd gotten Bunder's objections and questions on the record, and she hoped the story would ignite more discussion about the issue and its implications.

The Response: Run It and Wonder

Watling's story, which ran on the front page of the next Sunday paper,[3] introduced Bunder's blog post and his observation about "clubbiness" in the third paragraph. It then quoted from the blog and from the city hall reporter's interview, including this criticism from Bunder: "I don't see where all the nickels add up to making a big difference for the school corporation [district]." The story said Bunder questioned projections about cost savings as well as what he saw as a rush to study the proposal.

Though this particular story was done, ethics questions about quoting from blogs continued to nag at Watling. Seeking feedback, she took to her personal blog, where a cross-section of journalists, editors and professors regularly commented on her posts. Under the title "Public officials blogging, do you quote?"[4] Watling wrote the following:

> I get that you wouldn't (or probably shouldn't) just take it and run with information . . . posted in perceived confidentiality. This is for any number of reasons, not the least of which is the same as when you deal with inexperienced sources who aren't as press-savvy: They shouldn't be harmed because they're naive. . . .

---

3. Meranda Watling, "Merger Doubts Simmer in WL," *Journal & Courier*, Lafayette, IN, Feb. 24, 2008, A1.

4. Meranda Watling, "Public Officials Blogging, Do You Quote?" Merandawrites.com, http://merandawrites.com/2008/02/19/

Now, tell me what you think about a scenario like this: An elected official in your community has a blog. The blog identifies the official . . . and discusses issues related to that office as a means of reaching out to constituents. You have confirmed it is that person writing the blog. Would you consider that blog fair game?

Watling's personal blog entry continues:

My stance is that blog post is more than fair game. My only concern is to confirm the material was posted by the individual and isn't some type of hoax. Once you have that, why wouldn't you use it—if only for a jumping-off point for further reporting on issues raised. . . .

I think that if you're going to stamp your name on a blog, tout you are a public official and use that as the topic of your blog, then you have no reason to not expect people to hold you accountable for what you say, the same as if you'd mailed out a flier with that message or said it during an open meeting. I could be wrong, but I don't think I am.

Five people responded to Watling's question. All five said, in effect, that using blog posts by public officials is fair as long as the elected official is positively confirmed as the author. Among the other guidelines her correspondents recommended were asking the blogger to elaborate on the post, telling the audience that the quotes came from a blog and copying the original post as backup source material in case it is changed or deleted after your story appears.

In online journalism ethics as in traditional journalism ethics, privacy and fairness are important. In general, an elected official is always on the record unless he or she specifically requests otherwise in advance. Public officials have, or should have, no expectation of privacy when commenting on public matters.

Fairness is another matter. To be fair, journalists must not only strive for accuracy—verifying who said or wrote something and quoting it accurately—but also try to provide context and tell all sides of a story. Part of the issue for Watling's editor and coworker involved whether the councilman would consider it fair to quote from his blog and how readers would react to his somewhat sarcastic comments. In this case, fairness and accuracy required asking for elaboration of the points in the blog post.

TOOL FOR THOUGHT:
Day's SAD Decision-Making Model

Making ethical decisions takes time and thought because you have so many perspectives to consider: audience, sources, co-workers and your organization, among others. The deadline-every-minute online world adds pressure as you attempt to balance your loyalties. Using an ethical decision-making model can help you sort through your motivations and consider the consequences of your actions. Of the many models available, one created by Louis Alvin Day could work well to guide you to a resolution[1] in a case like the one Meranda Watling faced.

Day, a Louisiana professor and author of several books on media law and ethics, calls his decision-making model SAD: Situation, Analysis and Decision. Briefly, SAD advises you first to define the situation. Identify the person who must make the final decision (that person is called the moral agent), and identify the ethical values at stake—for example, protecting the vulnerable or keeping a promise to a source. In Watling's case, she was the agent, and among the values she considered were truth, loyalty and privacy. Day suggests framing the issue or question as narrowly as possible to help with critical thinking about ethics.

In the second step, analysis, you consider the competing values and principles that make up the dilemma. Is it a question of truth versus privacy? Public service versus damage to reputation? Most situations involve multiple issues and external values, so which

(Continued)

(Continued)

seem most important in this particular case?

Consider the stakeholders, the people or organizations affected by the issues you're reporting on. What impact could your decision have on each of them? You might imagine conversations in which you try explaining your decision to the stakeholders. You can also look for moral theories that might apply, such as Immanuel Kant's Categorical Imperative or W. D. Ross' pluralistic theory of duty.

Applying the SAD model to the questions about the city councilor's blog post would mean weighing Watling's duty to the audience against her loyalty to her co-worker, the city hall reporter who regularly covered Bunder. She might also have considered the accuracy of Bunder's post versus possible harm to his reputation if she quoted the post verbatim. Another possible "value" could have been the consequences to her, to the paper and to the public if she did nothing at all. What might have happened if

Bunder's blog comments were not reported?

Finally, SAD directs you to make a decision and to frame it as a statement, so you can work through the advantages and disadvantages that might result. For example, Watling's statement might have been the following:

> I want to report the councilman's blog post, but he and others might consider a blog private. I think his status as an elected official makes the post public, and his ideas will add to public understanding of this issue.

The beauty of the SAD model is that the directive to formulate a statement may help you defend your decision later, when audience members or sources or co-workers question you.

***

1. Fred Brown, "SAD Formula Can Turn Happy Ethical Results," Society of Professional Journalists, Oct. 2006, http://www.spj.org/rrr.asp?ref=4&t=ethics.

THE AFTERMATH: BLOGS GO MAINSTREAM

Meranda Watling believes her story with Bunder's blunt comments helped influence public perceptions and spark debate about the idea of combining the city and the schools. After the story ran, other concerns about the merger came to light, and some community residents began speaking against it at board meetings. The paper ran many more stories exploring the issue and reaction to it.

"This was really a lot bigger mess than the superintendent wanted to handle," Watling said. "He didn't expect so much pushback." While the issue of saving money continued to trouble the West Lafayette Community School Corp., city and school officials never formed the committee to explore consolidation. The schools looked for cost savings elsewhere, and the merger idea eventually fizzled.

Watling left the newspaper in August 2010 and is an associate editor for a magazine in Indianapolis. In the two-plus years between the Bunder blog and her departure, she said, the growth of social media changed attitudes in the newsroom. The newspaper and its staff are more tech-savvy now, routinely using the web and social media for reporting and developing ideas and sources. As in most newsrooms, J&C reporters now use Twitter, blogs and Facebook to communicate with the audience and issue alerts about upcoming stories or breaking news.

Would she do anything differently now?

"I would have quoted more extensively from his [Bunder's] blog," Watling said. "I still think what we did was right. And, if I had Twitter at that point, I would have tweeted it in 2.5 seconds."

Thinking It Through

1. Meranda Watling's initial concern about using the city councilor's blog post was making sure he was the one who had written it. Was that question alone enough? If not, what else should reporters do or think about when considering quoting from a blog?

2. Once you've decided to use a blog post in a story, should you quote it exactly? In its entirety? What, if any, guidelines would you suggest for "cleaning up" the language or grammar in a blog post? Try to frame your response as guidelines that could go into a policy for your news organization on how to use online material in reporting.

3. In tough budgetary times, elected and appointed officials at all levels consider a wide variety of ways to save money, but only a few of those ideas will ever be seriously pursued. What are the media's responsibilities in reporting on these ideas? When Watling had decided that covering the city-school consolidation proposal was important, did that make Bunder's blog post an essential source? If Watling, her editor and the city hall reporter had decided *not* to use any material from Bunder's blog, would their coverage of the issue still have been accurate?

4. Who could potentially be helped by the newspaper using Bunder's blog post as a source? Who could be harmed? Outline the possible positive and negative consequences of a story that quotes the blog. If you were facing this dilemma today, with more technological tools at your disposal, what options beyond waiting to assemble a full story might you consider?

What If?

Meranda Watling found a blog in which a public official wrote about public issues in a somewhat sarcastic way. What if you came across a blog by an elected official in your town, or by an administrator at your university, that contained important information about his or her views on issues important to your audience, but some of the posts libeled other public figures or accused them of crimes? What if the blog included obscenities or racist or sexist remarks?

Are there circumstances under which you would use those comments? What argument would you make to your editor, and how would you respond later when people who read your story called to complain? What if the blogger himself or herself complained? Does it matter whether you're quoting the blog in your story or just linking to it?

In the case in this chapter, the city council member confirmed that he'd written the blog entry, and he elaborated on his comments for the reporter's story. What would you do if an elected official in your town had a blog described much the way that Bunder described his, but then claimed he did not write the one post that you wanted to quote? Would you use it anyway? What would you do if the official confirmed that he did write the post, but then he took it down as soon as you asked him about it? If you'd saved the post, would you still use it? Why or why not? Would you report its removal?

Looking back at this incident from early in her career, Watling said that if she'd had today's technology in 2008, she would have tweeted the blog post immediately. Would you? If so, how would you explain that action to someone who disagreed? What are the advantages of tweeting small slices of information in an ongoing story? What are the dangers? Do you think journalists have a responsibility to educate the audience about how social media differ from a fully researched, "finished" story?

Go Online for More

Many news organizations and professional groups are developing reporting guidelines for the internet in general and social media in particular. Here are a few sets of guidelines; you can find many more online.

American Society of Newspaper Editors 10 Best Practices for Social Media:
http://asne.org/portals/0/publications/public/10_Best_Practices_for_ Social_Media.pdf

Radio Television Digital News Association social media guidelines:
http://www.rtnda.org/pages/media_items/social-media-and-blogging- guide lines1915.php?g=37?id=1915

Reuters Handbook of Journalism: Reporting From the Internet:
http://handbook.reuters.com/index.php/Reporting_from_the_internet

The Guardian:
http://www.guardian.co.uk/info/2010/oct/19/journalist-blogging- commenting-guidelines

Los Angeles Times:
http://asne.org/article_view/articleid/317/los-angeles-times-social-media-guidelines.aspx

National Public Radio:
http://www.npr.org/about/aboutnpr/ethics/social_media_guidelines.html

CHAPTER 25

On the Record or Off?

The Case of the Cranky Professor

K. Tim Wulfemeyer

I t's not unusual for reporters, especially beginning reporters, to have problems with the people they interview. Ideal communication between reporter and source can be short-circuited by a variety of factors—misunderstandings, technical breakdowns, different expectations, even semantics.

One student journalist experienced an unexpected short circuit when a professor at her university agreed to a recorded interview with her on a sensitive subject, and then later told her that she could not use anything he had said. The fact that she had explained multiple times, on tape, that she needed his comments for a newspaper story didn't matter to him. The reporter knew she had behaved correctly, yet at a university it can be dangerous to burn any source you might need again or a source who might see fit to spread negative views about you or student media in general.

What should she do? Because of the controversy surrounding what happened, the people involved in this story asked that their names, as well as the name of the university and the newspaper, be changed for this chapter.

The Situation: Late Professor, Angry Students

Early one February at Santana University, several unhappy students contacted the student newspaper, The Sun, to complain that their geology professor still had not filed his grades from the previous semester. All professors' grades had been due within two weeks of the end of final exams in mid-December. Grade deadlines are a big issue for students because late grades can keep them from registering for advanced courses, delay their graduation, delay grad school enrollment and even jeopardize potential jobs. Reporter Jennifer Collins wasn't convinced that one professor's missed deadline warranted a story, but she decided to do a little digging.

To ensure that the students' complaints were legitimate, she interviewed them and asked to see their notes from professor Robert Peterson's classes. She looked at their grade reports to confirm that Peterson had actually failed to file grades for his three courses. Only one student, Henry Chen, agreed to be quoted in the newspaper. The other students said they had to take future classes from Peterson and didn't want to get on his bad side; however, their complaints and allegations were similar to Chen's.

Even after checking with the students, who were obviously upset about not getting their grades, Collins still wasn't positive she wanted to do a story for The Sun. "I thought there was probably a simple explanation for why he was late with his grades," Collins said. "There might be a medical reason, a family issue, a vacation or sabbatical, or something like that."

Despite her reservations, Collins decided that since Peterson was more than a month late in reporting grades, she'd contact him to hear what he had to say. She left phone messages and sent emails to Peterson in an effort to arrange an interview. After a couple of days without response, she went to Peterson's office.

When the professor opened the door, Collins identified herself as a reporter for The Sun, told him she was working on a story because students had reported that his grades were late, and asked if he'd be willing to talk to her.

"Yeah, I'll tell you exactly what's going on," he said. "Come on in."

Collins sat down and took out her notebook and audio recorder. "I'm going to record our interview, if that's all right with you," she said.

"Go ahead," he responded.

Since Peterson's tone seemed defensive to Collins, she decided to start with a few general, relatively safe questions before asking the more sensitive ones.

"I figured if I started out slow, I'd at least get some statements from him before he might get mad at me and end the interview." Periodically during the interview, Collins prefaced her questions with comments like "for the record" and "just for the record." She wanted to be sure that Peterson was clear that she was gathering information for a Sun news story.

She'd done enough background research to know that Peterson had been interviewed by student and professional journalists a couple of times for stories related to his research. "But I was still concerned that since he wasn't really a public figure, he probably wasn't that used to dealing with reporters and the news media," she said. "I wanted to be sure that he understood that his comments were on the record."

During the 15-minute interview, Peterson said he was withholding grades as a protest over what he perceived as mistreatment, poor facilities and lack of support by the university and the chairman of his department. He also was unhappy about the lack of time to determine grades and report them, in light of all his other university-related obligations, especially the expectation that faculty publish groundbreaking research findings in refereed academic journals.

Several times during the interview, the professor asked the reporter to give him the names of the students who had complained about the late grades. Collins refused each time.

"The final question I asked was, 'When do you plan to file your grades?' He told me he'd filed his grades right before I knocked on his door and that he was done talking about the matter. I thanked him for his time and left to go write my story."

Now that she knew that Peterson was deliberately withholding his grades as a protest, rather than simply being late, Collins had a bigger story. Because Peterson was criticizing the geology department for what he saw as lack of support, she knew it was important to get the perspective of the department's chairman.

The chairman of the geology department, Marco Valenzuela, told her that to his knowledge, Peterson had not yet submitted grades for the 73 students who had been in his classes the previous semester. In response to one of Peterson's claims, that he was not given office space, Valenzuela acknowledged that because of a construction project, Peterson had had to temporarily change offices and lab space, and that the move had caused some problems. The chairman expressed deep concern over the impact that the late reporting of grades was having on students. According to him, some students could not begin graduate school, or take jobs for which they'd been hired, because a missing geology grade from the previous semester was keeping them from officially graduating.

"We've tried to help professor Peterson as much as we can, especially with the reporting of his grades," Valenzuela said. "He just keeps saying he needs more time."

THE CHALLENGE: "I RETRACT ALL MY COMMENTS"

Collins had just begun to organize her notes when she got a call from Peterson. "I don't want anything I said to you to be used in your article," the professor said. "I retract all my comments to you."

Collins was stunned. She had clearly identified herself as a reporter for The Sun who was working on a story. She had obtained the professor's permission to record the interview, and the recording showed that several times she had reminded him that he was speaking on the record.

"I told you I was working on a story, and you agreed to be interviewed," she said to Peterson on the phone. "You said it was OK to record the interview, and I made it clear that we were on the record."

Peterson said he didn't care about any of that. He threatened to sue Collins, The Sun and the university if any of his comments appeared in The Sun.

"I'll have to check with my editor," Collins said.

Peterson hung up on her.

Collins immediately went to her editor, Courtney Wylie. Collins told her the timeline and explained what she had said to Peterson at the beginning of her interview with him.

"Let's check with professor Lewis in the journalism department," Wylie suggested.

Collins called Eric Lewis, told him what had happened, and asked what he'd advise her to do.

"Well, if you're sure professor Peterson understood that he was on the record and he agreed to be interviewed, you're on pretty solid ground," Lewis said. "If you're a little uneasy about things, I guess you could let him review the comments that you plan to use from him to be sure you quoted him accurately. I might do that, especially if I thought I might need to use him as a source in the future. It's almost never a good idea to burn a source if you don't have to. Besides, if he gets a chance to see what you plan to use, he might feel better about the whole thing. He knew he was being recorded, right?"

"I made it very clear that I was recording the interview and that I was likely to use some of his comments in the story I was planning to write," Collins said.

"Sounds to me like you did everything right. I think legally and ethically you're good to go. I'd use his comments, but it's really your call on whether to use them or not. I don't think your story will be as good without his comments, though."

TOOL FOR THOUGHT:
Combining Codes and Theory

When the professor demanded that his comments not be used in her story, and then threatened legal action if they were, reporter Jennifer Collins used a variety of tools and methods to decide what to do. She consulted her own conscience, asked others for help, reread her newspaper's code of ethics and—either knowingly or unknowingly—followed the elements of several traditional theories of ethics.

The Society of Professional Journalists ethics code, the Associated Press Statement of News Values and Principles and the National Public Radio News Code of Ethics and Practices all contain provisions relevant to this case. Collins looked at the ethics code of her own student newspaper, The Sun, which states, "'Off the record' is an agreement that is made very clear and prior to the answering of the question at stake. A source may go off the record only with the expressed agreement of the reporter." Later in the code comes this advice: "If a source says something on the record and then says that the previous statement was off the record, you, as the journalist, should inform the source that since the statement was on the record, you have the right to decide whether or not to use it in a story."

The code was a good tool for thinking about the specific question, but Collins also needed to think more broadly in order to be sure she had all the information she needed to create a balanced, accurate story on a subject that was important to her readers. She and her editor and a journalism professor discussed various options, from not running the story to the other extreme of including everything they had, then looked at other possible courses of action that fell between those two extremes. That's Aristotle's Doctrine of the Mean in action.

In her clarity about her journalistic purpose, Collins

in many ways followed the steps outlined by Sissela Bok. She first thought about the dilemma. She then discussed her ethical concerns with others who had the knowledge, experience and expertise to discuss alternative courses of action and help her work through her dilemma. She also thought about the various stakeholders and analyzed the legitimacy of their motives for speaking out, and she considered the likely impact her story would have on the stakeholders.

In the end, she was sure she had done enough things right that, if necessary, she'd be able to justify her actions and decisions to others—including the court system if it came to that, but more likely to her fellow journalists; her sources; and, most importantly her audience.

THE RESPONSE: WEIGH THE OPTIONS AND CHOOSE

Collins thanked Lewis for his advice and then met with her editor again. They decided that they had five possible courses of action:

1. Run the story with Peterson's comments.

2. Run the story without Peterson's comments.

3. Give Peterson a chance to verify the accuracy of the comments that were going to be used in the story.

4. Run the story with Peterson's comments and an editor's note explaining what had happened during the reporting process.

5. Don't run the story.

Collins and her editor quickly dismissed the option of not running the story at all. Grading practices were an important issue for everyone in the university community; this was just the kind of story the student newspaper should be publishing. They also knew that without the professor's comments, the story would be incomplete. Although they were absolutely sure that the comments from Peterson were accurate and fair, they were a bit uncomfortable with simply printing the story without giving him a chance to confirm and clarify.

Collins decided to call Peterson and read him the statements that would be attributed to him in her story. When she reached him, however, he refused to listen, criticized her and reiterated his threat to sue if any of his comments appeared in The Sun.

"He said he didn't think his comments were that relevant, and he was sure I wouldn't quote him accurately or fairly," Collins said. "Looking back on it, I think that his asking me over and over again for the names of the students who complained about him, his angry tone and his threats to sue were all part of his trying to bully me."

After another brief consultation, Wylie and Collins decided that the story would run with Peterson's comments in it, along with an editor's note at the beginning of the story explaining why the story was being printed and what had happened during the reporting process.

"Our main concern was how to best serve our readers," Collins said. "We decided that we had to include professor Peterson's comments to be fair and balanced in our reporting. We also wanted our readers to know why we were including his comments even though he didn't want his comments used."

While Collins was writing her story, she got a call from professor Valenzuela, the geology department chairman. "I just wanted you to know that we just got a call from the Registrar's Office," the chairman said. "Professor Peterson just filed his grades. I guess the 'power of the press' really works."

Collins noted the time: 4:15 p.m. She had ended her interview with Peterson at 2 p.m. She finished her story at 6:30 p.m. after making a quick call to Henry Chen to get his reaction to finally getting his grade.

Here is Collins' story as it ran in the newspaper, but with the names changed as in the rest of the chapter.

Professor Withholds Grades

Jennifer Collins

Staff Writer

Editor's Note: The comments made by Prof. Robert K. Peterson in this article are essential to its clarity and completeness. Jennifer Collins introduced herself as a student journalist and recorded her interview with Prof. Peterson to ensure accuracy; however, shortly after the interview, Peterson retracted his statements and requested we not print them. He questioned the accuracy, completeness, and relevance of his comments. The Sun chose to include his comments to provide readers with a complete story.

Last semester, geology students enrolled in G400, G420, and G470 at Santana University had to wait more than a month and a half to receive their grades. Prof. Robert K. Peterson delayed posting these grades until late yesterday, causing some graduating seniors to miss job opportunities and stopping other students from going to graduate school, because they couldn't receive their diplomas without these grades. In addition, some students were blocked from enrolling in courses this semester via online registration, because they did not have grades in the required prerequisite courses.

The chairman of the Department of Geology, Dr. Marco Valenzuela, said during a telephone interview at 3:45 p.m. yesterday that he was still waiting for Peterson to submit grades for the approximately 73 students enrolled in the three classes.

According to the SU Faculty Policy Guide, "Faculty members are expected to submit final grades in a timely fashion. Grading practices and patterns are expected to meet the highest professional standards of objectivity, fairness, and accuracy."

"Professor Peterson has not submitted the grades from last semester and he will not allow me access to the coursework to

(Continued)

(Continued)

assist him in getting the grades submitted," Valenzuela said. "But he has not refused to post the grades, he just keeps asking for a couple of days of extension. I'm trying to work with him as much as possible to get the grades to the students."

Shortly after making the above comment, Valenzuela was informed by university officials that Peterson had posted his grades at approximately 4:15 p.m. Peterson had told The Sun that he had posted grades prior to 2 p.m. and did not want to discuss the matter further.

The three classes are required for graduation in the geology department, but Peterson is the only professor who teaches the courses.

"It's completely unprofessional," geology senior Henry Chen said about Peterson's delay in posting grades. "You have faith in your professors, and they're supposed to be very moral and responsible, but if they pull something like this, it's totally unethical."

Chen said he was afraid Peterson would retaliate against him by giving him a C in the class for speaking to The Sun, but he wanted other students to know what was going on.

"I wouldn't recommend him ever, but we're forced to take his classes," Chen said. "He opens the textbook up and flips through it for class. And that's just when he shows up."

Chen said that Peterson missed class the entire first week of school last semester, he didn't teach the last week of school before finals, and he missed about three to four other days during the semester.

Peterson had canceled his classes yesterday, and during an interview with The Sun, he repeatedly requested the names of the students who had informed the newspaper about his failure to submit grades.

Peterson has had more than a decade of internationally recognized research in his field. He explained his actions as a response to what he called "unfair treatment."

"My research endeavors have been essentially terminated by the university. My lab space has been reduced. It took more than half the semester before I got my email access restored, and I still don't have a phone in my lab."

Valenzuela said about seven or eight graduating students were drastically inconvenienced by the situation because they went on job interviews and couldn't produce proof that they had obtained degrees.

"The effects on the students were sometimes significant," Valenzuela said. "Some of them are going on job interviews and I have to write something for each of them individually to let prospective employers know that they have satisfied all the requirements for their degree, but they're waiting for the grades from a class before they can receive their diploma."

Valenzuela added that some students were trying to begin graduate school this semester, but they were denied admission because they couldn't establish competency without their undergraduate degree.

Chen reported that though he never received more than half of his graded coursework for the class, including two 20-page papers, take-home portions of a midterm and a final, plus multiple homework assignments, he did receive an A.

"We're really hoping that this kind of thing never happens again," Valenzuela said.

SOURCE: The Daily Aztec, San Diego State University. Used with permission.

THE AFTERMATH: INSTITUTIONAL AND INDIVIDUAL IMPACT

Professor Robert Peterson continues to teach at Santana University. He did not sue Jennifer Collins, The Sun, the university or anyone else mentioned in or involved with the story. Partly as a result of The Sun story, the university's faculty guide was changed to include specific sanctions for professors who do not submit their grades by the posted deadline each semester. The sanctions include censure and probation for a first offense, the docking of pay for a second offense and possible termination for a third and subsequent offenses.

Jennifer Collins graduated and now works as a multimedia reporter for a major metropolitan newspaper. In all her reporting, she makes extra sure that both she and her sources know when they're on the record. "I'm probably more careful about 'on and off the record' situations than I need to be, but the Peterson story taught me that you really can't be too careful about being sure that sources know that what they say to you can show up in the newspaper or online," she said.

The Peterson story had an impact on the journalism department at Santana University, too. Professors in reporting classes and in the law and ethics class stress even more the importance of ensuring that all of the people involved in the information-gathering process understand the difference between being on the record and being off the record and exactly what those terms mean. The professors also regularly counsel reporters and editors for The Sun about the importance of ethical and professional conduct.

Thinking It Through

1. If you were Jennifer Collins and your source called to retract his comments, what would you have done? Would you have added any steps to the process that Collins and her editor followed? To flip the situation around, what if you gave an interview to a reporter as a source and then later realized that publication of that interview might cause you big problems? Can you think of an argument you might make to a reporter that would allow you to retract your comments? Or should that never happen?

2. In your view, did Collins do enough during the interview to make sure the professor knew he was speaking on the record? If you were running a newsroom, what guidelines would you give reporters for making the reporting and publishing process clear to sources? Does publishing a story online require any different sorts of cautions to sources from print publication or TV or radio airing of a story?

3. Should guidelines on being named in stories be the same for everyone, or different for different kinds of people—students versus professors or administrators, the governor versus a clerk in a state office, adults versus children? Do you think it matters whether someone is a one-time-only source or a person you'll be speaking with repeatedly on your beat? When a person says he doesn't mind being named in a story (like the student who complained about the professor), is his permission to be quoted enough? Does the reporter have any obligation to make sure the person understands what might happen after the story is published and becomes permanently available on the internet?

4. Reread the editor's note that ran with the story. Does the note cover what you consider the most important points for conveying the staff's thinking to the audience? What else might you have added or deleted? Would anything else about the published story concern you as an editor?

5. From the decision-making process the newspaper staff used in this case, what guidelines might you create for your own newsroom about how to make tough ethical decisions on deadline? Are there any procedures you think would apply no matter what type of question you were debating?

What If?

You are a reporter for a medium-sized news organization, working on an investigative story about alleged misuse of public funds by some members of the city council. A staff member for a councilwoman suspected of misusing funds is willing to talk to you, but she wants to remain anonymous and wants you to use her comments only as background.

What could you do to try to get the staffer to speak on the record? If you can't persuade her to go on the record, what steps would you take to ensure that both you and your source have a clear understanding of what the terms "off the record" and "as background" mean, so that you're sure what information can be used and how?

What would you do if you promised your source anonymity, but then your editor demanded that you name the source in your story? What if your editor agreed to run the story without naming the source, but only if you tell him first who the source is? Would you be willing to quit your job rather than reveal the name of your source to your editor or anyone else?

After completing the interview with the source who provides you with information for background use only, you interview another source who gives you the same information. He says you can use it, but you can't attribute it to him in any way. What obligation, if any, do you have to your original source?

You decide to let your original source know that you have obtained the same information from elsewhere and plan to publish it. She begs you not to do that, saying that people will assume the information came from her, and she's afraid she'll lose her job. What would you tell her?

What would you do if you were asked to reveal the name of your anonymous source by a judge during a criminal trial? Would you be willing to go to jail rather than reveal the name?

Go Online for More

McBride, Kelly. "Questions to Ask Before Going Off the Record," the Poynter Institute:
http://www.poynter.org/uncategorized/25191/questions-to-ask-before-going-off-the-record/

"Offering Anonymity Too Easily to Sources"—edited text from a symposium at Harvard's Nieman Foundation for Journalism:
http://www.nieman.harvard.edu/reportsitem.aspx?id=101110

Individual news organizations provide their employees varying amounts of guidance about what should be on and off the record. Here are some examples:

Guidelines on sourcing from the Reuters Handbook of Journalism:
http://handbook.reuters.com/index.php/The_Essentials_of_Reuters_sourcing

CHAPTER 26

Giving Voice to the Voiceless

The Case of Telling the Story of the Other

Beth E. Concepción

The subject of the lack of diversity in newsrooms has been a hot topic for journalists and news managers for some time. News managers seldom hire people without a college degree, and comparatively few minorities earn a college education. Journalists often find themselves reporting the stories of people who have different education, experiences and values than their own. Yet the purpose of reporting is to uncover the information that the public wants to know and needs to know.

After taking a news writing course, a student grappled with gender, race and class issues when interviewing people for a collaborative multimedia project. She had long questioned her place in society and how she came to be in a position of privilege, and struggled with how best to tell the story of people whose lives were very different than her own.

The Situation: A New Project Causes Unexpected Concerns

Astoria Jellett did not particularly want to take News Writing and Editing, but it was a required course for her creative nonfiction major. During the course of the quarter, though, she found herself coming up with story idea after story idea and getting excited about local news. Her newfound interest in politics even inspired her to vote for the first time. She enjoyed the process of telling true stories about people she met and began to carry a voice recorder with her to record conversations. "I was obsessed with recording everything," she said.

After the quarter ended, she wanted to continue honing the new story-telling skills she learned. Jellett joined with a local photographer who was working on a project that involved photographing African-American businesses on Waters Avenue, an economically challenged street in Savannah, Georgia. The photographer had developed contacts in the community because she had been working as a photographer for an all-black church in the neighborhood. Jellett's role was to conduct interviews with the business owners, record the interviews, and also record the ambient sound of the businesses. The goal of the project was to produce a multimedia installation for a group exhibition at a Savannah gallery.

Her first assignment was to interview some people in a barbershop. One of the participants, a 23-year-old, talked about how most of the people his age grew up without fathers. The barbershop became a place where boys could go for male guidance.

It was a great interview, but Jellett felt out of place. Not only were she and the photographer the only white people in the barbershop but they were the only women. Jellett came to Savannah, Georgia, from Daphne, Alabama—a city that is 84 percent white. Savannah is 55 percent African-American and 38 percent white. "I felt uncomfortable almost immediately," she said. "I was very aware of our differences. I felt like the customers in the barbershop were thinking, 'They don't belong here.' I felt like we were taking advantage of them."

She thought back to a documentary she had watched as part of the News Writing and Editing class. The film was "Stranger With a Camera," a 2000 documentary film by director Elizabeth Barret that examined the reaction and aftermath of the murder of a documentary filmmaker in rural Kentucky in 1967. In the documentary, filmmaker Colin Low of the National Film Board of Canada said, "A camera is like a gun." That line stuck with Jellett as she asked for personal stories and thoughts from the various participants in the photographer's project—participants who had a completely different economic status and life experience than she did.

THE CHALLENGE: "WHO AM I TO TELL THIS STORY?"

Some background: In her documentary, Barret wrestled with the objectification of the residents of Eastern Kentucky, located in America's so-called Poverty Belt. It was something the residents struggled with as well, as evidenced by the mixed reaction to landowner Hobart Ison shooting filmmaker Hugh O'Connor. The U.S. Department of Commerce had commissioned O'Connor to depict life in the United States for the 1968 HemisFair in San Antonio, Texas. During this time, the nation's attention was focused on the abject poverty of Appalachia. Countless media outlets had documented the War on Poverty in the late 1960s. While many residents appreciated the media scrutiny, hoping that it would lead to more opportunities for work and better living conditions, others were horrified at what they felt was an intrusion for the purpose of judgment.

Perhaps unaware of the climate of dislike for outsiders, O'Connor and his crew had obtained permission to shoot footage of a coal miner who had just returned home from a long day in the mines. The miner rented one of Ison's houses. When Ison heard that someone was filming on his property, he raced over and shot O'Connor as he and the crew were packing up to leave. O'Connor died on the spot. The New Yorker reported his last words were, "Why'd you have to do that?" The reason Ison felt obligated to protect himself, the community and their way of life was the subject of Barret's documentary.

The film was included in the material for the News Writing and Editing course to remind students to be respectful of private space, conduct thorough research, and remember the reasons for trying to tell the story in the first place. It also served the purpose of sparking a discussion about the danger of labeling people as "Other," thus categorizing and limiting.

The tension between public information and private space is not a new one, but it is one that Jellett had not considered so carefully until she began the project with the photographer one month after the News Writing and Editing class ended. Jellett began to think about "Stranger With a Camera."

Jellett went to an all-white private Christian school in Mobile, Alabama. As a student, she volunteered at an orphanage next door and noticed the stark difference between her life of privilege at the private school and the life of the African-American children in the orphanage. "I'm adopted," she said. "I began to wonder, 'Why am I so privileged?' I struggled with questions of chance, race and class. It was because of other people's decisions that I had this privileged life." When she conducted the interviews in the barbershop after the News Writing and Editing class, these issues came to a head. "I was very aware of that disparity [between her life and theirs] and being an outsider to black culture," she said.

"I wondered, and continue to wonder: 'What right do I have to talk about these people?'" she said. "What right do I have to write about their lives when I'm obviously so far removed? I just feel I don't have the authority to report on this. But then does that mean I can only report on the lives of middle-class white women? I don't think that's right either."

TOOL FOR THOUGHT: Rawls' Social Contract View of Justice

American philosopher John Rawls (1921-2002) drew on the philosophies of John Locke and Jean-Jacques Rousseau to create a "justice as fairness"[1] model for ethical behavior. His philosophy also echoes that of Immanuel Kant in that people should not be used as a means to an end. Rawls believed that people in a society should ensure that primary goods or social values benefit all unless an unequal distribution would benefit the least advantaged of the society. Rawls advocated for social contracts based on two principles of justice:

1. Each person has the same extensive set of basic liberties.

2. Social and economic inequalities are allowed only if they benefit the least advantaged party.

To eliminate bias that would cause people to make decisions based on wealth, power or social standing and to ensure that each person enjoys the same basic liberty, Rawls advanced the idea of the "veil of ignorance." Behind the veil, all parties are stripped of their "real" positions and begin in an "original position," creating a level playing field. With all qualifiers removed and equality artificially created, Rawls believed that people always will seek to protect the most vulnerable parties and seek to minimize risk.

In Jellett's case, she recognized that she was in a privileged position in terms of economic status and education, and she was conducting the interview as part of a larger project that benefitted herself and the photographer. Perhaps they did not benefit monetarily, but they each planned to use the project to gain more experience, draw attention to their work, and enhance their resumes. Behind the veil of ignorance, however, she was simply one person speaking with a different person. Not knowing the difference in race or economic background, the parties are on equal footing. With that being the case, who will benefit from proceeding with conducting the interview for the project? Will anyone suffer? Is this project giving "voice to the voiceless" or

(Continued)

(Continued)

is it exploiting someone for personal gain? Is the project an altruistic one or is it selfish?

1. J. Rawls, *A Theory of Justice* (Cambridge, MA: Harvard University Press, 1971).

THE RESPONSE: SEEKING COUNSEL

Jellett considered carefully her feelings regarding the photographer's project. She sought counsel from her News Writing and Editing professor, who noted that Jellett's awareness of difference was in itself a positive step toward making sure she was representing her subjects appropriately and with respect. "It sounds like your project is simply revealing what you heard and saw. It isn't like you were undercover or trying to do some kind of expose," her professor said. "The people knew you were there and agreed to be recorded/interviewed, yes? You may be far removed, but as long as you are portraying the situation accurately and with humanity, I think you are fine."

Jellett continued to work on the project with a sense of purpose. "Everyone has their own story to tell, but not everyone has the podium," Jellett said. "They don't have the education or opportunity to give their story to the world. I saw my duty as being the messenger."

Jellett and the photographer decided to simply record conversations around them for the gallery exhibition. In this way, they felt they were preserving the integrity of the interactions in each business and communicate what it is like to be in each place.

"I decided I should never editorialize or speak for them but I should be the conduit," Jellett said. "I decided not to give them my voice but to let them tell their stories through me."

The preamble to the Society of Professional Journalists Code of Ethics[1] states that "public enlightenment is the forerunner of justice and the foundation of democracy."

Three of the tenets in the "seek truth and report it" section relate to Jellett's experience:

1. Be vigilant and courageous about holding those with power accountable. Give voice to the voiceless.

2. Boldly tell the story of the diversity and magnitude of the human experience. Seek sources whose voices we seldom hear.

3. Avoid stereotyping. Journalists should examine the ways their values and experiences may shape their reporting.

Reporters may face two challenges when seeking diverse sources: finding the sources in the first place and becoming the "Other" themselves when they do. To the first point, Jellett was fortunate in that she was able to work with a photographer who had already secured permission from the businesses on Waters Avenue. For others who are perhaps not so well connected, SPJ offers several resources to help reporters find a wide range of experts. The link for the Journalist's Toolbox is http://www.journaliststoolbox.org/archive/expert-sources/. In addition to actively seeking diverse voices, reporters need to thoroughly vet all sources to ensure their credentials are accurate. Additionally, reporters must develop contacts in a variety of organizations—the chamber of commerce, for example, at various levels. For example, a reporter covering the court beat should be on good terms with administrative assistants all the way to the judges themselves. In this way they can actively seek out those who are typically not heard.

As for the second point, it can be challenging for reporters when they become the "Other." It's important to remember why the story is worth covering in

(Continued)

(Continued)

the first place. The goal of the reporter is to tell stories about real people, their hopes, dreams, successes and challenges. When reporters are up front with their sources about that goal, sources are usually more than happy to share information that will help the reporter better understand the context of the story and the source's personal experience. The ultimate goal is to produce stories that have impact. Sources want to help in that goal.

_____

1. http://www.spj.org/ethicscode.asp

THE AFTERMATH: "EVERYTHING IS STORYTELLING"

The exhibition was a success. Many of the subjects of the photos and ambient recordings came to the opening. For many, it was their first time ever being in an art gallery. Jellett said she believed she had accomplished something positive for many reasons, the primary one being that the participants were pleased.

"They were very happy with it, and that was very rewarding," she said.

Jellett is now conducting an internship as an instructional designer at the United Nations Institute for Training and Research. She creates e-learning courses regarding sex- and gender-based violence to help train U.N. police and peacemakers. When the internship concludes, she plans to head to Nicaragua to kick-start a nonprofit that teaches sustainable farming to the people of the Matagalpa region. She uses her writing degree in many ways in all these endeavors.

"Everything is narrative," she said. "Everything is storytelling."

Her experience with the photographer gave her new perspective on her responsibility to give voice to the voiceless.

"Our very position as people of privilege (class, race, education) not only enables us to tell stories that would otherwise go untold, but also gives us the responsibility to tell those stories," she said. "I think we really owe it to people without a voice to lend them our megaphones (and our pens). Because without them—without the historical exploitation of other people—we wouldn't have that privilege to begin with."

Thinking It Through

1. Do you think Jellett had cause to worry about being the right person to be assisting the photographer on this project? How could she have alleviated her concerns?

2. What are best practices to employ when approaching sources of a different economic status, race or ethnicity? Does there need to be thought about an approach in the first place or does it not really matter?

3. Think about the lack of diversity in newsrooms. What are some ways hiring managers and news managers can increase the percentage of minorities in newsrooms? Why is it important to have different voices represented? Is the field narrowed too much by the sheer fact that reporters typically are people with a college degree, and 40 percent of white people have a bachelor's degree compared with 23 percent for African-Americans and 15 percent for Hispanics?[1] Interestingly, 60 percent of Asian-Americans have a bachelor's degree, but they make up only about 3 percent of the newsroom staff across the country.[2]

What If?

You are a new reporter at a small market television station. The city in which you live now is 51 percent white and 49 percent black. You grew up in a small town that was 98 percent white. Your assignment editor asks you to cover a story about frequent traffic stops by the local police department. Of 100 traffic stops over the past month, more than 75 of

---

1. http://www.cbsnews.com/news/record-numbers-earning-college-degree/

2. http://www.poynter.org/news/mediawire/218189/having-more-diverse-newsrooms-wont-always-prevent-errors-like-ktvus-but-it-would-help/

the drivers are African-American. The head of the local NAACP chapter gave this information to the assignment editor as evidence that the local police are guilty of racial profiling.

You learn that your next-door neighbor is one of those African-American residents pulled over by the police. She is a teacher at a local elementary school and is embarrassed by the citation. She agrees to an interview. During the interview, she says she had taken the day off, but was driving past her school on the way to run some errands. She was pulled over for driving 5 miles per hour over the speed limit outside her school, but claims she was driving within the limit and that it was the person in the car next to her who was speeding. She says that the police officer who pulled her over had been her school's resource officer. Your neighbor says she heard the officer had been removed from the school because he falsely accused an African-American student of being a gang member.

Moments after you wrap the interview, she tells you that she changed her mind and does not want you to use her interview in your piece. She says she fears repercussions at her school and in the community. You know that her interview provides evidence in support of the NAACP representative's theory of racial profiling. It also will make a great story for the resume reel you are compiling to help you move to a larger market when your contract ends in two months. It also is late in the day and your story is slated to run in the 6 p.m. broadcast.

Would you use the interview in your story?

Use Rawls' concept of the "veil of ignorance" to decide how to proceed. Make a list of all the people who would be affected by the decision, including yourself, the audience, officials, those who received a citation, the officers involved. Put your position aside and assume the identity of all the various stakeholders in this scenario. What path gives "voice to the voiceless" but minimizes harm? What path best allows you to fulfill your job duties as a reporter and meets the expectations of your assignment editor, producer and news director? What path provides the best story for your demo reel? What path allows you to maintain a positive relationship with your neighbor? What path best allows your neighbor to maintain her reputation at the school and standing in the community?

Go Online for More

Bob Steele wrote an article about challenges one reporter faced while giving voice to the voiceless: http://www.poynter.org/news/mediawire/747/holding-the-powerful-accountable-giving-voice-to-the-voiceless/

One of the challenges of showcasing diverse voices is the lack of diversity in newsrooms. The annual census released by the American Society of News Editors reveals that the percentage of minority journalists at daily newspapers is just over 12 percent: http://asne.org/content.asp?pl=121&sl=415&contentid=415

The Columbia Journalism Review tackled that issue in an article titled "Why aren't there more minority journalists?" Read it here: http://www.cjr.org/analysis/in_the_span_of_two.php

Nieman Reports considered the idea of news departments adding a "black beat" in an article titled, "Making Black Lives Matter": http://niemanreports.org/articles/making-black-lives-matter-in-the-news/

CHAPTER 27

Along Came a Better Offer

Two Cases of Job-Hunting Ethics

Scott R. Hamula

As graduation approaches, students hunt for helpful resources and sage advice on how to land that entry-level position. On the internet and in the career services office, they find an avalanche of material: job search checklists, professional networking tips, guidelines on cover letter wording and resume writing, and ideas for interview preparation.

Usually, however, job hunters won't find advice on what to do once they receive an offer. What if the job you're offered isn't the one you really want? And what if you say yes, or even start working, and then get a better offer?

Two integrated marketing communications graduates of Ithaca College faced this dilemma and chose to handle it in different ways. Because they've reassessed their actions in light of professional standards, and they don't want to hurt their futures or the companies involved, Emily

Parnell and Josh Murray will be referred to by those pseudonyms. The names of the companies have also been changed, but the descriptions of what happened are accurate—which the author of the chapter knows because he was the professor whom the students consulted during these events.

THE SITUATION: "I GOT THE JOB, BUT . . ."

EMILY PARNELL

Emily Parnell is a classic Type A personality: competitive, impatient and driven to do everything promptly and perfectly. She was a top student in her class, with an excellent GPA, leadership positions in extracurricular activities, solid internship experiences and a strong record of community service work. A few weeks before graduation, however, she didn't have a job, and she was feeling the pressure.

The same thoughts kept bouncing around in her brain: "I'm going to graduate. I'm going to have bills." In her mind, it was essential to have that job in the pocket before graduation day. Accordingly, she had begun her search six months earlier. She was methodical and focused, creating a spreadsheet that tracked her applications by position type and location and also served as a handy place to keep her research notes. Her dream was a job in account management at an advertising agency, preferably on the East Coast.

Weeks and months went by with plenty of "informational meetings" but no job interview. Finally, she got an interview, but no follow-up invitation. Dead end. Then it happened: Parnell received an email from a professor about Connectiv, an online marketing services firm in Boston that had an entry-level sales position available. While selling wasn't on her employment radar, it was a job opportunity nonetheless. She secured a first interview and a second, and during the second interview she got the job offer right there in person.

Though Parnell was excited to have an offer at last, something about the job didn't feel quite right. Sure, it was in the field of advertising, but the agency didn't seem to have that energized, creative vibe. Still, she felt almost obligated to say yes. "I'd taken two trips to Boston, paid for hotels, investing so much time and money into this relationship that it seemed way harder to just walk away from it without a commitment," she said.

Back on campus, still uncertain about what to do, Parnell sought advice from one of her professors and her school's career services office. Both said it was a good offer—and because it was her only offer and graduation was looming, she signed and mailed the Connectiv statement of intent saying that she intended to start work there a few weeks after graduation. Not to take the job, she said later, would have made her feel like all her hard work had been for nothing.

A few days later, while preparing for finals, Parnell began to experience cognitive dissonance or "buyer's remorse," constantly questioning her decision. Conflicting thoughts swirled around her mind. Why had she taken a job that involved sales, when she didn't like sales? Why had she taken a job that would send her 400 miles away from her family, to a city with which she was unfamiliar and to an office that looked like "cubicle land"? The more she asked herself these questions, the more Parnell came to the conclusion that she had made a mistake.

JOSH MURRAY

Josh Murray has a Type B personality: relaxed, laid-back, patient. Because he'd wanted to spend an extra semester studying at his college's program in Los Angeles, he graduated not in May with his peers but in December. He'd thought about jobs now and then but didn't really start searching until November. What followed was months of rejection. He sent resumes to all sorts of companies and managed to get five interviews, but no one offered him a job. He wanted to work in New York City at an advertising agency in either media planning/buying or account management. He came very close to getting a job with an agency, Direct Message Advertising, but the offer never materialized.

Then, about eight months after graduation, a ray of hope appeared. He told his professor about it in emails:

On Aug. 24, 2010, at 1:57 p.m., Murray wrote, "I just had an interview today at InterAd Media. I believe it went well (I can only hope)."

On Aug. 30, 2010, at 9:23 a.m., he wrote, "Late last week I got a call from InterAd Media and . . . I got a job there! I start September 7th as a sales coordinator. Thank you for all your help. The hard work finally paid off."

This job wasn't the sort of thing Murray had been hoping for; he went into it excited to have an offer but somewhat resigned about the actual duties of the position. He reviewed his written offer with his parents, signed it, sent it in and began working at InterAd Media. During his first days there, he filled out a lot of paperwork for human resources and went through daily training sessions so that he would be fully prepared to perform his duties as a new sales coordinator. With one eye looking forward to the challenge, the other was looking out for better opportunities.

THE CHALLENGE: DEALING WITH SECOND THOUGHTS

EMILY PARNELL

Within days of agreeing to work at the Boston firm, Parnell received a telephone call from a recruiter who had found her information on LinkedIn. She told Parnell that Nova Associates, an advertising agency in Rochester, N.Y., was looking for a marketing coordinator and that she would recommend Parnell for the job. Feeling uneasy about her upcoming move to Boston, Parnell, who had grown up in Rochester, agreed to an interview with Nova. She arrived for her interview, walked through the door and immediately sensed the funky, fun, creative atmosphere that she was looking for in her first job. This was definitely the type of place she wanted to work.

During her interview, which went very well, she disclosed to her interviewer and potential future boss that she had already accepted an offer with a firm in Boston. "Nova was very gracious about this situation and cut me a break," she said. The company called her with a verbal offer and position overview, and then followed up with the offer in writing. Nova offered Parnell the job on the condition that she rescind her employment agreement with Connectiv.

Parnell had a very tough decision to make. She had already accepted, in writing, a position in Boston. However, the Nova job was in her hometown, a more comfortable place to live at this point in her life, and it was more advertising-focused, with no selling involved. Before making a decision, she wanted advice. Her parents told her, "You don't want to take a job that you don't want. Better for the employer to know the truth." Her professor, in contrast, focused on the potential legal aspects of her having signed an agreement and the possibility of "burning a bridge," usually not a wise move; he also tried to point out the positive aspects of the job in Boston.

A representative of her career services office told Parnell that backing out of a job you've already agreed to take is generally frowned upon. "I wouldn't do it," the representative said, "but if you want to, if you absolutely know that you don't want to go there, go ahead."

JOSH MURRAY

After about two weeks of working at InterAd Media as a sales assistant, Murray was liking the job and the company. Then something happened, which he described in an email to his professor.

On Sept. 16, 2010, at 4:05 p.m., Murray wrote,

Can I ask you some advice?

I am on my second week at InterAd. It is great and all ... people here are amazing and truly nice and great to work with.

Now get this, I got a call from Direct Message Advertising asking if I was still interested in an AAE [Assistant Account Executive] position. I lied of course just to see what the situation was. Didn't tell them I was working. The HR lady said she was talking to the team and financial department but that, according to her, [they] were "really, really interested" in me. They also have two media positions open.

Let's say I am offered the AAE job or can try for the media job ... what should I do? I know I just started at this company and that looks bad, but, I am also young so I basically shop around and see where I can go.

One of my career goals (I know I have a few lol) is to eventually be an AE and work up from that. You know I was always interested in an AE field. Should I continue to pursue it? If so, does that look bad if I get it and in maybe two weeks tell this job I am done?

I am trying to weigh all the pros and cons. This job offers salary plus overtime. Account doesn't. This is routine, no meetings, and in account at least I get to participate in meetings.

I'm just at a loss, so if you can give me a direct and honest answer, I would really appreciate that.

Thanks so much!

The professor replied,

You're already working for InterAd and things are going well. I recommend you stay there for six months to a year. You'll be even more marketable, and other agency offers will come. Tell Direct Message Advertising that, while you are still interested, you started in a position with InterAd Media and feel that it would not be ethical to leave so soon.

On Sept. 21, 2010, at 12:53 p.m., Murray wrote,

Direct Message hasn't contacted me yet, but I think I am going to stay at my current job for now. My benefits kick in next week and I do get overtime, so it's good right now for my student loans. But, who knows what they'll say. Will keep you informed.

When the human resources department at Direct Message did contact Murray, however, he began to waffle.

On Sept. 23, 2010, at 3:06 p.m., he wrote,

Direct Message called for that AAE position. They asked for a list of references. That's usually good news. You are on that list. . . . THANKS lol.

I still don't know what to do. I got my current job through someone who put their foot out there for me. Isn't it bad if I leave because it would be bad for her? Why is this so frustrating, ugh?

Thanks!

TOOL FOR THOUGHT:
The Millennial Generation

Cultural researchers continue to examine the characteristics of Generation Y, or the millennials, the approximately 75 million people in the United States born between 1977 and 1998.[1] Renna Nadler, coauthor of the book "Millennials in the Workplace," believes Gen Yers are "pressured and programmed" and that they "fear risk and dread failure."[2] In a radio interview, she referred to a 2009 Pew Research Center study that found "a majority of older Americans believe today's young adults are inferior to them in moral values, work ethic, and respect for others."

Nadler, though, believes that contrary to the negative stereotype among baby boomers, the millennials have a lot to offer America's workplaces. A 2010 Pew study showed that they possess positive characteristics like being confident, self-expressive, liberal, upbeat and receptive to new ideas and ways of living.[3]

If you're one of the millennials, chances are you like that list of positives and you don't agree that your parents' generation is superior to yours. But what you feel isn't the point. What's important about the study of generational characteristics is realizing that this may be the lens through which bosses or potential employers are viewing and judging you.

One key difference between millennials and the generations that preceded them is a syndrome known as FOMO: Fear

(Continued)

(Continued)

of Missing Out.[4] The theory is that people who are constantly texting and tweeting and checking Facebook can't stop doing those things because if they do, they might miss hearing about something better and cooler than what's happening to them right now. Now take that idea in the direction of careers. On the one hand, a new college graduate who receives a job offer, even in a bad economy, might be afraid to take it—because what if a different, better offer is just days away? FOMO. Or the new grad might take the job but keep thinking every day about what else might be out there, at a company that offers a better environment or a higher salary.

For those millennials now entering the job market for the first time, patience and realistic expectations can help. Though it may be difficult to see at first, what's bothering you about your job today is not going to last forever. The problem is not so much that you and your boss come from different generations, as that your boss's experience enables him or her to take the long view, while you don't yet have enough experience to do that. Try hard to think beyond today. In a few months, someone will quit, opening an opportunity for you to be promoted or take on new responsibilities.

Other preconceptions that companies may have about millennials include that they want instant gratification; blurt out whatever they're thinking, even at inappropriate times; need to be constantly reminded of the details of projects they've promised to complete; and tend to do so many things at once that their bosses think they have attention deficit disorder. If right now you're indignantly saying, "Those are not true," then great. Being aware that an interviewer or supervisor might have those unfair stereotypes in mind can help you be extra careful to behave in ways that show how professional you really are.

By the way, if you want to find out if you fit the Gen Y stereotype, check out http://pewresearch.org/millennials/

quiz/ and take the Pew Research "How Millennial Are You?" quiz. Or read about the generational research here: http://pewresearch.org/millennials/.

1. Diane Thielfoldt and Devon Scheef, "Generation X and the Millennials: What You Need to Know About Mentoring the New Generations," *Law Practice Today*, August 2004. http://apps.americanbar.org/lpm/lpt/articles/mgt08044.html.

2. Chris Farrell, "Flip Flops and Facebook Breaks, the Millennial Generation Invades the Workplace," March 4, 2011. http://www.marketplace.org/2011/03/04/life/makin-money/flip-flops-and-facebook-breaks-millennial-generation-invades-workplace.

3. "The Millennials: Confident. Connected. Open to Change," Feb. 10, 2010. http://pewresearch.org/millennials/.

4. J. Walter Thompson, "JWT Explores Fear of Missing Out Phenomenon," May 4, 2011. http://www.jwt.com/content/447047/fomo-jwt-explores-fear-of-missing-out-phenomenon.

THE RESPONSE: MAKING A QUICK SWITCH

EMILY PARNELL

Parnell knew that having already accepted the first offer should weigh heavily in her decision about the second. But no matter how she looked at it, the job she'd accepted just wasn't the one she wanted. All she could think of was being alone in a strange city, far from her family, and facing the challenge of learning a new discipline in a company with a workplace culture that didn't fit her personality. She knew her proposed role at Connectiv wouldn't build her career the way her role at Nova would, and a misstep this early in her career could put her at a competitive disadvantage for future opportunities.

She decided to accept the second offer at Nova Associates, but she knew that to be ethical and professional, she had to contact Connectiv first and rescind her acceptance of their offer. She dreaded the phone call and sought several people's advice on what to say.

Parnell spoke with Steve, the person she had worked with the most during the hiring process. She told him it was a very tough call to make, she felt horrible and she appreciated everything the company had done for her. They were great people, but she'd had a job offer in her hometown and she just couldn't move to Boston. She asked to be released from her contract, and Parnell was relieved by Steve's reaction.

"Connectiv took it very well; they were very supportive and very nice," she said. "Steve told me that it was OK, they understood, and that if I changed my mind, the position will be here for me for a week more." Surprised and elated, Parnell called Nova Associates and accepted the marketing coordinator job.

JOSH MURRAY

Again, Murray's thinking was communicated through emails. For a second time, Direct Message was pursuing him for a position he really wanted in account management.

On Sept. 27, 2010, at 9:25 a.m., Murray wrote,

> So Direct Message gave me the offer on Friday. I thought about it and . . . I took the offer. I sent them my signed offer letter this morning. I know it was quick at InterAd Media, but Direct Message Advertising offered a very competitive salary and it definitely is something I want to pursue.
>
> Thanks for helping me out on everything.

That same day, at 2:13 p.m., Murray wrote,

> I told my supervisor this morning. I basically told her that Direct Message called me out of the blue and fast tracked everything and really wanted me to come work for them. The offer was such a competitive salary and it is definitely an area I want to pursue.
>
> The operations executive didn't take it so well. She actually cut me and made my last day today. But it's fine. I start Direct Message next week. Just got a mini break haha.
>
> I apologized and told them this was unexpected but something I did not want to pass up.

If you want to avoid facing the kinds of tangled loyalties that Parnell and Murray struggled with, your best bet is to do some tough thinking early in your job search process. When it comes to your career, what do you really want? Sit down and come to grips with what your ideal job would include.

Then, since almost no one gets a dream job right out of school, think about what you should realistically expect, and what you would be willing to do, in your first or second job. For instance, what's more important to you right now, where you're living or where you're working? Whatever the job title may be, what skills do you need to develop as you aim for your ultimate goal? Answering these kinds of questions can go a long way in helping you make a logical choice when you get your first offer—especially if you're dealing with a bad economy that makes any job offer seem like a gift from on high.

Career counselors sometimes recommend creating a Benjamin Franklin Balance Sheet, a tool favored by salespeople who are trying to help clients reach a decision. Simple as it is, a balance sheet is a great technique for making "go" or "no go" decisions—like whether to turn down one job offer to take another—and you don't have to be an accountant to use one effectively. Simply take a blank sheet of paper and draw a line down the center. Label the left side "Go" and the right side "No Go."

Now, consider the details of your job offer: company, location, hours, specific duties, salary and benefits, co-workers, chance for advancement, even intangibles like whether you'd fit in well at the company and whether you had a good feeling being there. Can you picture staying at the company awhile? Does the work done there seem worthwhile? When you've thought about these categories and questions, grab the balance sheet. In the left column, list everything that appeals to you about the job. On the right, list everything you dislike or that gives you pause.

(Continued)

After you've finished, count the number of arguments for the decision on the left side of the paper, and compare it with the number of arguments against the decision on the right side. Often, just the exercise of making the list will make the best decision obvious.

THE AFTERMATH: TWO APPROACHES, TWO RESULTS

Parnell's and Murray's stories are similar in that they both accepted jobs and then changed their minds, quickly switching their allegiances to a different employer. There, however, their stories diverge. While Parnell maintained a good relationship with the first company by being honest about her thoughts and feelings before starting work, Murray's approach of working for a short period while still communicating with another company created a strained relationship with his first employer, which had already invested time and resources in training him. Possibly there's no good way to avoid problems when leaving a job you've just started, but honesty—and especially keeping an employer informed in as timely a manner as possible—can go a long way in creating a win-win situation.

EMILY PARNELL

After a little over a year of working at Nova Associates, Parnell believes she made the right decision. "The culture was a better fit, the job description was spot on, I admired my boss immediately and their goals complemented my strengths and interests very well," she said. "So I knew my opportunity for career growth in a creative agency—a business I've really loved since my early internships in college—was much higher than my opportunity for growth at an online marketing agency where the location would've been an adventure, but I wasn't as passionate and would've encountered a learning curve that would've prevented me from starting on a level playing field with my peers."

Of course, no decision feels 100 percent perfect 100 percent of the time. "There were some brief moments of 'What if' a couple months ago, when I read in *PROMO* magazine that the company I'd left in Boston was doing quite well, and its Groupon-esque product was right up there with the big players in the daily deals category," Parnell said. "I thought, 'Where would I be in my career if I'd gone to Boston instead?' But then those feelings quickly passed as the articles about daily deals companies dropping left and right started popping up."

Not long ago, Parnell took her first business trip, accompanying the agency's CEO to Advertising Week in New York. "Milestones like these completely reaffirm my choice to take the job in Rochester with Nova Associates," she said.

JOSH MURRAY

Murray, who is enjoying his job with Direct Message Advertising, acknowledges now that quitting his first job after just two weeks wasn't the best move. "I have to completely take fault here and say I took the wrong approach," he says. "Anyone can tell you that it is your life and you have to find the best job that makes you happy, but you should also not burn that bridge to get to the perfect job you want."

The problem, he believes now, was accepting the InterAd Media job in the first place. Worried about the economy and his internship-only experience, "I just wanted to take what I could get," he says. Now he thinks "balancing and managing your approach is the best way to handle it. Don't be so quick to apply to everything just because the company is looking for a recent grad."

If given a second chance, Murray believes he would handle things differently. "The smart approach would be to narrow down your field of opportunities and focus on places you feel would be the best fit," he said. "I am happy where I am now, but I think it would have been easier to focus on [applying for] my current job at Direct right at the beginning."

Murray has had no further contact with InterAd Media.

Thinking It Through

1. If you were friends with Parnell or Murray as they were struggling with the decision about which job to take, what would you have told them? What ethical or professional standard can you think of that would help justify, or cast doubt on, what either of them did?

2. Practice makes perfect. With another person being the employer and you the employee, role-play how you would tell the company you were leaving to accept another offer, after just two weeks of working there.

3. A company is interviewing on campus and has only a limited number of interview spots available. Would you take one just for interview practice even if you were sure you didn't want to work there? Why or why not?

4. If you were working for a company you really liked, and you knew a fellow employee was interviewing for a job with a different company, would you tell your supervisor? What if the company was a direct competitor? What if you and the other person were both being considered for the same promotion?

5. While a good resume may open the door, it's your interviewing skills that will land you a job offer. Have you ever said anything during an interview that wasn't true, or said something just because you thought that's what the interviewer wanted to hear? If there's anything in your work history that you're hoping will not come up in an interview (getting fired, for instance), rehearse what you'll say if it does come up.

6. Like most jobseekers, both Parnell and Murray got help from people they knew. As an exercise, comb your university's alumni lists to find names of people working in the field you'd like to pursue. Also list every acquaintance you can think of who might be able to help you make contacts. If you're on a professional networking site like LinkedIn, look on your contacts pages to see who their contacts are. Hang onto this as an initial list for starting your job search.

What If?

Let's say that you've sent out 45 cover letters and resumes; received only three replies; and had only one first-stage telephone interview. It's been five months since you graduated, all but one of your close college friends has a job, and your parents keep hinting that it's time for you to move out.

Then you receive a call from a major advertising agency to interview for an entry-level assistant account executive position. At the end of your interview, the account supervisor leans in and says, "We'd like to offer you this position." You're so excited and relieved at the same time. Then the supervisor adds, "You'll be working with our newest client, Camel cigarettes."

You have never smoked and think big tobacco companies are the devil. Would you take the job? Why or why not? Could those big college loans hanging over your head change your answer? What if a close relative had died of lung cancer? Would your answer be more difficult if the job entailed promoting Camel products in developing countries? How about promoting them in inner-city neighborhoods?

If you're pretty sure you would not take the job, is there anything that might change your mind? What if the people at the agency said Camel was just your training account and offered to move you to another client after six months? What if they acknowledged that the account might be problematic and offered to raise your pay accordingly?

What if, instead of cigarettes, your client was a brewery—and you don't drink, and you've watched several friends or relatives struggle with alcoholism? What if the client were a network of "adult" websites? How about something less direct—a communications job with a power company that happens to run a nuclear plant, and you've always opposed nuclear power? What if the job involves working on the alternative energy side of the company, and you'll never have anything to do with nuclear power?

Go Online for More

A targeted search engine to find the job you want, where you want it:
http://www.indeed.com/

A resource for film and television broadcast production:
http://mandy.com/

Jobs for media professionals in everything from journalism to advertising:
http://www.mediabistro.com/

Entertainment jobs in film, television, music and animation:
http://www.entertainmentcareers.net/

Site for job advice, resources and listings:
http://www.careerbuilder.com/JobSeeker/Resources/CareerResources
.aspx

The internet is full of sites that can help with most questions and concerns regarding job searches and the like. One particular site, CareerBuilder.com, has an "Advices & Resources Articles" section that contains a number of papers on a variety of topics that could prove helpful to the newly minted college graduate, including articles that deal with many of the potential ethical issues you may face, such as, "Will Your Social Networking Profile Get You Hired or Fired?" and "Quiz: How Ethical Are You?"

Appendix
Links to Ethics Codes

Many codes of ethics, including some not directly from mass media organizations, are referenced in this volume. The following is a list of such codes.

American Marketing Association Statement of Ethics:
http://www.marketingpower.com/AboutAMA/Pages/Statement%20
of%20Ethics.aspx

American Society of Newspaper Editors roundup of ethics codes:
http://asne.org/key_initiatives/ethics/ethics_codes.aspx

Associated Press Statement of News Values and Principles:
http://ap.org/company/news-values

Dow Jones Code of Conduct:
http://asne.org/article_view/articleid/306/dow-jones-code-of-
conduct.aspx

Gannett Company Ethics Policy:
http://asne.org/article_view/articleid/298/gannett-company-inc-
ethics-policy.aspx

Hearst Newspapers Statement of Professional Principles:
http://asne.org/article_view/articleid/307/hearst-newspapers-statement-
of-professional-principles.aspx

International Code of Ethics for Sales and Marketing:
http://www.smei.org/displaycommon.cfm?an=1&subarticlenbr=16

Marketing Research Association Code of Standards:
http://www.mra-net.org/resources/documents/CodeMRStandards.pdf

National Press Photographers Association Code of Ethics:
http://www.nppa.org/professional_development/business_practices/
    ethics.html

National Public Radio News Ethics Code:
http://www.npr.org/about/aboutnpr/ethics/ethics_code.html

Pew Research Center's roundup of ethics codes:
http://www.journalism.org/node/125/print

Public Relations Society of America Member Code of Ethics:
http://www.prsa.org/AboutPRSA/Ethics/CodeEnglish/index.html

Qualitative Research Consultants Association Code of Member Ethics:
http://www.qrca.org/displaycommon.cfm?an=1&subarticlenbr=26

Radio Television Digital News Association Code of Ethics and
Professional Conduct:
http://www.rtnda.org/pages/media_items/code-of-ethics-and-profes
    sional-conduct48.php

Society for News Design Code of Ethical Standards:
http://www.snd.org/about/code-of-ethics/

Society of Professional Journalists Code of Ethics:
http://www.spj.org/ethicscode.asp

Word of Mouth Marketing Association Code of Ethics and Standards
of Conduct:
http://womma.org/ethics/code/

Index

on or off the record, 304–305
sexual harassment, 252–261
Ethics:
 codes of. *See* Codes of ethics
 defining types of, 2
 digital manipulation and, 48
 job hunting and, 324–339. *See also*
  Job hunting, ethics in
 personality and, 23
 protecting sources and, 153–156
Ethics, theories of:
 Doctrine of the Mean (Aristotle), 259
 ethics of care, 18–19
 duty-based (Kant), 9–11
 Plato, 5–7
 pluralistic moral (Ross), 278–279
 prima facie and actual duties (Ross),
  14–15
 sexual harassment, 255
 Socrates, 4–5
 utilitarianism (J. S. Mill), 11–14
 veil of ignorance (Rawls), 15–17
 virtue ethics (Aristotle), 7–9
"Ethics in Human Communication"
 (Johannesen), 80
Ethics of care, 18–19, 146–147, 157–158
Ethnic groups, stereotypes and, 16
Eudemian Ethics, 7
Eudemus, 7
Ewen, Michael, 217
Expert advice, seek, 232, 233
Expertise, 244

Facebook, 72, 139–144. *See also* Social
 media *entries*
Facts:
 confusion and, 126–128
 Potter Box and, 38–40
Fairness, 54, 64, 120–121, 244–245,
 292–293, 306, 316
Fallibility, moral sophistication and, 28
"Falling Man, The" graphic video, 205
False advertising, 185–188
False identity:
 difficult sources and, 105–107
 online, marketing and, 70–78
Falsifying data, 64
Farhi, Paul, 276–277, 282
Favors, 43

Feedback, reader, 131–132
Fidelity, 14, 165–166, 232
"Field Guide for Immersion Writing"
 (Hemley), 156
File footage, using, 92–93, 97
Fisher, Douglas J., 211
Flew, Anthony Garrad Newton, 20
Florida Journal, big story vs. top story at,
 271–278, 280
Focus group, rebranding, 59–66, 67
FOMO: Fear of Missing Out, 330–331
Food Lion, undercover case, 112–113
"Formula of the CI" (Kant), 10–11
Franklin, Benjamin, 334–335
Free expression, 54
Free press, on campus, 115–125
Freud, Sigmund, 18

Gandhi, Mahatma, 21
GateHouse media, 222
Gender:
 moral reasoning and, 19
 moral uniqueness and, 18–19
 newsroom diversity and, 313.
  See also Storytelling, of diverse/
  disadvantaged communities
 sexual harassment and, 257–258.
  See also Sexual harassment, intern
  and (ethical dilemma)
 women's voices, 147
Generation Y (Millennials), 330–332
Ghostwriters, 80. *See also* Social media,
 false identity online
Gifts, 43
Gilligan, Carol, 18–19, 25, 146–147,
 157–158
Glass, Stephen, xxvii
"Good and the Right, The" (Ross), 166
Google, xxvii–xxviii, 174, 177
Google +, 72
Google, unpublishing and, 206–225
Google Alerts, 287, xxvin2
Google Trends, 281, 283
Google trends, 212
Gossip websites, reporting on?, 150–151
Graphic visuals:
 breaking news and, 237–238
 "Falling Man, The" (video), 205
Grassroots Editor, 211

MEDIA ETHICS AT WORK

MEDIA ETHICS AT WORK

Reporters Without Borders, 176
Reporting vs. withholding, 88
Republic, The (Plato), 6
Research:
    background information, social media and, 143–144
    omitting results, 64
Respect, 43, 54
Restrictions on press. *See* Prior restraint, restrictions on press
Retaliation, fear of, 62
Reynolds Journalism Institute, 280
Rhew, Adam, 228–238
"Right and the Good, The" (Ross), 14–15
Right to know, privacy and, 162–167. *See also* Privacy, public's right to know vs.
Rodenberg, Cassie, 152–161
Rodriguez, Stacy, 271–281
Rosenstiel, Tom, 31
Ross, Kathy, 273
Ross, William Davie, 14–15, 165–166, 231–234, 278–279, 294
RTDNA. *See* Radio Television Digital News Association
Rumors, 142–143

Sabotage, 43
SAD (Situation, Analysis, and Decision) Decision–making model (Day), 293–294
Sagona, Lauren, 102–111
Scientific American (magazine), 153, 158, 159, 161
Search engine optimization (SEO), 275, 280, 281
Secondary moral principles, 14
Self-censorship, 265–266
Self-improvement, 14, 165–166
Sensitivity:
    social media and, 138–151. *See also* Social media, sensitivity and
    storytelling, of disadvantaged/diverse communities, 313–323
Sexism:
    culture of, 257
    defining, dealing with, 257–258

Sexual harassment, intern and (ethical dilemma), 252–261
    defining, dealing with, 257–258
    how to handle, 254
    leaving internship, 256–257
    moving forward after leaving, 259
    philosophical theories on managing, 255
    supervisor, unethical requests from, 252–254
    workplace rights, 261
Shelby, Jessica, 60–66
Siddiqi, Mohammad A., 21
Smith, Kevin, 115–125
Smith, Richard, 162
Snapchat, 254
"Sobering Up to Reality" (Nasseff), 208–210
Social contract view of justice (Rawls'), 316–318
Social media:
    audience behavior, web analytics and, 280
    dummy accounts, politics and, 51–53, 56–57
    ethical guidelines for use of, 148
    crowdsourcing information, 139–142
    false identity online, 70–78
    journalist's use of, ethics and, 236–237
    Millennials and, 331
    professional decision making, 147–148
    rumors/off-the-record information, 142–143
    trends on, 283
    using as source, 143–144, 288
    virtual focus groups and, 67
Social trust, 17
Society of Professional Journalists, 94, 105, 198, 214–216, 279
    Code of Ethics, 85–87, 156, 265, 304–305, 319–320
Socrates:
    critical thinking method, 256
    ethical theories of, 4–5
Software, analytics and, 280
Soley, Lawrence, 269

Solo journalism, 97. *See also*
Video journalism
Solutions, identify/evaluate, 75
Sources:
anonymous, 311–312
crowdsourcing information,
139–142
difficult, 103–104
diverse, 319–320
explain publication ramifications
to, 179
identifying, 237
limited, 144–146
loyalties to, 201
minimize harm to, 129–130
on/off the record, 299–312.
See also Record, comments
on or off the
paying, 43
people, just talk to, 158–159
protecting, balancing ethics and,
153–156
vulnerable populations, 155
Sources, disagreeing, 126–137
burning bridges, 130–131
criticisms, 128
facts and confusion, 126–128
reader feedback, 131–132
Sources, protecting, 168–182
foreign governments, dangers of
denouncing, 171–173
government reaction, remove story,
173–174
safety of foreign, 175–177
transparency and, 177–180
Source remorse, unpublishing and,
206–225
doing the right thing—
prepublication, 220–221
guiding questions, 217–219
minimizing harm and, 216–219,
223–225
police blotters, ethics of
publishing, 225
small paper, big audience, 210–212
"Sobering Up to Reality" (Nasseff),
208–210
student privacy and, 223
"sunset" policy, 223

unpublish for right reasons,
219–220
website publishing and, 221–223
Sparkman, Daniel, 90–96
Speak up, or stay silent, 40–41,
65–66
Special effects, ethical use of, 99
SPJ. *See* Society of Professional
Journalists entries
Sponsors, revealing, 74
St. Claire, Laura, 192
Staged events, politics and, 51–53
Staging video, 94
Steele, Bob, 3–4, 18, 173, 180, 323
Stepp, Carl Sessions, 200
Stereotype, 16
Storytelling, of diverse/disadvantaged
communities, 313–323
everything is narrative, 320–321
should I tell their story?, 314–316
seeking advice, 318
"Stranger With a Camera" (film)
(Barret), 314–316
Strategic thinking, 49
Student journalism:
prior restraint, restrictions on press,
114–125. *See also* Prior restraint,
restrictions on press
undercover, 102–113. *See also*
Undercover journalism
Student Press Law Center, 121
Students, privacy and, 223
Subject choice, immersion journalism,
152–153
"Sunset" policy, police blotter reports
and, 223
Supervisor, unethical requests from,
252–254
Suspects, identifying in news media,
82–87
Swanton, Patrick, 83

Taglines, focus groups, rebranding and,
59–66
Talamantes, Valerie, 195–197,
200–201
Targeted demographics, false identity
online, 70–78
Taylor, Michael Jamar, 162–167

Theory, moral development and.
  See Moral development theory
"Theory of Justice, A" (Rawls), 15–17,
  132–134
Thresher, Jim, 192
Timbs, Larry, 142, 211
Timeliness, 143
Title IX, 256
TommieMedia.com, 213–225
Tompkins, Al, 268–269
Transparency, ethics of, 156, 158,
  164–165, 288
  disclosure of associations and, 193
  protecting sources and, 177–180
Trump, Miles, 217, 223
Trust, 17, 62, 155, 245–246
Truth/truthfulness, 39, 54, 98, 156, 158
  follow orders or print, 185–187
  harming through, 198–199
  seeking, 120–121, 174–175
Twitter, 139, 150, 236, 283. *See also*
  Social media *entries*

Undercover journalism, 102–111
  difficult sources and, 103–104
  publication/policy changes,
    109–111
  using false identity to get information,
    105–107
Uniform Resource Locators
  (Google), 213
University of St. Thomas (Minneapolis),
  206–225
Unpublishing, post-interview source
  remorse and, 206–225
U.S. Department of Commerce, 315
U.S. Equal Employment Opportunity
  Commission, 257–258
U.S. Newspapers Average Daily
  Circulation, 211f
Usher, Nikki, 281
Utilitarianism, 11–14, 40

Valenzuela, Marco, 302, 307–309
Values:
  competing, 232
  Potter Box and, 38–40, 74
"Veil of ignorance" (Rawls), 15–17,
  132–134, 322

Vella, Vinny, 115–125
Verify, 143
Video journalism:
  case of fatal accident, 195–201
  ethical judgment calls, 96
  graphic footage, ethics and, 202
  guidelines for ethical video/audio
    editing, 98–99
  re-creating scenario, 91–92
  solo coverage, 89–90
  tornado and aftermath, 90–91
  tweaking reality, 94–96
Video news releases, 92–93
Virtue:
  ethics and (Aristotle), 7–9
  love of (Mills), 13–14
  Plato on, 6
Visual journalists, code of ethics,
  42–44
Visuals, graphic:
  breaking news and, 237–238
  "Falling Man, The" (video), 205

Wall Street Journal, The, website, 276
Wal-Marting Across America (blog),
  191–192
Washington Post, The, website,
  192, 276, 282
Watling, Meranda, 286–287,
  289–297
Watterson, Henry, 3
Web 2.0, 177
Web analytics, clicks vs. judgment,
  270–284
  big story not a top story, 271–274
  choosing between competing duties,
    278–279
  increased use of, 279–281
  journalistic judgment and,
    281–282
  traffic conversion, 277–278
  traffic-driving strategies, 282–283
  who decides what is news?,
    274–277
Weinstein, Bruce, 53–54
Wheeler, Janet, 83–87
Whitehouse, V., xxvi–xxvii
Wilder, Deontay, 90–96
Wired magazine, 211

SAGE was founded in 1965 by Sara Miller McCune to support the dissemination of usable knowledge by publishing innovative and high-quality research and teaching content. Today, we publish over 900 journals, including those of more than 400 learned societies, more than 800 new books per year, and a growing range of library products including archives, data, case studies, reports, and video. SAGE remains majority-owned by our founder, and after Sara's lifetime will become owned by a charitable trust that secures our continued independence.

Los Angeles | London | New Delhi | Singapore | Washington DC | Melbourne